Using Film and Media in the Language Classroom

NEW PERSPECTIVES ON LANGUAGE AND EDUCATION
Founding Editor: Viv Edwards, *University of Reading, UK*

Series Editors: Phan Le Ha, *University of Hawaii at Manoa, USA* and Joel Windle, *Monash University, Australia.*

Two decades of research and development in language and literacy education have yielded a broad, multidisciplinary focus. Yet education systems face constant economic and technological change, with attendant issues of identity and power, community and culture. This series will feature critical and interpretive, disciplinary and multidisciplinary perspectives on teaching and learning, language and literacy in new times.

All books in this series are externally peer-reviewed.

Full details of all the books in this series and of all our other publications can be found on http://www.multilingual-matters.com, or by writing to Multilingual Matters, St Nicholas House, 31-34 High Street, Bristol BS1 2AW, UK.

NEW PERSPECTIVES ON LANGUAGE AND EDUCATION: 73

Using Film and Media in the Language Classroom

Reflections on Research-led Teaching

**Edited by
Carmen Herrero and
Isabelle Vanderschelden**

MULTILINGUAL MATTERS
Bristol • Blue Ridge Summit

DOI https://doi.org/10.21832/HERRER4481
Library of Congress Cataloging in Publication Data
A catalog record for this book is available from the Library of Congress.
Names: Herrero, Carmen, editor. | Vanderschelden, Isabelle, editor.
Title: Using Film and Media in the Language Classroom: Reflections on
    Research-led Teaching/Edited by Carmen Herrero and Isabelle Vanderschelden.
Description: Bristol; Blue Ridge Summit: Multilingual Matters, 2019. |
    Series: New Perspectives on Language and Education: 73 | Includes
    bibliographical references and index.
Identifiers: LCCN 2019003614 (print) | LCCN 2019014491 (ebook) | ISBN
    9781788924498 (pdf) | ISBN 9781788924504 (epub) | ISBN 9781788924511 (Kindle)
    | ISBN 9781788924481 (hbk : alk. paper) | ISBN 9781788924474 (pbk : alk. paper)
Subjects: LCSH: Language and languages—Study and teaching—Audio-visual
    aids. | Language and languages—Study and teaching—Foreign speakers—
    Audio-visual aids. | Motion pictures in education.
Classification: LCC P53.2 (ebook) | LCC P53.2 .U75 2019 (print) |
    DDC 418.0078—dc23
LC record available at https://lccn.loc.gov/2019003614

British Library Cataloguing in Publication Data
A catalogue entry for this book is available from the British Library.

ISBN-13: 978-1-78892-448-1 (hbk)
ISBN-13: 978-1-78892-447-4 (pbk)

Multilingual Matters
UK: St Nicholas House, 31-34 High Street, Bristol BS1 2AW, UK.
USA: NBN, Blue Ridge Summit, PA, USA.

Website: www.multilingual-matters.com
Twitter: Multi_Ling_Mat
Facebook: https://www.facebook.com/multilingualmatters
Blog: www.channelviewpublications.wordpress.com

The policy of Multilingual Matters/Channel View Publications is to use papers that are natural, renewable and recyclable products, made from wood grown in sustainable forests. In the manufacturing process of our books, and to further support our policy, preference is given to printers that have FSC and PEFC Chain of Custody certification. The FSC and/or PEFC logos will appear on those books where full certification has been granted to the printer concerned.

Typeset by Deanta Global Publishing Services Limited.
Printed and bound in the UK by Short Run Press Ltd.
Printed and bound in the US by Sheridan, Inc.

Contents

Acknowledgments

Numerous people have helped in the creation of this book. Needless to say, the volume would not have been possible without the contributions of an outstanding team of international researchers. We are most grateful for all of the positive responses, professionalism and collegiality during the publication process.

Kim Eggleton and Anna Roderick and other editorial members at Multilingual Matters have supported us throughout the production of this volume. The book reviewers provided insightful comments that have been extremely helpful.

For their ongoing support, we are very grateful to the Faculty of Arts and Humanities and the Department of Languages, Information and Communications at Manchester Metropolitan University, particularly Berthold Schoene, Derek Bousfield and colleagues from the French and the Spanish sections. Special thanks to India Morgan, Alicia Sánchez-Requena, Laura Ripper and Marta Suarez for their critical comments, editing help and their enthusiastic support.

We are very grateful to the language teachers and students who have participated in numerous courses, INSETs, CPDs, workshops and film study session days. Their input and feedback over the last two decades have helped us nuance the ideas and arguments that have led us to explore this interdisciplinary research field.

This book is dedicated to Ana and Jim.

Carmen Herrero and Isabelle Vanderschelden
Manchester, UK

Contributors

Rosa Alonso-Pérez works as a senior lecturer in Spanish at Sheffield Hallam University (UK). Her research interest lies in the field of language pedagogy through audiovisual translation (AVT). She holds a master's degree in AVT (Universidad Autónoma de Barcelona, Spain) and in teaching foreign languages (Universidad de Granada, Spain). Her other research interests include language learning motivation and intercultural awareness. Alonso-Pérez has successfully managed a short-film subtitling project with second-year undergraduate university students learning Spanish that culminates in a Spanish short-film festival designed to showcase students' work to an international audience. The film directors take an active part during the project and participate in Q&A sessions at the festival. The project was awarded the Pedagogic Innovation Fund from the Sheffield Business School in 2015. She has also worked as a voice-over and subtitling assistant for a specialist translation company in Sheffield. Currently, Alonso-Pérez is co-organising events with international guest speakers and lecturers for the series 'Translation & Interpreting at SHU' for applied purposes that enhance employability skills.

Jelena Bobkina lectures in the Department of Linguistics Applied to Science and Technology at the Technical University of Madrid (UPM), Spain. She has co-supervised graduate students with Elena Dominguez during her years in the Department of English Studies at the Complutense University of Madrid and still shares academic interests in higher education and EFL/ESL, with co-authored publications in journals and edited volumes. They both belong to the Manchester Metropolitan FLAME research group and the Visual Arts Circle and are active members of numerous Complutense and Politécnica research projects on innovative teaching.

Eva Cerviño-Povedano is a PhD candidate and lecturer in the Department of Modern Languages and Literatures and English Studies in the University of Barcelona. She is a member of the GRAL research group on language acquisition (http://www.ubgral.com/). She is currently completing her PhD on the relationship between L2 vowel discrimination and phonological short-term memory. Her topic interests include the relationship between cognitive ability, L1 crosslinguistic influence, input and L2 phonological acquisition.

Melissa Cokely is a PhD Candidate, EFL instructor and researcher. She has taught adults and children in both Spain and the United States. Her interests lie in foreign language acquisition through television series, action research methods, and bilingualism. She holds an MA in Applied Linguistics from the Universitat de Barcelona and a BA in English from Boston University. Her PhD thesis deals with focused language instruction and language related episodes using film and television as sources of input.

Kieran Donaghy is a freelance award-winning writer, international conference speaker and trainer. He is the author of books for students and teachers of English as a foreign language. His publications include *Film in Action* (Delta Publishing), *Writing Activities for Film and Video* (ELT Teacher2Writer) and *The Image in ELT* (ELT Council). His website Film English (http://film-english.com/) has won a British Council ELTons Award. Kieran is the founder of The Image Conference and co-founder of the Visual Arts Circle. He is a fellow of the Royal Society of Arts. You can find out more about Kieran at his author website http://kieran-donaghy.com/.

Anne-Laure Dubrac is associate professor at the University of Paris XII (UPEC) where she teaches general and legal English. Her research analyses how cinema and theatre can stimulate the development of linguistic and cultural skills. Incorporating research from fields as diverse as neuroscience, arts and education, she is investigating the links between language, body and mind. Her teaching methodology explores the physicality of English with students, especially in relation to promoting students' understanding of physical gestures as semantic aids in the learning process.

Anca Daniela Frumuselu is currently a project manager of a European-funded Erasmus project and lecturer of English at Rovira i Virgili University, Tarragona (Spain), which she joined in 2011. She has been module convenor and lecturer for undergraduate and postgraduate (taught) modules. Her research interests include the areas of English as a foreign language (EFL) and teaching and learning methodologies, such as new technologies in the EFL classroom, e-learning and audiovisual translation. She has attended several international conferences in the last years and she has published chapters and peer-reviewed articles on the implication of captioned and subtitled audiovisual materials upon colloquial language learning in EFL settings.

Mark Goodwin is in the final year of a PhD (part-time) in Spanish and Education at the University of Manchester, under the supervision of Professor Chris Perriam (Spanish/Film) and Dr Alex Baratta (Education). His thesis (due for completion in Summer 2019) is titled 'Spanish cinema studies: Methodology and practice at GCSE, A level and undergraduate level'. During the PhD, he has presented papers at the FLAME international conference (2015) at Manchester Metropolitan University, the Childhood and Nation conference (2016) at Royal Holloway University and the UK LINGUA Colloquium (2016) at the University of Durham. He works full-time as head of languages at a boarding school in Lancashire and has previously been head of languages at a state school in Hertfordshire and head of Spanish at an independent school in Greater Manchester.

Carmen Herrero is a principal lecturer and Spanish section lead in the Department of Languages, Information and Communication at Manchester Metropolitan University. She is the director of FLAME (Research Centre for Film, Languages and Media Education) (https://www2.mmu.ac.uk/languages/flame/) and co-founder of the Film in Language Teaching Association (www.filta.org.uk). She has been part of the European project Communication for Mobile and Virtual Work (CoMoViWo) (http://www.comoviwo.eu). Her research focuses on film pedagogy (the use of film and audiovisual media to enhance language learning and teaching) and contemporary Spanish film. Recent publications include 'Medios audiovisuales' (2018) in *The Routledge Handbook of Spanish Language Teaching: metodologías, contextos y recursos para la enseñanza del español L2*; and 'Film in Language Teaching Association (FILTA): A multilingual community of practice', *English Language Teaching Journal* 70:2 (2016). Her current line of research explores the use of transmedia practices in language learning and teaching as part of the AHRC-funded OWRI programme Cross-Language Dynamics: Reshaping Community.

Joan C. Mora is associate professor in the Department of Modern Languages and Literatures and English Studies in the University of Barcelona. His research has examined the role of contextual and individual factors in the development of L2 speech and oral fluency, and the acquisition of L2 phonology. His current research interests include the role of bimodal input in the development of L2 pronunciation, phonetic training methods and task-based pronunciation teaching and learning.

Carmen Muñoz is professor of applied English linguistics at the University of Barcelona (Spain). Her research interests include the effects of age and context on second language acquisition, young learners in instructed settings, individual differences, bilingual/multilingual education and multimodality in language learning. She has coordinated a dozen research projects, among them the BAF Project (*Age and the Rate of Foreign Language Learning*, Multilingual Matters, 2006) and more recently the SUBTiLL Project, on the effects of captions/subtitles on second language learning ('The role of age and proficiency in subtitle reading: An eye-tracking study', *System*, 2017).

Juan-Pedro Rica-Peromingo is senior lecturer of English–Spanish translation and English language and linguistics at the Universidad Complutense de Madrid (UCM, Spain). His recent research focuses on corpus linguistics and audiovisual translation, specifically on the field of linguistic accessibility (subtitling for the deaf and audio description for the blind), and the use of corpus linguistics for teaching and learning audiovisual translation. He has taught in the master's degree on audiovisual translation (METAV) at the Universitat Autònoma de Barcelona and is currently teaching in the master's degree on English language and linguistics at the UCM, where he has also been the director and academic coordinator.

Elena Domínguez Romero is senior lecturer in the Department of English Studies at the Complutense University in Madrid, Spain. Her research interests include higher education and EFL/ESL. She is currently working on evidential perception and visual literacy. Her research publications include over 60 papers in national and international journals and book chapters published by Peter Lang, Routledge, Multilingual Matters and Equinox. She is an active member of numerous research projects on innovative teaching.

Ángela Sáenz-Herrero holds a PhD in English linguistics from the Complutense University in Madrid, Spain. Her research primarily focuses on the adaptation and translation of mockumentaries and cinema. She is a lecturer in English and specialised language for the degrees of audiovisual communication and film studies at different universities. She has received various grants as an academic visitor at EFAP, Ècole de Communication, Paris, France, Imperial College, London, UK and University of Helsinki, Finland among others. She has also been an audiovisual and freelance translator for over 15 years.

Isabella Seeger looks back on her comprehensive experience teaching EFL and ESP/ESAP as well as French and German as foreign languages at secondary and tertiary level and in adult education. She completed a master's degree in TEFL/SL at the University of Birmingham (UK) in 2011 and subsequently taught in the teacher education programmes at the Universities of Bielefeld and Münster (DE) for six years. Currently, she runs the languages and further education programmes at the VHS Gelderland, an adult education centre in Germany, and enjoys sharing her experience through teacher training seminars. Her special interest lies in involving learners in the selection of authentic materials such as film and web content to elicit meaningful language production, foster plurilingual learning and address cultural and linguistic classroom diversity. She is a member of the FLAME research group (Manchester Metropolitan University), FILTA and the Materials Development Association (MATSDA).

Stavroula Sokoli, PhD, is a researcher in audiovisual translation and language learning. She has initiated and coordinated the EU-funded projects 'Learning via Subtitling' and 'ClipFlair – Foreign Language Learning through Interactive Revoicing and Captioning of Clips' (www.clipflair. net). She has also collaborated on numerous national and EU-funded projects, including the 'Academic and Research Excellence Initiative in Greece' (http://excellence.minedu.gov.gr), 'The Translation of Multilingual Films in Spain' (www.trafilm.net) and 'MOVEME – MOOCs for University Students on the Move in Europe' (http://movemeproject.eu). Sokoli teaches Spanish at the Hellenic Open University and subtitling at the Universitat Pompeu Fabra and Metropolitan College, Greece. She has designed and teaches online subtitling courses. http://www.linkedin. com/in/sokoli.

Brian Tomlinson has worked as a teacher, teacher trainer, curriculum developer, film extra, football coach and university academic in Indonesia, Italy, Japan, Malaysia, Nigeria, Oman, Singapore, UK, Vanuatu and Zambia, as well as giving presentations in over 70 countries. He is founder and president of MATSDA (The International Materials Development Association), an honorary visiting professor at the University of Liverpool, a professor at the Shanghai International Studies University and a TESOL professor at Anaheim University. He has over 100 publications on materials development, language through literature, the teaching of reading, language awareness and teacher development.

Isabelle Vanderschelden is senior lecturer and French section lead in the Department of Languages, Information and Communications at Manchester Metropolitan University. Her research focuses on different aspects of contemporary French cinema. She has published a film study guide on *Amelie* (IB Tauris 2007) and *Studying French Cinema* (Auteur 2013). She has co-edited with Darren Waldron *France at the Flicks: Issues in Popular French Cinema* (Cambridge Scholars Publishing 2007), and guest-edited a special issue of *Studies in French Cinema* on the French film industry (2016). She is currently completing a history of French screenwriters and their work with Sarah Leahy for Manchester University Press. She is also co-founder of FILTA, a website and community of practice for language teachers to promote the use of film critical thinking and film literacy in language teaching.

Patrick Zabalbeascoa is professor of translation studies at the Universitat Pompeu Fabra (Barcelona). His fields of investigation within translation studies are multilingualism in audiovisual fiction and humour. His recent publications (with Marta Mateo) are 'Translation and humour' in *The Routledge Handbook of Spanish Translation Studies* (2019) and (with Montse Corrius) 'Conversation as a unit of film analysis. Databases of L3 translation and audiovisual samples of multilingualism' in *MonTi Special Issue 4* (2018) *Multilingualism and Representation of Identities in Audiovisual Texts*. Zabalbeascoa has published various articles on the translation of multilingualism in film. He is principal researcher for the ClipFlair project, with a focus on foreign language learning through audiovisual translation.

Introduction

Carmen Herrero and Isabelle Vanderschelden

For almost 20 years, the languages team at Manchester Metropolitan University has been exploring innovative ways of using film and audiovisual media in the language classroom (e.g. videos, ads and short films). In 2015, the research group Film, Languages and Media in Education (FLAME: https://www2.mmu.ac.uk/languages/flame/) organised an international conference to bring together teachers, scholars and specialists of language, film education and applied linguistics from Europe and beyond. The aim was to showcase current good practice, to gather evidence of the positive impact of using films and audiovisual media in different forms of language education and to discuss new emerging trends and methodologies. This book is based on the some of the developed version of contributions presented during this event. *Using Film and Media in the Language Classroom: Reflections on Research-Led Teaching* was conceived in response to the fact that audiovisual media have become an integral part of the way that most language learners get access to their second (L2) and foreign language (FL) and culture. In the title of this volume, we have also used the word 'film' as a broader term, following the definition provided by the British Film Institute (2015: 3) suggesting that '*film* refers to all forms of moving images with sound (and without!), irrespective of the medium, be that digital or analogue, TV, online or cinema'. Film's ubiquity, complexity and cultural richness, as well as its relevance in learners' lives, provide a further justification for our interest as L2 and FL teachers, material designers and researchers.

In the last two decades, many language pedagogy models, projects and books have promoted the use of film and audiovisual materials in the language classroom (e.g. Altman, 1989; Hill, 1999; Sherman, 2003; Stempleski & Tomalin, 2001). Most of these works adopt communicative cultural models primarily applied to English teaching (English as a foreign language/English language teaching/teaching English to speakers of other languages [EFL/ELT/TESOL]) (Donaghy, 2015; Thaler, 2014, 2017). This area has also been explored by specialists of FLs: French as a foreign language (FLE) (Vanderschelden, 2012, 2014) and Spanish as a foreign language (ELE) (Amenós Pons, 1999; Brandimonte, 2004;

Castiñeiras & Herrero, 1999; Cea Navarro, 2010; Herrero, 2018a, 2018b; Junkerjürgen *et al.*, 2016; Toro Escudero, 2009); and, more recently but to a lesser extent, extended to other European and non-European languages (Chan & Herrero, 2010; Yang & Fleming, 2013). Some of these approaches have focused more specifically on a range of teaching methods/modes to address cultural learning as part of language teaching. Some pedagogical and education specialists have demonstrated the value of using film and moving images to promote (inter)cultural awareness and develop specific strategies to improve intercultural competence (Barrett *et al.*, 2013; Chan & Herrero, 2010; Herrero & Valbuena, 2011; Pegrum, 2008; Pegrum *et al.*, 2005; Sturm, 2012; Vanderschelden, 2012, 2014). New technologies are increasingly used in language teaching and they are creating opportunities for teachers and students to make use of various semiotic resources. Yet, few language education publications have so far fully addressed the use of film and audiovisual media and new techno tools (e.g. use of iPads, tablets and smartphones in the classroom, audiovisual subtitling and filmmaking in an FL).

In an attempt to bring forward new research and models in this field, this book presents a series of pedagogical approaches by international contributors, who are experts in modern language education, to demonstrate how to integrate new technologies, multimodality and interculturality into FL classes. It is aimed primarily at teachers and language students of English, French and Spanish, but the methodologies and outcomes are easily transferable to other language learning contexts.[1]

Overview of the Book

The chapters in this volume make practical suggestions based on tested methods of teaching with authentic resources and integrating research into teaching. They answer the need for new innovative pedagogical approaches, gathering evidence through the research conducted on this interdisciplinary field by scholars from different countries. The book aims to build discussion on film, multilingualism, cultural and intercultural awareness and competence. Another objective is to explore the intersection between audiovisual translation and language teaching with contributions covering a wide range of audiovisual translation modes (interlingual subtitling, subtitling for the deaf and hard-of-hearing, audio description, etc.). Finally, the volume provides language teachers with elements of professional knowledge on this area with practical ideas for exploring the huge potential of film and audiovisual media as teaching tools.

The opening chapter, 'Using Film to Teach Languages in a World of Screens', addresses the rise of visual media in our society and its impact on language education. Pointing out the potential benefits of using film in the language classroom, Kieran Donaghy offers valuable guidelines for enhancing the integration of film into the language syllabus, drawing on his experience as an English language teacher and author of books and teaching resources based on short films (Film English: http://film-english.com).

The second part of the book focuses on multilingualism, the development of intercultural awareness and the acquisition of related skills and competences. These competences have been actively promoted at European institutional level in the training of language students and teachers (Byram, 1997, 2008; Puren, 2002; Sercu, 2004, 2006; Shaw, 2000; Windmüller, 2011). Directly drawing from a number of European Common Reference Framework (ECRF) guidelines, the chapters in this part are concerned with the current plurilingual and multicultural context. They discuss the benefits of using moving images and films to develop intercultural awareness. In 'Developing Intercultural Awareness through Reflected Experience of Films and Other Visual Media', Brian Tomlinson defines the concept of intercultural awareness based on his EFL teaching experience and teacher training practice and examines different examples of quality materials using videos and films that can contribute to develop language acquisition and intercultural awareness. In 'Addressing "Super-Diversity" in the Language Classroom through Multilingual Films and Peer-Generated YouTube Content', Isabella Seeger adopts Vertovec's (2007) term 'super-diversity' to describe the impact of the multi-ethnic and multicultural influx on secondary schools in Germany. In Chapter 4, 'Playing the Part: Media Re-Enactments as Tools for Learning Second Languages', Anne-Laure Dubrac calls for making more use of the moving image in modern language curricula, particularly as a tool to develop learners' oral skills and gestural communication.

Part 3 focuses on audiovisual translation and subtitling (AVT), a growing area of research in the field of audiovisual media in applied linguistics. This includes activities such as audio description, dubbing, subtitling and voice-over. An increasing number of empirical studies assess the benefits of AVT applied to L2 teaching and learning, all the more since the wide availability of information technology (IT) tools has enabled wider use of AVT. Intralinguistic (from oral to written message in the same language) and interlinguistic subtitles (using two different languages) facilitate vocabulary acquisition, reading comprehension, oral production and student motivation (Díaz-Cintas, 2012; Vanderplank, 2010, 2016). So far, research on audiovisual media and its application to FL acquisition has focused mainly on the use of subtitles for L1 or L2 for the development of oral/aural comprehension and lexical acquisition, with subtitles acting as a bridge between reading and aural comprehension. The last 17 years have seen a significant growth in interest in the use of subtitles for FL teaching purposes (Borghetti, 2011; Bravo, 2008; Incalcaterra McLoughlin & Lertola, 2011, 2014; Sokoli, 2006; Talaván, 2010, 2013; Williams & Thorne, 2000). As pointed out by Talaván

(2010: 286), 'subtitling as a task' (the production of subtitles by students) complements the use of 'subtitles as support' helping learners to improve their oral comprehension and fostering autonomous learning. Dubbing is valued for its capacity to enhance motivation and active participation by students (Danan, 2004). Chiu (2012) and Sánchez-Requena (2016) have used dubbing to improve pronunciation, intonation and fluency in English and Spanish, respectively. Dubbing can increase learners' motivation (Navarrete, 2013) and aids the language learning process. Audio description tasks also help learners to develop their linguistic skills (Ibáñez Moreno & Vermeulen, 2014). The chapters in this part provide empirical research and show how audiovisual translation can provide additional benefits, such as the acquisition of a wide range of tools, and cultural and intercultural competences while encouraging the aesthetic appreciation of films as cultural objects (Herrero *et al.*, 2017; Herrero & Escobar, 2018). In the first case study included in this part of the volume, 'Captioned Video, Vocabulary and Visual Prompts: An Exploratory Study', Melissa Cokely and Carmen Muñoz explore an under-researched area, namely the use of captioned videos and the effect of intentional learning combined with pre-viewing tasks that offer learners the meaning of the target vocabulary. The next chapter by Joan C. Mora and Eva Cerviño-Povedano, 'The Effects of Bimodal L2 Input on the Processing of Function Words by Spanish EFL Learners: An Eye-Tracking Study', develops existing research on the impact of exposure to audiovisual media to support the development of perceptual phonological competence and pronunciation skills for EFL learners. Anca Daniela Frumuselu's chapter pursues the pedagogical exploration of the effective use of audiovisual input in EFL in the context of higher education. In 'A Friend in Need Is a *Film* Indeed': Teaching Colloquial Expressions with Subtitled Television Series', she redefines the notion of *authenticity* and lists the benefits of using authentic videos as teaching resources in language teaching using two longitudinal case studies. Rosa Alonso-Pérez's chapter, 'Enhancing Student Motivation in Foreign Language Learning through Film Subtitling Projects', focuses more specifically on the positive effects of integrating AVT techniques into L2 acquisition with a project-based formative assessment. Finally, in 'Audiovisual Translation Modes as L2 Learning Pedagogical Tools: Traditional Modes and Linguistic Accessibility', Juan Pedro Rica Peromingo and Ángela Sáenz Herrero evaluate the use of professional and non-professional software available for AVT with two different groups of higher education language learners.

Part 4 is devoted more specifically to teacher training issues and resources available to (trainee) teachers for language teaching and advice on assessment strategies. It is particularly important to consider current types of assessments appropriate for the use of film in language education to evaluate their success and infer training needs. As many teachers find it challenging to develop their own resources (i.e. lack of time and training) and to optimise the multimodal potential of films, it is important to give visibility to innovative tested projects that develop resources and/or provide examples of best practice and guidance on technological tools. A range of valuable websites are already available to language teachers who wish to use films in their classes: ClipFlair (http://clipflair.net); Film English (http://film-english.com); Film in Language Teaching Association (http://www.filta.org.uk); Lessonstream (http://lessonstream.org); Video for all (http://videoforall.eu/); among others. As part of the teaching resources discussed in this book, we have included three chapters that should be valuable to language teaching trainees and their trainers, regardless of the languages they work with, because they bring together the use of film and language teaching. In this part, the chapter 'Towards an Inclusive Model for Teaching Literature in Multimodal Frameworks: The Case of a Film-Based Workshop in the Complutense EFL/ESL Teacher Training Programme' presents a research project based on a film workshop with EFL and ESL master's students at the Universidad Complutense de Madrid. Jelena Bobkina and Elena Domínguez discuss the application of multimodal theories to support the teaching of literary texts. Mark Goodwin's 'An Analysis of the Success of the "Cultural Topic" at A Level through the Study of Spanish Film Directors' explores the integration of Spanish films in the cultural component of the language curriculum in UK secondary schools. In the final chapter 'Audiovisual Activities and Multimodal Resources for Foreign Language Learning', Stavroula Sokoli and Patrick Zabalbeascoa Terran present the ClipFlair project, a free resource aimed at supporting and guiding language teachers on the use of video and film to enhance language learning, funded under the Lifelong Learning Programme of the European Commission.

The volume advocates different theoretical backgrounds, practices and research studies for the use of film and audiovisual media, including television, and the impact of the accessibility of online video. It outlines some of the main reasons for using audiovisual media in the language classroom. It highlights the importance of elaborating video and audiovisual media pedagogies that are conceived within interdisciplinary theoretical frameworks and thoroughly investigated through primary research carried out in the international language classroom. It gathers related research-based articles, which demonstrate the scope of video use for language teaching and learning across different languages, age groups and curricular areas. It also illustrates a range of approaches to video creation for the language classroom, working with the three dimensions of the media literacy model, also known as the '3Cs': cultural access, critical understanding and creative activity (British Film Institute, 2015). The interdisciplinary nature of the work presented here will be extremely useful for researchers, language teachers and teacher trainees. It will do justice to the current and future potential power of film and video for language teaching and learning.

Note

(1) We will use the terms 'student' or 'learner' on the understanding that the terms can apply to primary or secondary school pupils studying a modern language, as well as higher education students or adult learners who study a language for more personal or professional purposes.

References

Altman, R. (1989) *The Video Connection: Integrating Video into Language Teaching*. Boston, MA: Houghton Mifflin Company.

Amenós Pons, J. (2000) Largometrajes en el aula de ELE. Algunos criterios de selección y explotación. In M. Franco Figueroa, C. Soler, M. Rivas and F. Ruiz (eds) *Actas del X Congreso ASELE* (pp. 769–783). Cádiz: Universidad de Cádiz. See http://cvc.cervantes .es/ensenanza/biblioteca_ele/asele/pdf/10/10_0765.pdf (accessed 2 February 2017).

Barrett, M., Byram, M., Lázár, I., Mompoint-Gaillard, P. and Philippou, S. (2014) *Developing Intercultural Competence through Education*. Strasbourg: Council of Europe Publishing.

Borghetti, C. (2011) Intercultural learning through subtitling: The cultural studies approach. In L. Incalcaterra McLoughlin, M. Biscio and M.A.N. Mhainnín (eds) *Audiovisual Translation: Subtitles and Subtitling: Theory and Practice* (pp. 111–138). Bern: Peter Lang.

Brandimonte, G. (2004) El soporte audiovisual en la clase de E/LE: el cine y la televisión. In H. Perdiguero and A. Álvarez (eds) *Medios de comunicación y enseñanza del español como lengua extranjera. Actas del XIV congreso de ASELE* (pp. 870–881). Burgos: Servicio de Publicaciones Universidad de Burgos.

Bravo, C. (2008) Putting the reader in the picture: Screen translation and foreign-language learning. PhD dissertation, University Rovira i Virgili. See https://www.tesisenred. net/bitstream/handle/10803/8771/Condhino.pdf?sequence=1

British Film Institute (2015) *A Framework for Film Education*. London: British Film Institute.

Byram, M. (1997) *Teaching and Assessing Intercultural Communicative Competence*. Clevedon: Multilingual Matters.

Byram, M. (2008) *From Foreign Language Education to Education for Intercultural Citizenship*. Clevedon: Multilingual Matters.

Castiñeiras, A. and Herrero, C. (1999) Más allá de las imágenes: El cine como recurso en las clases de español. In T. Jiménez Juliá, M.C. Losada Aldrey and J.F. Márquez Caneda (eds) *Español como Lengua Extranjera: Enfoque comunicativo y gramática* (pp. 817–824). Santiago de Compostela: ASELE and Universidad de Santiago de Compostela.

Cea Navarro, M.B. (2010) El cine en clase de ELE para estimular el desarrollo de la competencia intercultural. Master's dissertation, Universidad de León. See https://blogs.f uniber.org/formacion-profesorado/2010/12/16/los-elementos-extralinguisticos-claves-para-comprender-una-nueva-lengua (accessed 7 January 2017).

Chan, D. and Herrero, C. (2010) *Using Film to Teach Languages*. Manchester: Cornerhouse Education. See https://goo.gl/MhScf7 (accessed 2 February 2017).

Chiu, Y-H. (2012) Can film dubbing projects facilitate EFL learners' acquisition of English pronunciation? *British Journal of Educational Technology* 43 (1), 24–27.

Danan, M. (2004) Captioning and subtitling: Undervalued language learning strategies. *Meta: Journal des traducteurs. Meta: Translators' Journal* 49 (1), 67–77.

Díaz-Cintas, J. (2012) Los subtítulos y la subtitulación en la clase de lengua extranjera. *Abehache, Revista da Associação Brasileira de Hispanistas* 2 (3), 95–114.

Donaghy, K. (2015) *Film in Action: Teaching Language Using Moving Images*. Peaslake: Delta Publishing.

Herrero, C. (2018a) El cine y otras manifestaciones culturales en ELE. In M. Martínez-Atienza de Dios and A. Zamorano Aguilar (eds) *Iniciación a la metodología de la enseñanza de ELE* (Vol. IV; pp. 65–85). Madrid: EnClaveELE.

Herrero, C. (2018b) Medios audiovisuales. In J. Muñoz-Basols, E. Gironzetti and M. Lacorte (eds) *The Routledge Handbook of Spanish Language Teaching: metodologías, contextos y recursos para la enseñanza del español L2* (pp. 565–582). London/New York: Routledge.

Herrero, C. and Valbuena, A. (2011) Cultura participativa y alfabetización multimodal aplicadas a la enseñanza de lenguas. In M. Buisine-Soubeyroux and J. Seguin (eds) *Image et éducation* (pp. 277–286). Lyon: Le Grihm/Passages XX-XXI and Université Lumiere-Lyon 2.

Herrero, C. and Escobar, M. (2018) A pedagogical model for integrating film education and audio description in foreign language acquisition. *Special Issue of Translation and Translanguaging in Multilingual Contexts. Audiovisual Translation in Applied Linguistics: Beyond Case Studies* 4 (1), 30–54.

Herrero, C., Sánchez-Requena, A. and Escobar, M. (2017) Una propuesta triple: Análisis fílmico, traducción audiovisual y enseñanza de lenguas extranjeras. *inTRAlinea Special Issue on Building Bridges between Film Studies and Translation Studies.* See http://www.intralinea.org/specials/article/una_propuesta_triple_analisis_filmico _traduccion_audiovisual_y_ensenanza (accessed 7 January 2018).

Hill, B. (1999) *Video in Language Learning.* London: CILT.

Ibáñez Moreno, A. and Vermeulen, A. (2014) La audiodescripción como recurso didáctico en el aula de ELE para promover el desarrollo integrado de competencias. In R. Orozco (ed.) *New Directions in Hispanic Linguistics* (pp. 264–292). Newcastle upon Tyne: Cambridge Scholars Publishing.

Incalcaterra McLoughlin, L. and Lertola, J. (2011) Learn through subtitling: Subtitling as an aid to language learning. In L. Incalcaterra McLoughlin, M. Biscio and M.A.N. Mhainnín (eds) *Audiovisual Translation Subtitles and Subtitling: Theory and Practice* (pp. 243–263). Bern: Peter Lang.

Incalcaterra McLoughlin, L. and Lertola, J. (2014) Audiovisual translation in second language acquisition. Integrating subtitling in the foreign-language curriculum. *The Interpreter and Translator Trainer* 8 (1), 70–83.

Junkerjürgen, R., Scholz, A. and Alvárez Olañeta, P. (eds) (2016) *El cortometraje español (2000-2015). Tendencias y ejemplos.* Madrid: Iberoamericana-Vervuert.

Navarrete, M. (2013) El doblaje como herramienta de aprendizaje en el aula de español y desde el entorno de CLIPFLAIR. *MarcoELE* 16, 75–87.

Pegrum, M. (2008) Film culture and identity: Critical intercultural literacies for the language classroom. *Language and International Communication* 8 (2), 136–154.

Pegrum, M., Hartleym, L. and Wechtler, V. (2005) Contemporary cinema in language learning: From linguistic input to intercultural insight, *Language Learning Journal* 32 (1), 55–62.

Puren, C. (2002) Perspectives acionnelles et perspectives culturelles en didactique des langues cultures; vers un perspective co-actionnele-co-culturelle. *Les Langues Modernes* 2, 55–71.

Sánchez-Requena, A. (2016) Audiovisual translation in teaching foreign languages: Contributions of revoicing to improve fluency and pronunciation in spontaneous conversations. *Portalinguarum* 26, 9–21.

Sercu, L. (2004) Assessing intercultural competence: A framework for systematic test development in foreign language education and beyond. *Intercultural Education* 15 (1), 73–89.

Sercu, L. (2006) The foreign language and intercultural competence teacher: The acquisition of a new professional identity. *Intercultural Education* 17 (1), 55–72.

Shaw, S. (ed.) (2000) *Intercultural Education in European Classrooms*. Stoke on Trent/ Sterling, VA: Trentham Books.

Sherman, J. (2003) *Using Authentic Video in the Language Classroom*. Cambridge: Cambridge University Press.

Sokoli, S. (2006) Learning via subtitling (LvS). A tool for the creation of foreign language learning activities based on film subtitling. In *EU-High-Level Scientific Conference Series MuTra 2006: Audiovisual Translation Scenarios: Conference Proceedings* (pp. 1–5). See http://www.sub2learn.ie/downloads/2006_sokoli_stravoula.pdf (accessed 7 January 2017).

Stempleski, S. and Tomalin, B. (2001) *Film*. Oxford: Oxford University Press.

Sturm, J.L. (2012). Using film in the L2 classroom: A graduate course in film pedagogy, *Foreign Language Annals* 45 (2), 246–259.

Talaván, N. (2010) Subtitling as a task and subtitles as support: Pedagogical applications. In J. Díaz-Cintas, A. Matamala and J. Neves (eds) *New Insights into Audiovisual Translation and Media Accessibility* (pp. 285–299). Amsterdam: Rodopi.

Talaván, N. (2013) *La subtitulación en el aprendizaje de lenguas extranjeras*. Barcelona: Octaedro.

Thaler, E. (2014) *Teaching English with Film*. Paderborn: Schöningh.

Thaler, E. (ed.) (2017) *Short Films in Language Teaching*. Tübingen: Narr Franke Attempto.

Toro Escudero, J.I. (2009) Enseñanza del español a través del cine hispano: Marco teórico y ejemplos prácticos. *MarcoELE* 8, Suplemento. See http://marcoele.com/descargas/china/ji.toro_cinehispano.pdf (accessed 2 February 2017).

Vanderplank, R. (2010) Déjà vu? A decade of research on language laboratories, television and video in language learning. *Language Teaching* 43 (1), 1–37.

Vanderplank, R. (2016) *Captioned Media in Foreign Language Learning and Teaching: Subtitles for the Deaf and Hard-of-Hearing as Tools for Language Learning*. London: Palgrave.

Vanderschelden, I. (2012) Filmer l'école: un révélateur des identités langagières et des manifestations interculturelles dans la France d'aujourd'hui. In A. Lachkar (ed.) *Langues et médias en Méditerranée: Usages et réception* (pp. 227–234). Paris: L'Harmattan.

Vanderschelden, I. (2014) Promotion de l'interculturel par le film dans la classe de langue au 21e siècle: une approche multimodale. In A. Lachkar (ed.) *Langues cultures et médias en Méditerranée* (pp. 224–236). Paris: L'Harmattan.

Vertovec, S. (2007) *New Complexities of Cohesion in Britain: Super-Diversity, Transnationalism and Civil-Integration*. Wetherby: Communities and Local Government Publications.

Williams, H. and Thorne, D. (2000) The value of teletext subtitling as a medium for language learning. *System* 28 (2), 217–228.

Windmüller, F. (2011) *Français langue étrangère: L'approche culturelle et interculturelle*. Paris: Belin.

Yang, L.H. and Fleming, M. (2013) How Chinese college students make sense of foreign films and TV series: Implications for the development of intercultural communicative competence in ELT. *The Language Learning Journal* 41 (3), 297–310.

Part 1
Film Literacy and Languages

1 Using Film to Teach Languages in a World of Screens

Kieran Donaghy

The moving image is rapidly becoming the primary mode of communication in the world. The ascendance of the moving image has important consequences for society and education. In this chapter, I examine the changing nature of literacy in the 21st century and the importance of film in society and education. I look at the benefits of using film in language teaching and examine how we can successfully integrate film into the language classroom. In doing so, I offer guidance on using feature-length films, film clips and, in particular, short films, in critical and creative ways in language education. In addition, I consider the increasingly important role of student-generated media.[1]

Introduction

The increased ease of capturing moving images with digital cameras and mobile devices, the development of inexpensive, accessible and user-friendly video-editing tools, the appearance of video-distribution sites (such as YouTube, Daily Motion and Vimeo) and the ubiquity of screens have all led to the increasing presence and even predominance of the moving image in society. As Apkon (2013) notes:

> What we are now seeing is the gradual ascendance of the moving image as the primary mode of communication around the world: one that transcends languages, cultures and borders. And what makes this new era different from the dawn of television is that the means of production – once in the hands of big-time broadcasting companies with their large budgets – is now available to anyone with a camera, a computer and the will. (Apkon, 2013: 24)

As Apkon points out, anyone who owns a camera and a computer – or, indeed, even a mobile phone or tablet – is, potentially at least, a filmmaker. That is, they are no longer just a consumer of media, but they also have the capability to create their own films. Given that the majority of young people now have access to technology that allows them to become media producers in their own right, it would seem to make sense for schools to focus on visual media and capitalise on young people's knowledge of and enthusiasm for moving-image media in the form of films, television series, videos and computer games. However, on the whole, our educational systems have been slow to respond to the ascendance of visual media in our society. In the words of Goodwyn (2004: 1): 'given the prominence of the moving image in twentieth century culture, and the current evidence that it seems to be even more dominant in the twenty-first, it may seem more peculiar that its study is not at the heart of a postmodern education'.

To get a better understanding of the slow reaction of schools to the dominance of the moving image in society, we have to explore the changing nature of literacy in the 21st century, in addition to the concept of multiliteracies and its impact on our educational systems. The term 'multiliteracies' was coined by the New London Group (1996), a group of scholars who argue that literacy pedagogy should be linked to the rapidly changing social, cultural and technological environment. The group calls for a much wider and more inclusive view of literacy than is portrayed by traditional language-based approaches. According to Kress (2003: 9), a prominent member of the New London Group, '[the] former constellation of medium of book and mode of writing is giving way, and in many domains has already given way, to the new constellation of medium of screen and mode of image'. In *Literacy in the New Media Age*, Kress (2003) offers a new theory of literacy. He argues that our previous dependence on linguistic theories to define literacy is now inadequate and obsolete, and that we should combine language-based theory with semiotics (the study of signs and symbols and their use or interpretation) and other visual theories, if we are to give an adequate and contemporary meaning to the term 'literacy' in the 21st century.

Literacy now reflects a wider cultural competence that goes far beyond the three Rs (reading, writing and arithmetic); therefore, film, which plays a vital role in culture and society, should be integrated into our educational systems. One of the leading proponents of integrating film in schools is the British Film Institute, which argues that 'film literacy' is integral to literacy as a whole in this new age of the image. The British Film Institute (2013: 3) defines film literacy as 'the level of understanding of a film, the ability to be conscious and curious in the choice of films; the competence to critically watch a film and to analyse its content, cinematography and technical aspects; and the ability to manipulate its language and technical resources in creative moving image production'. In the seminal report *Film: 21st Century Literacy: A Strategy for Film Education across the UK*, the case for film literacy is stated eloquently:

> We live in a world of moving images. To participate fully in our society and its culture means to be as confident in the use and understanding of

moving images as of the printed word. Both are essential aspects of literacy in the twenty-first century. In the same way that we take for granted that society has a responsibility to help children to read and write – to use and enjoy words – we should take it for granted that we help children and young people to use, enjoy and understand moving images; not just to be technically capable but to be culturally literate too. (British Film Institute, 2011: 3)

The importance of visual literacy in education is becoming more widely acknowledged. There is an increasing acceptance that education needs to develop students' skills in and their ability to interpret images and communicate visually: in many schools, there is a move away from a reliance on print as the primary medium of instruction towards moving-image media and the screen. Furthermore, an increasing number of educational theorists stress that film literacy is fundamental to literacy in the 21st century, if young people are to be able to participate fully in a rapidly changing world in which moving images are increasingly predominant. Nonetheless, despite this increased awareness of the importance of visual literacy, policymakers fail to understand the importance of moving-image media in young people's lives and, consequently, in our educational systems. There is also a scarcity of structured, systematic opportunities for students to watch, analyse and understand films, and there are even fewer opportunities for students to make their own films.

If students are to become fully participative citizens, they need to be able to read and write in all forms of communication, not just the written word. Lucas (2004) asks the question: 'If students aren't taught this new language of sound and images shouldn't they be considered as illiterate as if they left college without being able to read and write?'. In our schools, we need to introduce structured, systematic opportunities for students to 'read' the screen (to watch, analyse, interpret and understand films) and 'write' the screen (to make their own films). Educational programmes that make use of visual tools and media, help students to understand moving images and show them how to create their own films will better prepare students for life in a rapidly changing world. This is because filmmaking develops many of the life skills that are increasingly valued in the 21st-century workplace, such as communication, creativity, collaboration, innovation, conflict management, decision-making and critical thinking. As Theodosakis (2009: 7) argues, 'we need filmmaking in our classrooms, not to graduate filmmakers, but to graduate problem solvers, critical thinkers and passionate people who can work with others to make that which does not yet exist, real'. Part of the reason for the absence of film education in our schools is the feeling among many educators that curricula are already bulging at the seams: there is simply no room for any more subjects or tasks. For that reason, it is vital to understand that film literacy should not be treated as an add-on subject. Every school subject, including foreign languages, needs to take responsibility for helping students to acquire the skills and knowledge they will need in our media-saturated society.

Despite the fact that our educational systems have been slow to embrace film, more and more teachers are using films to motivate and engage students in the classroom, and to contextualise various areas of the curriculum. Using film can also encourage disaffected students to participate more in class and increase their self-confidence. Beeban Kidron is a film director and co-founder of the charity Film Club, which gives approximately 200,000 children a week in more than 7,000 schools throughout the UK the opportunity to watch, discuss and review films from around the world (about 6,000 reviews are uploaded onto the Film Club website each week). Kidron (2012) comments on how film inspires and motivates students in different ways:

> We guessed that film, whose stories are a meeting place of drama, music, literature and human experience, would engage and inspire the young people participating in Film Club. What we could not have foreseen was the measurable improvements in behaviour, confidence and academic achievement. Once-reluctant students now race to school, talk to their teachers, fight, not on the playground, but to choose next week's film – young people who have found self-definition, ambition and an appetite for education and social engagement from the stories they have witnessed.

When students are given opportunities to create their own films and videos, they are usually even more motivated and enthusiastic. Even students who are usually disaffected and disengaged are prepared to put in a great deal of work on film projects, and they often achieve outstanding results. It is obvious that the ability of film to motivate also applies in language education. Students constantly engage with moving images outside school; they are knowledgeable about them and enjoy watching them. As watching films and television series is an integral part of our students' lives, it makes perfect sense to bring them into the language classroom. The motivational qualities of film in language education are even more enhanced if students are given opportunities to create their own films and videos. In a world where the moving image is rapidly becoming the dominant medium of communication, producing their own media is intrinsically motivating for many students. As Goldstein and Driver (2014: 2) ask: 'How much more motivational if the learners produce the videos themselves?'.

Although motivation is the most frequently cited reason for using film in the language classroom, it is by no means the only one. Another vital benefit of using films in language education is that they are a source of authentic language, as films are authentic materials and provide students with genuine input in which they can see and hear the foreign language being used in 'real' situations. Film also provides students with authentically interactive language. 'Interaction' is recognised in the Common European Framework of Reference for Languages (Council of Europe, 2001) as one of the major areas of language competence, along with production, reception and mediation, yet interactive language is still not usually covered thoroughly in published language learning materials. As a consequence, many students are often unable to produce natural-sounding spoken language, and they have a limited range of colloquial and idiomatic expressions and functional language. Film exposes students to the language of everyday conversation and the natural flow of speech. As Sherman (2003: 14) states, students 'need such exposure because to learn to speak to people they must see and hear people speaking to each other'.

In addition, the ability of film to help students acquire this conversational language, and vocabulary in general, can be enhanced if the films are subtitled. When students regularly watch films subtitled in their first or second language, they receive information from three different channels – film, sound and text. Therefore, they are exposed to large quantities of multimodal input, which may lead to greater vocabulary acquisition (Mishan, 2005).

Another benefit of using film in language education is its visual nature. When students watch a film, they often comprehend more, because language is interpreted in a full visual context, which supports the verbal message. Film may also contribute to the development of learning strategies (such as predicting or guessing from the context, and inferring ideas) and give students an opportunity to activate their background schemata, due to the wealth of visual information and stimuli that film provides (Sherman, 2003).

As films are cultural artefacts, using film is a highly effective way to communicate the values, customs, attitudes and beliefs of the target language culture. Film has a capacity to bring a wide range of cultural concepts into the language classroom and develop intercultural communicative competence – the ability to understand cultures and use this understanding to communicate effectively and appropriately with people from other cultures (Landis et al., 2004). It is increasingly recognised that learning a foreign language involves fostering not only linguistic competence but also intercultural communicative competence. The Common European Framework of Reference for Languages (Council of Europe, 2001) stresses that teachers should develop not only their students' communicative language competences but also their intercultural competence. Using films from the target language culture in the language classroom is a powerful way to help language students understand different cultures and intercultural relationships. As Chan and Herrero (2010: 11) argue: 'films are perfect vehicles for introducing students to different types of popular culture and engaging them with critical questions about the relationship between information and power, through the critical analysis of sociopolitical issues and intercultural relationships'.

Another advantage of film is that it can bring more variety to the language classroom. The different roles that films can play in the language learning classroom supply the teacher with a variety of techniques. Willis (1983) identifies four main roles of moving images in language teaching. The first of these is to provide a language focus when new or recently introduced words are encountered in context in a film. The second role is skills practice, when a film is used to practise listening and reading or as a model for speaking and writing. The third role is that of a stimulus, where film acts as a springboard for communicative follow-up tasks, such as discussion, debate and role play. The fourth role is that of a resource, when a film provides students with the content for subsequent projects, such as making their own films. It is also possible to bring further variety to the language learning classroom by screening a diverse variety of films – different genres of feature-length films, short sequences of films, short films, adverts and a whole range of digital video content.

Integrating Film into Language Teaching

Benefits of using film in the classroom

Given the many benefits of using film in the language learning classroom, it is not surprising that many teachers are keen to use film with their students. Indeed, increasing numbers of teachers are successfully integrating film into the language learning syllabus and using film in pedagogically sound ways to engage their students. As with all educational technologies, the value of film relies on how it is implemented in the classroom. It is important to remember that film, like any other technology, is a tool and not a learning outcome. However, effective language learning is greatly enhanced when a film is integrated into the syllabus and the learning outcomes of the class.

Effectively integrating film into the language classroom involves the teacher carefully selecting the topic and content, deciding on clear pedagogical goals and then thoughtfully deciding on and preparing staged activities for before, during and after viewing. We will look briefly at each of these implementation stages.

Selecting films and setting pedagogical goals

Selecting an effective film is an essential component of integrating film into the language classroom. When choosing a film, teachers should consider if the theme of the film fits into the syllabus, is age-appropriate and is relevant to the interests and backgrounds of their students. It is also important to consider the level of the language and factors that may hinder comprehension, such as:

- a lot of dialogue and relatively little action;
- more than one character speaking at the same time;
- loud soundtracks, which make the dialogue difficult to understand;
- complex storylines.

At the same time, it is essential to consider factors that aid comprehension, such as:

- dialogue with a high degree of visual support and a close connection between speech and action;
- clearly enunciated speech;
- only one character speaking at a time;
- clear, conventional storylines;
- titles, graphics and animations. (Sherman, 2003; Donaghy & Whitcher, 2015)

Having selected a film that is appropriate for and appealing to their students, the teacher has to decide on the pedagogical goals that they want to achieve through using the film. The value of a film is closely correlated with how well the content and pedagogical objectives fit with the syllabus and the overall structure of the class. The pedagogical goals may be, for example, to use a film to introduce or raise awareness of a topic at the beginning of a class, to give the students a chance to see a language point in a 'real-life' conversation in a scene or short film or to provide a prompt for written or oral communication.

Activities and tasks

After selecting the film and clearly defining the pedagogical goals, the teacher has to decide on the activities and sequence of activities that will accompany the film. In the language classroom, teachers have traditionally sequenced the use of film in terms of pre-viewing, while-viewing and post-viewing tasks. As this practice has worked effectively for many years, this model does not need to be altered. However, what the teacher can change is the relative emphasis on each of the three stages and the kinds of activities used with the film. They can extend a stage in order to achieve their pedagogical goals, and choose activities that depend on the content of the film and the learning outcomes of the lesson. For the sequencing to work well, it is necessary for the teacher to try to connect the stages of a pre-viewing/while-viewing/post-viewing sequence to one another – and, perhaps, to previous and subsequent sequences.

It is important that the pre-viewing activities selected by the teacher prepare the students for the actual viewing by helping them to follow the film and understand the narrative and characters. If the pedagogical goal of the viewing is language based, pre-viewing tasks could include pre-teaching vocabulary or expressions that appear in the dialogue. If the pedagogical goal of viewing is mainly communicative, pre-viewing activities may include discussion tasks that generate prediction and speculation and give students an opportunity to activate their background schemata about the topic, content or narrative of the film.

The viewing tasks that the teacher selects will depend on the pedagogical goals of the lesson. If the pedagogical goal is comprehension, typical tasks are to set multiple-choice or True/False comprehension questions and to give the students the dialogue with some vocabulary and expressions taken out. If the pedagogical goal is language based, a typical activity is for students to complete fill-in-the-blank texts with the target language; for example, grammatical structures and vocabulary.

While these comprehension and target language activities are legitimate, it is preferable that not all the tasks are comprehension based or language based. It is also important to include tasks that focus on and exploit other facets and modes of the film – such as the visual, sound, culture and narrative aspects. If the pedagogical goal is developing visual skills, the teacher may show the film with no sound and ask the students to focus exclusively on what they see in order to understand the narrative of the film. If the pedagogical goal is to raise the students' intercultural awareness, the teacher may ask them to notice any aspects of the target language culture illustrated in the film that are different from their culture.

Post-viewing activities often involve getting the students to extract the main ideas or concepts of the film or to do production tasks. If there is a clear language goal, the teacher may want the students to use the target language that they have encountered in the film in speaking or writing tasks. If the pedagogical goal is communicative, the teacher should try to select follow-up activities that encourage the students to reflect on and explore the concepts or ideas contained in the film and to get a personal response from the students. Among the many possibilities for post-viewing activities are research projects on ideas and themes brought up in the film, discussions in small groups on the ideas and issues raised in the film and creating their own moving-image texts in response to the film.

Feature-length films vs short films

It is obvious that the type of tasks teachers choose to use will depend on the type of moving-image text they select for use in class. Feature-length films have been used by language teachers for many years and, in general, they have been used in two ways. The first approach is to show the whole film in one sitting. The pre-viewing tasks may include language work on words and expressions contained in the film's dialogue or discussion on the themes with which the film deals. However, students are often not asked to perform any tasks beyond trying to understand the film and enjoy it. A possible advantage of showing the whole film is that it offers students extensive exposure to authentic language, and they may pick up useful interactive language. A clear disadvantage of this approach is that students may find it difficult to concentrate for up to two hours, leading to cognitive overload and students watching the film passively. Sometimes, this method is used with little or no preparation, and often no pre-viewing, while-viewing or follow-up activities. Showing a whole film in this way is sometimes justified as a 'treat' after a hard week or at the end of term, or to calm down young students when they become agitated. Showing a film in this way – without any clearly defined pedagogical goals and with no preparation – should be avoided, as it fails to integrate film effectively into the language learning curriculum. An alternative approach is for the students to do the pre-viewing activities in class but view the film at home, where they can pause the film and rewatch any scenes that they do not understand. After viewing the film, the students do the post-viewing activities in class. This approach makes more optimal use of class time.

In the second common approach, the students view the whole film in short sequences over a number of sessions. There are two types of tasks that teachers typically use to exploit these clips. First, the teacher gives the students viewing sheets (which they have often prepared themselves) that focus on language and cultural features of the film. The students have to complete the sheets. This method is also used as a tool to aid listening comprehension. The students watch the film and carry out listening comprehension exercises and activities based on what is said by the characters or the narrator, in very much the same way as with an audio text. These exercise types are usually exactly the same as those used in a listening comprehension task. There are two main advantages to this approach. First, as the film is shown in short sequences, it is cognitively less challenging for the students than viewing a whole film. Secondly, as the sequence can be shown several times, students may understand more.

Although this approach uses the full visual context to aid listening comprehension, a drawback is that it fails to exploit the other rich visual details of film. It is a wasted opportunity not to have any tasks that focus on what the students have seen. As film is primarily a visual medium, optimal educational use capitalises on its visual richness. Film becomes much less effective as an educational tool in language learning if the activities the students are asked to do depend largely on non-visual elements. Another disadvantage of this approach is that the students have to do so much work on vocabulary, grammatical structure and content that it may take away their enjoyment of watching the film.

Instead of using whole feature-length films, many teachers find and use film clips that fit the grammatical point, vocabulary or theme they want to present and practise in class. The emergence of YouTube in 2005, where we can find hundreds of thousands of film clips, makes it easier for teachers to find just the clip they are looking for and allows for greater flexibility. There are a number of advantages to using film clips. The main advantage is that because the clip is short, the students can watch it several times, study it in greater depth and engage with it more meaningfully. Another advantage is that it allows teachers greater spontaneity, as they can find and show clips as themes come up in the class. A drawback is that when the teacher finds and shows a clip during a class, there is little or no preparation and there are no clear pedagogical aims.

Most language teachers realise that feature films are too long to be viewed and discussed in ordinary classroom sessions. Many language teachers are now ignoring feature-length films and film clips and turning to short films. Short films are an excellent resource in the language classroom for a number of reasons. First, as we have already seen, viewing an entire feature film in one sitting may lead to cognitive overload and is often not possible, given timetable constraints. In contrast, whole short films can be shown within one class. These can have a greater dramatic impact than feature films do, as feature films often lose their impact when they are viewed over a number of sessions. As most short films are under five minutes long, they can be shown several times in a single class, and students are able to acquire detailed familiarity with them.

Secondly, short films are excellent for grabbing and holding students' attention. This can be exploited to capture the students' curiosity at the beginning of a session, to motivate them when their interest is flagging or to make an impact to promote discussion and debate. Thirdly, short films are especially useful to exploit in a single lesson, as they offer a complete narrative in a short space of time. Students enjoy narratives, and because makers of short films are usually independent and not tied to big film studios they often have greater scope for innovation and creativity, which leads to more imaginative narrative structures. These departures from more familiar narrative structures very often provoke stronger responses from students than the more traditional narratives of feature-length films do. Finally, as many modern short films are silent or have very little dialogue, comprehension is much easier. The teacher can get the students to supply the dialogue by imagining what the characters are thinking or what they would say.

Resources available

Whichever form of moving images – whole feature-length films, film clips or short films – the teacher decides to use in class, preparing their own activities and tasks around film is very time-consuming. The internet now offers a wealth of ready-made, pedagogical sound film-based resources for language learning, which teachers may like to access before creating their own material. The Film in Language Teaching Association (FILTA; http://filta.org.uk/) is an association of language teachers, film educators and researchers that encourages teachers to design and share their own film-related materials on the association's website. Teachers can find a wide range of study guides for Arabic, Chinese, French, Italian, Spanish and Urdu feature-length films and short films, which can help their students develop linguistic, cultural and intercultural, and visual skills. For teachers who prefer to use film clips, Berkeley Language Centre's (http://blcvideo-clips.berkeley.edu/) library of foreign language film clips is a tagged, structured collection of 14,500 clips drawn from 415 films in 23 languages. The film-clip database is available free of charge to faculty at other institutions through institutional agreement. Teachers who want to use short films can access the author's resource site, Film English (http://film-english.com/), which offers more than 150 free lesson plans designed around short films. The site is aimed primarily at English language teachers but because many of the short films used are silent, they can be used with any foreign language. Teachers should also encourage their students to watch films from the target language culture in their own time. There are a number of free websites where students can watch films in English with subtitles; one of the best is Speechyard (http://speechyard.com/), where students can click on unknown words in the subtitles, see their translation and add them to their own vocabulary library for further study.

As we have already seen, if we carefully select the topic and content of the film, have clear pedagogical goals and thoughtfully prepare pre-, while- and post-viewing activities, we can successfully integrate film into the language syllabus and help students to improve their knowledge and use of the foreign language. However, in addition to this, there should be an emphasis on developing a critical film literacy through the medium of the foreign language; in other words, to help students analyse and interpret moving images so as to encourage them to think critically about the film itself. What is more, in addition to helping our students 'read' the screen, we should also encourage them to 'write' it – that is to say, to create their own moving-image texts in the form of videos and short films. We have already suggested – when we looked at the changing nature of literacy in the 21st century – that young people need to be able to read and write in all forms of communication, not just the written word. As mentioned previously, creating moving images is intrinsically motivating for students, and it helps them develop the types of skills (such as collaboration, decision-making, conflict resolution, critical thinking and creativity) that are in demand in the modern-day workplace through the medium of the foreign language.

Filmmaking projects

As the moving image becomes ever more dominant in our society, student-created film and video will become a central focus in the language classroom. Expensive equipment is no longer needed to make a film, and students can create good short films with a mobile phone or tablet. They can also edit them by using a mobile device or computer, so it is not necessary to invest in expensive editing software. Although filmmaking is no longer prohibitively expensive it is still a complicated process, so it is best to start by keeping students' films short and simple. Making films that are just a few minutes long will involve a lot of time-consuming work. It is best to start with tight filmmaking criteria and limit choice to help students focus on what they have to do. As students become more proficient in their filmmaking, teachers can set looser criteria to allow them greater creativity.

We will now look at three simple filmmaking projects (Donaghy, 2015) that can be easily integrated into the syllabus. Students start with the simplest project from a logistical perspective: making a film promoting or telling the history of their school. They then move out of the school to their home, where they create a film about their family or a member of their family. Finally, they make a film about an artist in their local community. All of the film projects take the students out of the classroom, aim to bridge the gap between the curriculum and the world outside the classroom and may help to build bridges between the students and their school, family and wider community (Figure 1.1).

These filmmaking projects aim to develop the students' reading, writing, speaking, paralinguistic, presentation, research, visualisation, problem-solving, critical-thinking, planning and coordinating skills. The major decisions about creating the films should be left to the students, either individually or in pairs or groups. They explore and develop an original idea, prepare their own scripts, rehearse and perform their

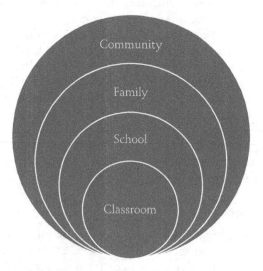

Figure 1.1 Film chronicles (Donaghy, 2015)

scripts, and direct and edit their films. However, the teacher is not passive. They support students in a number of ways, such as:

- helping them write their scripts;
- making sure their subtitles and captions are understandable;
- advising them on their pronunciation when they are rehearsing their scripts;
- advising them on paralinguistic features, such as body language, gestures and facial expressions;
- evaluating their performance in the process of making a film and evaluating their final products – their films; and giving feedback on their language errors.

In the first project, the students have to create a two-minute film to promote or tell the history of their school. There are three main advantages to this project: first, the logistics are relatively easy, as all the locations are within the school building; secondly, as students are familiar with the school they may find it easier to research, plan and coordinate the project; and thirdly, the film can be used as a promotional tool for the school.

In the second project, students make a two-minute film about their family. The main objectives are to raise students' awareness of their own families and their stories and, as the project is deeply personal, for the students to engage meaningfully with language. As the project criteria are fairly loose, students can be creative in the way they tell their families' stories. Some may interview siblings, parents, grandparents or other relatives, while others may use photos and video footage to tell their stories.

In the third project, students work in pairs to create a five-minute documentary film about an artist who lives in their community. The principal idea behind the project is to create meaningful engagement with language through engagement with the students' local community. As the project criteria are loose, the students are given opportunities to explore their own interests and creativity.

Conclusion

In this chapter, we have tried to show the benefits of using film in language teaching and we have offered guidance on how teachers can successfully integrate moving images in the form of feature-length films, film clips and (especially) short films into the language classroom. We have also examined the increasingly important role of student-generated media in language education.

There are four principal conclusions that we can draw from this chapter. First, when we use film in the language classroom we need to design activities that develop students' linguistic, cultural and intercultural skills in addition to tasks that help to develop their film literacy. Secondly, feature-length films are too long to be viewed and discussed in ordinary classroom sessions; showing short film clips or short films, which students can engage with on a more meaningful level, is a more optimal use of classroom time. Thirdly, short films are the perfect vehicle for using moving images in the language classroom because of their brevity, dramatic impact and innovative narrative forms. Finally, language students should be given the opportunity to create their own moving texts, as this helps them to acquire such skills as collaboration, decision-making, conflict resolution, critical thinking and creativity, which are in demand in the modern-day workplace, through the medium of the foreign language.

Note

(1) Part of this chapter is a revised version of the introductory chapter of *Film in Action: Teaching Language Using Moving Images* (Donaghy, 2015).

References

Apkon, S. (2013) *The Age of the Image: Redefining Literacy in a World of Screens*. New York: Farrar, Straus and Giroux.

British Film Institute (2011) *Film: 21st Century Literacy: A Strategy for Film Education across the UK*. British Film Institute, Film Club, Film Education, First Light Movies, UK Film Council and Skillset. See http://www.bfi.org.uk/sites/bfi.org.uk/files/downloads/bfi-film-21st-century-literacy.pdf (accessed 30 December 2015).

British Film Institute (2013) *Screening Literacy: Film Literacy in Europe*. See http://edition.pagesuite-professional.co.uk//launch.aspx?pbid=25c57922-2908-45b5-b752-e891849e520f (accessed 30 December 2015).

Chan, D. and Herrero, C. (2010) *Using Film to Teach Languages: A Teacher's Toolkit*. Manchester: Cornerhouse Education.

Council of Europe (2001) *Common European Framework of Reference for Languages: Learning, Teaching, Assessment*. See http://www.coe.int/t/dg4/linguistic/Source/Framework_EN.pdf (accessed 30 December 2015).

Donaghy, K. (2015) *Film in Action: Teaching Language Using Moving Images*. Peaslake: Delta Publishing.

Donaghy, K. and Whitcher, A. (2015) *How to Write Film and Video Activities* (Kindle version). ELT Teacher 2 Writer.

Goldstein, B. and Driver, P. (2014) *Language Learning with Digital Video*. Cambridge: Cambridge University Press.

Goodwyn, A. (2004) *English Teaching and the Moving Image*. London: Routledge.

Kidron, B. (2012) The Shared Wonder of Film, TED talk. See http://www.ted.com/talks/beeban_kidron_the_shared_wonder_of_film/transcript (accessed 30 December 2015).

Kress, G. (2003) *Literacy in the New Media Age*. London: Routledge.

Landis, D., Bennett, J. and Bennett, M. (2004) *Handbook of Intercultural Training*. Thousand Oaks, CA: Sage Publications.

Lucas, G. (2004) Life on the Screen. Edutopia, The George Lucas Educational Foundation (article). See http://www.edutopia.org/life-screen (accessed 30 December 2015).

Mishan, F. (2005) *Designing Authenticity into Language Learning Materials*. Bristol: Intellect Books.

Sherman, J. (2003) *Using Authentic Video in the Language Classroom*. Cambridge: Cambridge University Press.

Theodosakis, N. (2009) *The Director in the Classroom: How Filmmaking Inspires Learning*. Penticton, BC: Tech4Learning.

Willis, J. (1983) Implications for the exploitation of video in the EFL classroom. In J. McGovern (ed.) *Video Applications in English Language Teaching* (pp. 29–42). ELT Documents Series 114. London: Pergamon Press.

Part 2

Multilingualism, Intercultural Awareness and Competence

2 Developing Intercultural Awareness through Reflected Experience of Films and Other Visual Media

Brian Tomlinson

This chapter uses a personal approach to define intercultural awareness in the context of language teaching, and more particularly for English as a foreign language (EFL). It explains why intercultural awareness is valuable for language students and how pedagogical research on the use of film in language teaching can help students to develop intercultural competence by encouraging them to reflect on their experience of watching films and other visual media that portray cultures in action. The discussion is based on the author's 50 years' experience of teaching English all over the world and draws on his teacher training practice. It includes a number of examples of materials for developing language courses.

Introduction

This chapter presents a personal view of what intercultural awareness is, why it is valuable for language students and how we can help students to develop it by getting them to reflect on their experience of watching films and other visual media that portray cultures in action. It is based on my 50 years' experience of teaching English in nine countries, training teachers of many languages all over the world and contributing to the development of language learning courses for many different institutions and in many countries.

Intercultural awareness, in my view, is accepting that cultures (whether they be national, regional, ethnic, religious or social) differ in their beliefs and behavioural norms. It also means not being judgemental about the perceived differences between your own and other cultures. It results eventually from considered and open-minded reflection on actual and/or vicarious experience of cultures in action and requires an initial tolerance of ambiguity when you do not understand why people from the other culture (or cultures) seem to be behaving in different ways from yourself. It involves being curious about your own and other people's cultures, seeking experiences of those cultures and reflecting on those experiences. The process of developing intercultural awareness also contributes to the acquisition of the target language by facilitating exposure to rich, meaningful and comprehensible input and by helping to develop positive attitudes towards the language and its associated cultures (Tomlinson, 2016a).

There are two types of intercultural awareness. One involves awareness of the culture or cultures associated with the target language of a second or foreign language learning course, and the other involves a predisposition to develop awareness of any culture that is encountered. It is obvious that the first is important for students of a second or foreign language. The second is important for users of a language as a lingua franca (Tomlinson, 2016c) with people from many different cultures; for example, a Thai businessperson conducting business in English in the UK, the USA, Australia, India and Japan, or a French television documentary maker using Spanish or Portuguese for interviews throughout South America.[1] Although the terms are sometimes used interchangeably in the literature, I would say that intercultural awareness is different from intercultural competence, but intercultural awareness is an important aspect of intercultural competence and is a prerequisite for developing it.

Whereas intercultural awareness is an aptitude and attribute, intercultural competence is an ability. It is an 'ability to interact effectively with people from cultures that we recognise as being different from ourselves' (Guilherme, 2000: 297). Such an ability takes a long time to develop and, in my experience of living in such countries as Japan, Indonesia, Malaysia, Nigeria, Singapore, Vanuatu and Zambia, it requires multiple encounters with the other culture (or cultures) and the making of and learning from many mistakes. I would say that intercultural awareness is a prerequisite of intercultural competence; however, real experience of other cultures is necessary in order for intercultural awareness to be activated in such a way as to lead to effective interaction with people from those and other cultures. There are two types of intercultural competence. First, there is effective interaction with people and contexts from the target culture of a language course; second, there is an ability to interact effectively with people and contexts from any culture that is different from your own.[2]

Can intercultural competence be gained on a language course? In my view, the answer is no. Intercultural competence requires the development of capabilities, not the gaining of knowledge or advice; and the development of such capabilities requires more time and more first-hand experience than most language courses can provide. Such courses can, however, contribute to the eventual development of intercultural competence by giving the students real and simulated experience of interacting with people and contexts from the target culture. This can be done through articulating responses to video encounters (e.g. after muting the voice of one of the interactants), through simulations, through scenarios with a potential for intercultural misunderstanding (Troncoso, 2010), through spontaneous intercultural dialogues, through inviting people from other cultures to the classroom and, ideally, through visits to other cultures.[3]

In my experience, it is possible for intercultural awareness to be gained on a language course if students are given enough time and the right sort of materials. The most effective types of materials are those that provide experience of cultures in action in addition to opportunities to reflect on this experience. Ideally, the experience should be first-hand through interaction with people from other cultures and through overseas visits. But valuable intercultural awareness can be developed through reflecting on vicarious experiences of reading, listening and especially viewing, providing that the 'texts' are sufficiently engaging and the attitudes, thoughts and behaviours are sufficiently typical of the cultures being portrayed. A number of reports of research studies investigate the effectiveness of materials produced to facilitate the development of intercultural awareness and/or competence, such as Gottheim (2010), Mason (2010) and Troncoso (2010), published in English by Tomlinson and Masuhara (2010).

Gottheim (2010) conducted an action research study of the development and use of materials designed to facilitate both the learning of Portuguese as a second language and a greater awareness of Brazilian culture. It is notable for its text-driven approach (Tomlinson, 2013b) and for its critical account of the composing of a textbook by a 'non-expert'. Mason (2010) evaluates the course of materials that he developed and used at a university in Tunisia to help students to develop greater awareness of British culture and reflects on the tasks he used for assessing the students' resulting intercultural competence. He achieved successful effects with the use of DVD clips of British television documentaries and satirical comedies. Mason's (2010) study is particularly valuable for its detailed exploration of what intercultural competence is and for its innovative development of principled materials that make use of reflection on actual and vicarious experiences of cultures in action. Troncoso (2010) also reports on the development of text-driven (Tomlinson, 2013b) materials for facilitating and assessing intercultural competence; in his case, for students learning Spanish at a university in the UK. He makes very effective use of photos for depicting culturally typical Spanish behaviour (e.g. photos of street scenes, markets and festivals) in order to stimulate readiness activities to activate learners' minds in relation to the topic or theme of a text that they are about to experience.

Examples of Materials Designed to Facilitate the Acquisition of Language and the Development of Intercultural Awareness

In this chapter, I am focusing primarily on the use of films and other visual media. In my experience of helping to develop intercultural awareness, I have found that they can have the greatest impact on altering misconceptions and getting learners to become more aware and appreciative of the value of other cultures. An example of such an impact is the response of students at Kobe University in Japan to extracts from the film *My Beautiful Laundrette* (Frears, 1985). The students were shocked – not by the nudity and homosexuality, but by the scenes of poverty suffered by squatters in an empty London flat and by the uneasy multicultural society that is portrayed. Their image of England had been created by textbooks portraying middle-class, prosperous, white couples living perfect lives with their children, cars and a dog in detached houses in suburbia. The film stimulated an animated discussion in English about social problems in the UK and Japan.

Female and Male

The following detailed example of a unit of material makes use of a short video to develop the intercultural awareness of learners of EFL. The video is entitled *Female and Male* (2011) and is a humorous cartoon contrasting stereotypical male and female behaviour in Italy.

---

(1) You're going to watch a video about the differences between the behaviour of men and women. Think about a typical difference in your culture.

(2) Tell a partner (ideally someone from a different culture from yours) about the difference you thought about in (1) above.

(3) Watch the video. For each difference, shout out YES if you think it is typical in your culture and NO if you think it is just a stereotype, which isn't actually true in your culture.
   (a) What did you think of the video?
   (b) Were you annoyed by it because it was stereotyping the behaviour of men and women? Were you amused by it?
   (c) Did it make you think about your own experience?

(4) Think back to the video you've just watched and try to see it again in your mind.

(5) As you watch the video in your mind, decide on:
   (a) the one behaviour that you think is most true in your culture;
   (b) the one behaviour that you think is most untrue in your culture.

(6) Share your decisions in small groups with people from other cultures.

(7) It's been decided to produce a sequel to *Female and Male*. In your group, draw four new behaviours of men and women that you agree are typical.

(8) Show and explain your drawings to other groups.

(9) In pairs, improvise a short dialogue in which a man and a woman are behaving typically.

(10) Perform your dialogue for another pair. Then discuss their reaction to it with another pair.

The unit of material proposed above exploits what I have found to be a very engaging video that stimulates thought about cultural stereotyping, differences between cultures and personal experience while providing learners with experiences of using the target language for communication. In my view, the main criterion for effective intercultural awareness is that the activity provides experience of a culture or cultures in action. It also needs to provide opportunities for reflection on that experience. It is important that the activity contributes to the acquisition of the target language and to the development of communicative competence. For example, this can be done by providing rich exposure to the target language in use, achieving affective engagement, achieving cognitive engagement, helping learners to make discoveries about how the target language is typically used and providing learners with opportunities to use the language for communication.[4]

I have found that these criteria can be achieved by motivating the students through providing different types of tasks that generate positive energy – possibly the most important prerequisite for the classroom acquisition of a language – and tasks that allow students to 'hide' (i.e. to participate mentally without having to risk public performance). These types of activities are most easily achieved using a whole-class approach in which the teacher interacts with the entire class rather than with nominated individuals (Tomlinson, 2016b). Other activities that can achieve the criteria above include:

- tasks that are bizarre, in the sense that they are strange but compelling;
- tasks that invite personal mental responses and stimulate the voluntary expression of these views and feelings; texts and tasks that take learners to other cultures at the same time as being related to their lives;
- tasks that set an achievable challenge;
- tasks based on emotive texts (especially those that spark controversy and discussion); texts and tasks that stimulate thought;

- tasks that stimulate discovery of how the target language is typically used and how people think and behave in the culture or cultures being portrayed;
- tasks that are open-ended.

I consider texts to be very important in helping to achieve the objectives outlined above. I have found that the most effective types of texts are accessible but ambivalent poems; extracts from affectively and cognitively engaging stories, novels and plays; and, in particular, short, bizarre and humorous videos (with television adverts from different cultures being especially valuable for the exploration of cultural norms). In addition, the key to the effectiveness of most of the tasks is teacher and learner creativity.[5]

Not Now, Bernard

Here is an example of a unit of material designed to achieve the above criteria. It is entitled 'Not Now, Bernard'. *Not Now, Bernard* is a children's book by David McKee (2005) in which a young boy is ignored by his busy parents and is consequently eaten by a monster in his garden.

---

(1) Write 'Not now'.

(2) Now add another word at the end to make a common expression.

(3) Listen to the story of *Not Now, Bernard* and as you listen, imagine the story as a cartoon.

(4) Watch and listen to the cartoon (McKee, 2015) and compare the pictures in your mind with those on the screen.

(5) Who was responsible for Bernard's death?

(6) What is the meaning of 'Not now' as it is used by the parents in the story? Do they use it in the same way every time?

(7) Write a poem or story called *Not Now* that raises issues about your culture.

(8) For homework, find other examples of 'Not now ...' from books, newspapers and the web and bring them to class for us to think about.

When I used this unit at Sultan Qaboos University in Muscat, Oman, it provoked an unusually vociferous whole-class debate in which the female students unexpectedly challenged the male students' assertion that Bernard's death was the fault of the mother because it was her responsibility to look after her son. The female students countered that the father should have been looking after Bernard because the mother was busy cooking the dinner. There then ensued a heated discussion in English about the respective roles of the mother and father in Omani culture before somebody suggested it was the teacher's fault for not teaching Bernard to respect his parents. Someone else then suggested that it was the fault of society for spoiling children and reducing their attention span. When I have used the unit with mixed-culture classes, similar debates have ensued, with students representing the norms of their own culture and exploring those of other cultures.

Gonna Be an Engineer

Finally, here is another example of a unit of material designed to contribute to the development of intercultural awareness, the acquisition of the target language and the development of communicative competence. It is based on the text-driven approach (Tomlinson, 2013b), which advocates the use of a potentially engaging core text (in this case, Wong's [2010] animated version of a song, 'Gonna Be an Engineer' by Peggy Seeger) to drive the materials. All the learning points and activities derive from the text rather than from a predetermined syllabus.

---

(1) Readiness activity
  (a) Think about the toys you had when you were a very young child. Try to see pictures of them.
  (b) Now picture the toys you had when you were about 10 years old.
  (c) What did you want to become when you were a child?
  (d) Talk to yourself about one of your toys and about what you wanted to become: about your ambition.
  (e) Tell somebody else about one of your toys and about your ambition when you were a child.
  (f) In a small group, talk about your answer to the following question: When you were a child, were you encouraged to do only things that were either typically male or typically female?
(2) Initial response. Activity 1
  (a) Listen to me reading a song by Peggy Seeger. As you listen, imagine pictures you would use in an animated version of the song.
(3) Intake response. Activity 1
  (a) In your group, discuss your answers to the following.
  (b) What is your attitude towards:
    (i) the woman?
    (ii) her mother?

(iii)   her husband?

(iv)   her boss?

(4)   Development. Activity 1

(a)   In your group, write your own song, poem or story starting:

(b)   When I was …

(5)   Input. Activity 1

(a)   Read the song together and point out to each other anything you hadn't noticed about the four people when you listened to the song.

(6)   Input. Activity 2

(a)   In your group, look at all the instances of 'but' in the song. For each one decide what it means.

(b)   Look at other texts and find other instances of 'but'.

(c)   Use your discoveries about 'but' to write a summary of the uses of 'but'.

(7)   Development. Activity 2

(a)   Revise your song, poem or story about 'When I was …'. You can make use of your discoveries about the use of 'but' and anything else from your copy of the song to help you.

(8)   Initial response. Activity 2

(a)   Listen to Peggy Seeger singing her song in an animated version of 'Gonna Be an Engineer' (Wong, 2010).

(b)   As you listen and watch, think again about your attitudes towards the people in the song.

(9)   Intake response. Activity 2

(a)   Would a girl who wants to be an engineer face similar difficulties with her mother, her husband and her boss in your country today?

(b)   Share you answers to (a) with people from different cultures.

(10)   Further reading

(a)   'Do all girls want to play with dolls and tea sets? Do all boys want guns and trucks? Of course not. Then why are toymakers so aggressive in marketing these stereotypes? Kira Cochrane charts the rise of the pink–blue divide – and the fightback by angry parents'. Think about these questions and then read 'Load of old pony' by Kira Cochrane (2014) from *The Guardian*. Decide if you think what she says is true for your country.

This is a deliberately long unit of materials, which leaves the decisions to the teacher (and possibly the students) as to how many of the activities to use. I would use all of them if the unit achieved and maintained engagement but would omit (or modify) some of them if it did not. The unit follows an experiential approach (Kolb, 1984) in which apprehension precedes comprehension, in addition to a text-driven approach (Tomlinson, 2013b) in which a core text drives and stimulates responses with the potential to facilitate learning. It includes multidimensional mental activities, such as visualisation and using the inner voice (Tomlinson & Avila, 2007a, 2007b); listening, reading and viewing activities; personal response activities; discussion activities; language discovery activities; text exploration activities; and creative writing activities. All of these are designed to engage learners and provide a rich and varied experience that is likely to contribute to language acquisition, the development of communicative competence and the eventual development of cultural awareness. Just as in my other two examples, there is no provision of information about the institutions, norms, beliefs and behaviours of a culture. Instead, there is an experience of a culture in action and the encouragement of reflection on and discussion about it. If I were teaching this unit, especially if the students were from different cultures from mine, I would take part in most of the activities as a participant rather than as a teacher. After all, probably the most authentic experience that students in a classroom can have of both the target language and another culture is their interaction with a teacher from another culture.

Conclusion

The main points I wish to make in this chapter are that we should take pleasure in helping our students to enjoy becoming more interculturally aware and that we can do so by providing them with opportunities for engaging in reflected experience of other cultures through the use of films and other visual media. This cannot replace real interactive experience of cultures in action but it does help to provide authentic experience, without which awareness cannot develop. Knowledge can be given to students externally by books and teachers, but awareness can only be developed internally by the students themselves. Student awareness is 'internal, gradual, dynamic, variable and learner driven' (Tomlinson, 1994). It is developed by paying (and results in an increased ability to pay) 'a lot of attention to the things that are around them' and being 'interested in why they are happening' (Sinclair, 1987). Becoming more interculturally aware – in the sense of paying more attention to what is happening in cultures and why – can help students to eventually develop intercultural competence. This is defined by Byram and Masuhara (2013: 150) as consisting of knowledge of self and others, awareness of self and others, attitudes towards self and others and the 'skills of exploring, interpreting, relating and interacting'. Such awareness can also help students to increase their communicative competence in their target language and to mature as human beings.

Notes

(1) For a discussion of different types of cultures and ways of helping students to develop their awareness of them, see Tomlinson and Masuhara (2004).

(2) For a detailed discussion of intercultural competence and ways of contributing to it through materials developed for language learners, see Byram and Masuhara (2013).

(3) For suggestions on materials that can contribute to the eventual development of intercultural competence, see Tomlinson (2016c).

(4) For a discussion about what facilitates acquisition and development, see Tomlinson (2011, 2013a, 2016a, 2016b).

(5) See Maley and Peachey (2015) for suggestions on stimulating and exploiting teacher and learner creativity in the classroom.

References

Byram, M. and Masuhara, H. (2013) Intercultural competence. In B. Tomlinson (ed.) *Applied Linguistics and Materials Development* (pp. 143–160). London: Bloomsbury.

Cochrane, K. (2014) Load of old pony. *The Guardian*, 23 April.

Female and Male (2011) YouTube video, added by 30MiscC [online]. See https://www.youtube.com/watch?v=C3f3V6X4Ez4 (accessed 5 April 2017).

Frears, S. (1985) *My Beautiful Laundrette* [DVD]. UK: Working Title Films, SAF Productions and Channel Four Films.

Gottheim, L. (2010) Composing textbooks as a non-expert. In B. Tomlinson and H. Masuhara (eds) *Research for Materials Development for Language Learning: Evidence for Best Practice* (pp. 224–236). London: Continuum.

Guilherme, M. (2000) Intercultural competence. In M. Byram (ed.) *Routledge Encyclopedia of Language Teaching and Learning* (pp. 297–300). London: Routledge.

Kolb, D. (1984) *Experiential Learning: Experience as the Source of Learning and Development*. Englewood Cliffs, NJ: Prentice Hall.

Maley, A. and Peachey, N. (eds) (2015) *Creativity in the Language Classroom*. London: British Council.

Mason, J. (2010) The effects of different types of materials on the intercultural competence of Tunisian university students. In B. Tomlinson and H. Masuhara (eds) *Research for Materials Development for Language Learning: Evidence for Best Practice* (pp. 67–82). London: Continuum.

McKee, D. (2005) *Not Now Bernard*. London: Andersen Press.

McKee, D. (2015) *Not Now, Bernard*, YouTube video. See https://www.youtube.com/watch?v=fiHGi7ZQyKM (accessed 5 April 2017).

Sinclair, J. (ed.) (1987) *Cobuild Collins Dictionary*. London: Collins.

Tomlinson, B. (1994) Pragmatic awareness activities. *Language Awareness* 3 (3–4), 119–140.

Tomlinson, B. (2011) Introduction: Principles and procedures of materials development. In B. Tomlinson (ed.) *Materials Development in Language Teaching* (2nd edn; pp. 1–31). Cambridge: Cambridge University Press.

Tomlinson, B. (2013a) Second language acquisition and materials development. In B. Tomlinson (ed.) *Applied Linguistics and Materials Development* (pp. 11–30). London: Bloomsbury.

Tomlinson, B. (2013b) Developing principled frameworks for materials development. In B. Tomlinson (ed.) *Developing Materials for Language Teaching* (pp. 95–118). London: Bloomsbury.

Tomlinson, B. (2016a) Achieving a match between SLA theory and materials development. In B. Tomlinson (ed.) *Second Language Research and Materials Development for Language Learning* (pp. 3–22). New York: Routledge.

Tomlinson, B. (2016b) Applying SLA principles to whole class activities. In B. Tomlinson (ed.) *Second Language Research and Materials Development for Language Learning* (pp. 33–49). New York: Routledge.

Tomlinson, B. (2016c) Current issues in the development of materials for learners of English as an international language (EIL). In W. Renandya and H.P. Widodo (eds) *English Language Teaching Today: Linking Theory and Practice* (pp. 53–66). Berlin: Springer.

Tomlinson, B. and Masuhara, H. (2004) Developing cultural awareness: Integrating culture into a language course. *Modern English Teacher* 13 (1), 5–11.

Tomlinson, B. and Avila, J. (2007a) Seeing and saying for yourself: The roles of audio-visual mental aids in language learning and use. In B. Tomlinson (ed.) *Language Acquisition and Development: Studies of First and Other Language Learners* (pp. 61–81). London: Continuum.

Tomlinson, B. and Avila, J. (2007b) Applications of the research into the roles of audio-visual mental aids for language teaching pedagogy. In B. Tomlinson (ed.) *Language Acquisition and Development: Studies of First and Other Language Learners* (pp. 82–89). London: Continuum.

Tomlinson, B. and Masuhara, H. (eds) (2010) *Research for Materials Development in Language Learning: Evidence of Best Practice*. London: Continuum.

Troncoso, C.R. (2010) The effects of language materials on the development of intercultural competence. In B. Tomlinson and H. Masuhara (eds) *Research for Materials Development for Language Learning: Evidence for Best Practice* (pp. 83–102). London: Continuum.

Wong, K. (2010) Peggy Seeger's 'Gonna Be an Engineer' – unofficial animation by Ken Wong. YouTube video, added by KenKYW [online]. See https://www.youtube.com/watch?v=qr8jFMXTioc (accessed 18 August 2016).

3 Addressing 'Super-Diversity' in the Language Classroom through Multilingual Films and Peer-Generated YouTube Content

Isabella Seeger

For many years, inter-European cultural and educational exchange has been the main aim of language curricula across Europe. However, due to recent global developments, European educational institutions have seen a rising influx of non-European learners with different motives for migrating and new goals in language learning, which represent a potential source of conflict in addition to enrichment in the classroom. While this new 'super-diversity' could be addressed within the four topic domains – personal, public, occupational and educational – suggested by the Common European Framework of Reference for Languages (CEFR), curriculum designers' and language teachers' personal experience and knowledge of migration are limited. This chapter discusses how topic-related films and student-created videos can be used in the language classroom to supplement curricular input. It presents some examples for the English as a foreign language (EFL) classroom – three multilingual films and two YouTube videos created by young migrants – to illustrate how these materials enhance plurilingual learning and intercultural language awareness, promote learner autonomy and involvement, and increase students' and teachers' insight into 'otherness' to enable teachers to address learners' needs and interests in an authentic way.

Introduction

For many years, language teaching in Europe has generally relied on the suggestions made by the Common European Framework of Reference for Languages (CEFR; Council of Europe, 2001). Its aim is to facilitate linguistic, cultural, educational and professional exchange throughout Europe while raising awareness of European cultural heritage and protecting and promoting that heritage (Council of Europe, 2001). This aim is currently being challenged by an ever-increasing influx of students from non-European countries, who bring to the classroom a variety of life experiences, perceptions and motives for language learning. The ethnic, cultural and linguistic differences found in some classrooms today make for a 'super-diversity' (Vertovec, 2007) that goes beyond any previous experiences or visions of European politicians, educationists, curriculum designers and teachers. This raises the question of the extent to which these stakeholders are prepared to appropriately address the needs of these changing target groups by introducing relevant topics and selecting and designing suitable materials to enhance plurilingual learning strategies, as suggested by the CEFR (Council of Europe, 2001).

According to the CEFR guidelines, topics in language teaching should be taken mainly from certain areas related to the students' personal, public, educational and occupational experiences and perspectives, which are called the 'four domains' (Council of Europe, 2001: 14). However, an analysis of current teaching materials used in secondary schools in Germany clearly shows some disparity between the topics presented in the standard teaching materials and the real-world experiences of discrimination, isolation and trauma among many students in 'super-diverse' classrooms, as described in sociological studies (e.g. Mansel & Hurrelmann, 1993; Reynolds, 2008). The number of teachers in Germany who share, or have reliable knowledge of, the real-world experiences of an increasing number of their students is limited. Another issue to consider is the fact that teachers can no longer rely on using their first language (L1) as a common basis to clarify difficult content or structures. This raises the questions of how the standard teaching materials may be supplemented with more authentic materials and how prepared teachers are to adapt to the evolution of target groups in terms of linguistic and cultural diversity and students' real-life experiences. Although most of the ideas presented below are applicable within various language contexts, this chapter focuses on English as a foreign language (EFL) as a mandatory subject in German schools. It discusses the following three main aspects:

(1) The enhancement of plurilingual learning strategies, as defined in the following section, and awareness of the role of English as a lingua franca.
(2) Learner involvement with regard to topic selection and materials design, in order to enhance authenticity, learner autonomy and motivation.
(3) Teachers' insight into their students' experiences, in order to enable them to address the four CEFR domains in an authentic way.

The first aspect will be addressed using multilingual films; that is, films featuring dialogue in two or more languages, giving three examples for different age groups. The second aspect will be approached through the introduction of student-generated YouTube videos chosen by the learners themselves. The third aspect is an outcome of the first two, as the joint exploration of these materials provides all participants – native and immigrant students and the teacher alike – with insights into the unfamiliar experiences and perceptions of others, for mutual growth.

Super-Diversity in the Language Classroom: Thinking Outside the Coursebook

Global political, technical and economic developments over the past 20 years or so have improved the accessibility of information and personal mobility. They have brought about an increasing eagerness to learn, move and exchange knowledge, not only within the boundaries of Europe but also in remote parts of the world where, for centuries, most of the population was isolated from the rest of the world. At the same time, and often caused by these developments, political, cultural and religious conflicts have developed in many areas of the planet. Despite technological progress and advances in know-how, the world has so far failed to prevent food crises. All of these factors motivate groups and individuals from distant countries to travel to Europe in order to broaden their minds, find employment, escape hunger or civil war, or join family members who have already arrived; thus, generally improving both their position and view in life. A substantial number of children and adolescents travelling alone reach Europe every year (according to BAMF [2016: 20], in Germany, the number of minors seeking asylum unaccompanied by an adult rose from 4,399 in 2014 to more than 14,400 in 2015; almost 85% of these came from non-European countries). Therefore, lately we have been observing an influx of non-European students into our classrooms, with a 'myriad of legal statuses' (Vertovec, 2007: 4) and a wide variety of life experiences shaped by the factors that pushed or pulled them to Europe. In addition, they have diverse levels of proficiency in different languages and various approaches to language learning. Thus, the classroom is becoming a melting pot of ethnicities, languages, cultures and religions, which naturally generates some tension with regard to a number of issues while also fostering opportunities for enrichment.

The diverse experiences of students coming to Europe for the reasons described above imply a number of linguistic and sociocultural issues. These concern the students' abilities and perceptions, their motivations for language learning, and cultural issues relating to classroom interaction among the students and between the students and their teacher. The students' previous experiences in language learning may differ considerably from the institutionalised language learning experience of most

European students. In addition to the fact that their levels of proficiency may vary greatly, language learning in their home country may have been entirely different from the CEFR concept of an interactive, communicative classroom. Furthermore, the main purposes of learning any of the foreign languages included in the local school curriculum – linguistic, cultural, educational and professional exchange – may be of limited relevance to these students, since their main priority will be to learn the language spoken in their new local environment. For example, despite the general usefulness of English as the lingua franca (and perhaps personal experience of this), a student having arrived in Germany may no longer be motivated to learn English (or continue their learning) because the perceived priority of learning German may be overwhelming. In a classroom of speakers with various mother tongues, language learning can no longer be facilitated through occasional use of the L1 by the teacher; although this is not encouraged in Germany, it is a much-used instrument in many foreign language classrooms.

Moreover, the impact of the multi-ethnic, multicultural influx on society and the emerging 'new complexities of cohesion' (Vertovec, 2007: 7) are naturally mirrored – and sometimes intensified – within the classroom (Reynolds, 2008). This may affect language learning. For example, social issues (such as ethnic, cultural, religious or political conflict in class), if not always openly acknowledged by schools, are a daily challenge for many teachers, as confirmed by my own experience of teaching secondary school students in Germany. In addition, many young immigrants, especially those with a history of traumatic experience, can be stressed or destabilised and they often suffer from low self-esteem (Beckmann & Metz, 1997; Deniz, 2004; Mansel & Hurrelmann, 1993). As will be shown later, none of these aspects are addressed by the standard language teaching syllabus, yet they affect the four CEFR domains. There is also evidence that learners' sense of identity and attitudes towards their peers may influence language learning (Gatbonton & Trofimovich, 2008).

However, super-diversity also offers possibilities for enrichment, mainly through opportunities to raise both linguistic and cultural awareness in all participants – native students, immigrant students and teachers. During their often long and winding travels to Europe, many students have used English (or other world languages) as a lingua franca and acquired additional languages, if only superficially; thus, they are likely to have developed plurilingual learning strategies, as promoted by the CEFR (Council of Europe, 2001). Canagarajah (2009: 7) describes these strategies as 'a highly fluid and variable form of language practice' in which the learner – intuitively rather than through institutionalised learning – develops different levels of competence in different languages according to the respective purposes for which these languages are used. In order to be able to communicate spontaneously in a foreign language, learners apply 'ad-hoc strategies' (Canagarajah, 2009: 18). In other words, they use all the linguistic and paralinguistic resources available to them; for example, detecting language similarities, code-switching, eliciting words from an interlocutor or using non-verbal means of communication, such as mime and gesture (Council of Europe, 2001). Notwithstanding the positive stance of the CEFR, most European language curricula and practitioners do not yet actively foster (and may even suppress) this language acquisition process that 'aims towards versatility and agility, not mastery and control' (Canagarajah, 2009: 18). Yet, the plurilingual abilities of immigrant students may increase linguistic and strategic awareness in students who have learned a foreign language in an isolated, institutionalised context only.

The potential causes of conflict in class may also become advantages and be channelled into positive discussion, intercultural awareness and increased class cohesion, in the spirit of the CEFR's guidelines: 'In an intercultural approach, it is a central objective of language education to promote the favourable development of the learner's whole personality and sense of identity in response to the enriching experience of otherness in language and culture' (Council of Europe, 2001: 1). A study conducted by Janmaat (2010) shows that, in Germany, school classes with a particularly high percentage of ethnic minorities share experiences and goals more readily and there is greater tolerance and cultural understanding of ethnic minorities than there is in less diverse schools, with the caveat that this result may depend on certain variables unique to Germany. However, Reynolds' (2008) study, carried out in British schools, also suggests that there may be more opportunities for classroom cohesion in multi-ethnic contexts than there are in bi-ethnic ones. Classroom discussion and argument, without focus on form, may in turn foster plurilingualism, especially in groups of learners with extremely varying levels of language proficiency.

The sociolinguistic and sociocultural aspects mentioned in this section are all highly relevant with regard to the selection of topics and materials related to the four CEFR domains. Therefore, it is necessary to analyse to what extent the changing target groups are reflected in the standard teaching materials. It has been observed in language teaching that coursebooks are 'a cost-effective way of providing the learner with security, system, progress and revision, whilst at the same time saving precious time and offering teachers the resources they need to base their lessons on' (Tomlinson, 2012: 158). At best, therefore, a coursebook facilitates teachers' tasks by giving them a structural foundation on which to build lessons and it may be extended or supplemented by other materials selected to address learners' specific needs and interests. At worst, teachers, especially less experienced ones, may be tempted to rely entirely on the coursebook, thereby delegating the responsibility for addressing specific classroom issues to the book designer's concepts, knowledge and

experience. While the coursebook may be a legitimate way of addressing various topics and linguistic structures in the course of an academic
year, there is the danger of neglecting opportunities to address specific
aspects that are crucial to language learning. Mishan (2005: 44) speaks of
'culture', 'currency' and 'challenge' ('the three Cs'), which, in the context
of this chapter, would provide insight into cultures that are relevant to
students in the class and the presentation and discussion of current events
and perceptions related to the four CEFR domains. At the same time,
teachers could tap into individual students' experiences of real-world
language use to enhance plurilingual learning in the classroom.

There is evidence of coursebooks around the world that include
various controversial topics from real-life experience (Tomlinson, 2012).
However, an analysis of current EFL coursebooks used in German secondary schools shows that none of the sociocultural issues mentioned
above, in particular with regard to the rising numbers of asylum seekers,
refugees and other groups with a non-European cultural background, is
focused on (Seeger, 2016). In the context of German secondary education, the highest percentages of students with a non-European background[1] are found in schools preparing students for vocational training
(Years 5–10) (Statistisches Bundesamt, 2015). Nevertheless, the small
range of approved coursebooks (for all school types) reflects what
Tomlinson (2012: 164) calls 'the publishers' taboo on inappropriate
topics and their insistence on discrete-item approaches'. The coursebooks for Years 5–7 do not feature any topics related to 'otherness',
and in Years 8–10 the topics related to migration and otherness – where
included – are almost always treated superficially and/or euphemised
(Seeger, 2016). This comes as no real surprise, since coursebook designers
are usually teachers and the number of teachers in German state schools
who have a migration background themselves is negligible. In the federal state of North Rhine-Westphalia, for example, where every third
15-year-old student has a history of migration, the current proportion of
foreign teachers is 0.6%, a large majority of whom are European (MSW,
2015); they are included in the estimated 1% of teachers with a history of
migration (Rotter, 2012). These small numbers can be linked to the fact
that the school types preparing students for higher education have by far
the lowest percentage of immigrant students (and, taking into account
recent developments, this percentage was even lower when today's teachers were students). Therefore 'the enriching experience of otherness in
language and culture' (Council of Europe, 2001: 1) postulated by the
CEFR is hardly enhanced by the curricular materials. Thirteen years ago,
Burwitz-Melzer (2003: 67) had already deplored that the language policy
of fostering and protecting European cultural heritage, which underlies
the national language curricula, actually limits intercultural awareness
and 'excludes non-European communities'. More recently, Tomlinson
(2012: 163) emphasised 'the need to help learners to personalise, localise

and make meaningful their experience of the target language, as well as the need for materials to be affectively engaging and cater for all learning style preferences'. In view of the steadily rising numbers of non-European students, with their complex linguistic, cultural and psychosocial backgrounds, this status quo calls for a shift from set coursebook topics and procedures to versatile materials that are tailored to the target groups and reflect the students' real-world experiences with regard to the four CEFR domains. The following section will, therefore, give examples of how multilingual films and peer-generated YouTube content may be exploited to address the issues and opportunities described above.

Otherness in Multilingual Films and Peer-Generated YouTube Content

The technical developments and globalisation mentioned before also effectively bring young learners' familiarity with media to an equal level across the globe. At the same time, filmmakers have begun to produce films that cannot be ascribed to only one language or culture and that present narrations of young people on the move and/or in search of their identity. For language teachers there is a 'treasure trove of films that deal with subjects like immigration, xenophobia, adjusting to a new culture, or the dilemmas faced when one belongs to two cultures' (Roell, 2010: 3). Moreover, it is no longer only professional film productions that we are presented with: owing to digitalisation, anyone can record a video and publish it on the internet via freely accessible platforms. For the purposes of this chapter, I will consider these materials authentic in line with Mishan's (2005) and Tomlinson's (2012) definitions of authenticity, since the materials were not produced for language learning and they enhance authentic classroom interaction. However, while film is authentic in terms of purpose and classroom opportunities, film content, settings and dialogues are at most quasi-authentic. Furthermore, as Mishan (2005) and Tomlinson (2012) note, the danger of presenting or reinforcing cultural stereotypes by showing a single full-length film has to be taken into account. YouTube videos, which are seldom scripted and mostly no more than a few minutes long, enable teachers to present a range of cultural aspects in an authentic way. Moreover, as I can say from personal experience, peer-generated content is apt to give a 'voice' to less proficient or minority students in class. It can also reduce classroom tension by detaching ethnic or cultural issues from the personal level and transporting them to a more general level of debate. Therefore, as will be shown in this chapter, both genres are suitable for the introduction of topics related to students' life experiences and for plurilingual learning activities that go beyond standard language learning procedures.

Under the Same Moon/La misma luna (Riggen, 2007) is a bilingual feature film (Spanish/English, available with English subtitles) about

Carlitos, a nine-year-old Mexican boy who lives with his grandmother while his mother, Rosario, works illegally in the USA. When Carlitos' grandmother dies, he sets out on his own to cross the border and find his mother in the USA. The film is suitable for Years 5–7 (CEFR competence levels A1–A1+) and features as its main themes illegal migration, separation, cultural variance and bilingualism. While one might object that these topics excessively challenge the intellectual and emotional capacities of 10- to 12-year-olds, it should be considered that some students in the class may in fact have had very similar experiences, notwithstanding their youth, as it is clear that the migrational developments previously described do not exclude younger age groups. An experienced teacher may use the film to inspire students to share such experiences in class. Furthermore, the generally optimistic tone of the film and its happy ending may help to mitigate any emotional shock.

The film offers various opportunities for interesting classroom activities that are apt to raise cultural and linguistic awareness and enhance language production, as described in detail in Table 3.1. Since for young learners, viewing a full-length film in two languages may be demanding, even with subtitles, one solution may be to use only short extracts and provide a simple plot summary that links these scenes, in order to avoid the decontextualisation raised by such pedagogy experts as Mishan (2005), Sherman (2003) and Thaler (2014). Even though most students of EFL may not understand any of the Spanish dialogue and (presumably) not much of the English, the visual support provided by actions and facial expressions will help them to understand roughly what is going on and 'give their best guesses, follow their hunches, endure ambiguity, and absorb the language input' (King, 2002: 2). This effort will develop their plurilingual competence and raise awareness of and empathy with those students in the class who are not proficient enough in either the L1 or second language (L2) to communicate without difficulty.

For older and more proficient students, the film *Welcome* (Lioret, 2009) is a good opportunity for plurilingual and pluricultural learning. I used it in Years 9 and 10, in which the majority of the students still had comparatively low levels of language competence (A1–A2+). The film tells the story of Bilal, a 16-year-old Kurdish refugee from Iraq who is stranded in Calais (France). Bilal wants to swim across the Channel to be reunited with his girlfriend in England and is supported by a French swimming instructor, Simon. The film presents the topics of asylum, illegal migration and separation with bleak realism (uncannily foreshadowing recent events at Calais), but it also expresses the dreams and hopes related to migration: real-life aspects that concern many students in super-diverse classrooms and reflect their experiences and perspectives in terms of the four CEFR domains. Being multilingual (French, English and Kurdish, with English subtitles), the film illustrates the use of English as a lingua franca and plurilingual communication strategies.

Table 3.1 Suggested activities using scenes from *Under the Same Moon/La misma luna*

Scene	Extract	Dur.	Topic-related aspects	Cultural aspects	Affective aspects	Linguistic aspects
Rosario and her friend cross the border illegally	00:00:29– 00:01:26	57 sec	• Danger incurred by illegal immigration and threat of deportation		• Fear of... ...discovery ... destruction of hope	
Rosario and Carlitos have breakfast at the same time	00:01:27– 00:04:10	4 min 43 sec		• Comparison of Mexican and American culture and standards of living • Preservation of culture by immigrants	• Separation of mother and son	*Language production:* Emotional language
Rosario phones Carlito	00:04:38– 00:08:20	3 min 42 sec		• Immigrant standard of living (public phone)	• Affection • Separation, loneliness	
Carlitos attempts to cross the border with the help of two American students	00:26:59– 00:31:36	4 min 37 sec	• Danger incurred by illegal immigration • Exposure to exploitation		• Fear of... ...discovery ...destruction of hope	*Language awareness:* Vital importance of being able to communicate in another language
Carlitos leaves the van	00:37:46– 00:38:30	44 sec	• Destitution		• Loneliness • Disorientation	
Carlitos at the Greyhound station	00:39:00– 00:41:00	2 min 00 sec	• Minority	• Transport in the USA	• Determination • Independence	*Language production:* Situational phrases *Language awareness:* Vital importance of being able to communicate in another language
The 'Migra' raid the greenhouse	00:52:52– 00:57:19	4 min 27 sec	• Necessity of working to survive • Treatment of illegal immigrants by the authorities	• Latino community and preservation of culture	• Fear of... ...discovery ...physical violence	*Language awareness:* Vital importance of being able to communicate plurilingually
Carlitos dreams of his mom	01:09:42– 01:10:35	53 sec			• Separation, loneliness • Courage, hope • Independence	

Figures 3.1, 3.2 and 3.3 show examples of these uses of communication strategies and propose ways of exploiting the scenes in a super-diverse classroom.

An anecdote from one of my classes may illustrate how observant these students become when deploying plurilingual strategies. Upon reading the script shown in Figure 3.3, which did not include the subtitles

Simon: You mean you want to go [to England] for a girl?	(1) After viewing the scene, some students act it out in class on the basis of prompts (keywords), speaking freely (not reciting). When a student has difficulties saying something in English, other verbal and non-verbal resources are encouraged (mime, facial expression, code-switching, dictionary, drawings, etc.) to enable successful communication.
Bilal: Yes. – Mina.	
Simon: Mina.	
Bilal: I met her three years ago. She's the sister of a friend of mine. A football friend. [takes out photo]	
Simon: Oh... She looks pretty. – She's very pretty.	
Bilal: Her father <u>works</u> in England for a long time. She got the visa six <u>month</u> ago.	
Simon: And she knows you're coming?	(2) After reviewing the scene and/or reading the script, the students replace the ***French phrases*** with plausible English ones, guessing from the visual/written context or comparing with other languages they might know.
Bilal: Yes. – But I <u>could not speak</u> to her since I left Iraq.	
Simon: [proffers his mobile phone] ***Vas-y, appelle.***	
Bilal: No, no, thank you.	
Simon: [nods affirmatively] ***Si, appelle.***	(3) The students find <u>non-standard English</u> in the script, discuss what might be standard language and 'correct' the non-standard language.
Bilal: No really. I <u>call</u> from the <u>cabin</u>.	

Figure 3.1 Scene from *Welcome* (Lioret, 2009: 0:50:01–0:51:18; my transcription)

First officer:	[reads aloud from passport] ***Kayani... K – A – i-grec – A – N – I... Bilal... Iraq.*** [Subtitled: Kayani... Bilal... Iraq.] ***Huit, douze, quatre-vingt onze.*** [Subtitled: December 8th, '91]	(4) Cf. 2 above. Non-L1 students are encouraged to replace the ***French phrases*** with expressions from their mother tongue; all languages can be collected on the board. Students discuss the meaning of the number on Bilal's hand, guessing from the information given in the subtitles.
Second officer:	[repeats] ***Huit, douze, quatre-vingt onze. Huit-cent douze.*** [writes '812' on Bilal's hand] [Subtitled: 812] [whistles, takes photo out of Bilal's wallet] ***C'est qui, ça?*** Girlfriend? [hands photo to third officer]	(5) The students speculate about how the scene might go on and write a dialogue in English.
Third officer:	***Ah, réponds, c'ta*** girlfriend?	(6) Cf. 1 above. With the help of the board list, the scene can also be acted out in various languages, according to the students' preferences and abilities.

Figure 3.2 Scene from *Welcome* (Lioret, 2009: 0:15:22–0:15:47; my transcription)

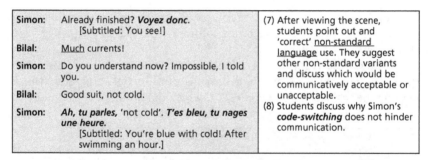

Simon:	Already finished? ***Voyez donc.*** [Subtitled: You see!]	(7) After viewing the scene, students point out and 'correct' <u>non-standard language</u> use. They suggest other non-standard variants and discuss which would be communicatively acceptable or unacceptable.
Bilal:	<u>Much</u> currents!	
Simon:	Do you understand now? Impossible, I told you.	
Bilal:	Good suit, not cold.	(8) Students discuss why Simon's **code-switching** does not hinder communication.
Simon:	***Ah, tu parles,*** 'not cold'. ***T'es bleu, tu nages une heure.*** [Subtitled: You're blue with cold! After swimming an hour.]	

Figure 3.3 Scene from *Welcome* (Lioret, 2009: 0:49:20–0:49:55; my transcription)

when used in class, a student who did not speak French asked if the French word *bleu* meant *blue* in English, partly because of the word similarity and partly because in her real life she automatically associated *swimming* and *cold* with *blue*. After watching these scenes, the students of all classes insisted on viewing the entire film, even though I told them that long stretches are in French – a language spoken by only a few students, and at a very low level. They were alerted to the fact that they would have to rely on the English subtitles, which represented a challenge for many students. It was surprising how much the students understood through non-verbal support. The film generated discussion in all classes, during which less confident students, who would not usually speak in class, also contributed, using compensation strategies (such as description or eliciting through L1) where necessary.

At a more advanced level of secondary education, it is even more possible to address the students' cognitive abilities in addition to their social and political interests. *The Other Son/Le Fils de l'autre* (Lévy, 2012) is a multilingual film using French, English, Hebrew and Arabic, with English subtitles available. Considering the complexity of its language and content and the age of its protagonists, the film is suitable for upper secondary students in Years 11–13 (competence levels B1–B2+). The Silbergs, a French-Jewish family living in Tel Aviv (where the father is a high-ranking army officer), and the Al-Bezaazes, a Palestinian family from the West Bank, find out that their respective 18-year-old sons, Joseph and Yacine, were switched at birth. It is probably easy to imagine the multifaceted problems and conflicts arising from this situation for everyone involved, and they are depicted fairly realistically.

Issues commonly found in multicultural classrooms, such as cultural and political conflict or the search for personal and religious identity, may be addressed through classroom discussion, and multilingualism through activities. To raise sociolinguistic awareness, for example, the students analyse an extract of the film (with the help of the script, if necessary) with regard to the speakers' purposes of using specific languages. A good example of this is the argument between the fathers, as shown in Figure 3.4. Despite the fact that his wife, Orith, has started the conversation in English, which so far has generally been used as the lingua franca, Alon Silberg almost immediately switches to French, one of his L1s, which he is aware the Al-Bezaaz family (their guests) are not very proficient in. However, when Saïd Al-Bezaaz replies in French, Alon abruptly switches to English, L2 to all; so in turn does Saïd. The conversation escalates into an argument until Saïd's wife, Leïla, stops him, to which he replies in Arabic, their L1, knowing that the Silbergs have only very basic knowledge of it. The students then analyse the entire film with regard to the different languages spoken by the individual characters, creating diagrams similar to the one presented in Figure 3.5. Thus, they can visualise the various possibilities of communication and interpret the purposes of the respective language use by the individual characters. On the basis of their diagrams, the students are expected to explore the following aspects:

- Virtual omnipresence of bilingualism/multilingualism.
- Virtual omnipresence of English as a lingua franca.
- Use of polite phrases in the interlocutor's language (otherwise unknown).
- Implications of the choice of a particular language to communicate with a particular person, and of changes in those choices.
- Acceptability of non-standard/incorrect language that does not affect communication.
- Role of non-verbal communication.

Characters	Spoken text	Subtitles	
Orith Silberg:	Joseph is an artist, he's a dreamer...		
Alon Silberg:	...Yes. *C'est un artiste, ce n'est pas un soldat. Au moins, il ne fera pas son service, c'est mieux comme ça.*	An artist, not a soldier. Thankfully he won't do his military service.	
Saïd Al-Bezaaz:	*Pourquoi ‹‹c'est mieux››? Parce qu'il est arabe?*	Why 'thankfully'? Because he's Arab?	
Alon Silberg:	Ah no, I mean it's hard to wait and to pray during three years that your kids stay alive. That's it.		
Saïd Al-Bezaaz:	Yeah. We also praying that our children stay alive.		
Alon Silberg:	Instead of praying, don't send your kids to the war.		**Language key:**
Saïd Al-Bezaaz:	Ha. A war. It's not a war. It's a destruction of a people.		English
Leïla Al-Bezaaz:	Saïd!		*French*
Saïd Al-Bezaaz:	<u>Anha alhqyqh.</u>	It's the truth.	<u>Arabic</u>

Figure 3.4 Example of multilingual dialogue in *The Other Son/Le Fils de l'autre* (Lévy, 2012: 00:53:54–00.54:40; my transcription)

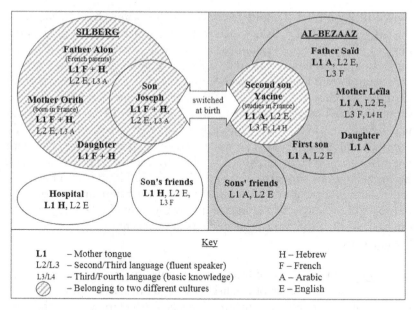

Figure 3.5 Multilingualism in *The Other Son/Le Fils de l'autre* (Lévy, 2012): Example of a diagram based on a film analysis

The analysis can then be linked back to the previously discussed aspects of the content, and the students can analyse how or to what extent individual language use influences the characters' attitudes and behaviour and vice versa. This approach not only increases the students' understanding of the significance of English as a lingua franca but also develops their insight into the plurilingual aim of using different languages at different levels of proficiency according to different purposes, as described by Canagarajah (2009) and mentioned above.

Student Productions on YouTube

Other suitable (if not necessarily multilingual) sources with which to address the needs and interests of super-diverse groups are student-created videos found online that deal with the authors' experiences of migration and/or otherness. Their main advantages over film are easy accessibility, constant availability, brevity and, most of all, authenticity in terms of the real-life experience of peers. Furthermore, due to the medium's huge popularity with students, it is easy to let the learners select the materials autonomously, thereby ensuring that the content is relevant and motivating (Lennon, 2008). Many videos are produced by teenagers or young adults and shared on open-access video platforms and social media (YouTube, Vimeo, Ooyala, Kaltura, Facebook and Instagram, to name just a few). Two examples from YouTube are briefly presented below.

Rap for Immigrants! (MinaLinda07, 2009), suggested by my Year 8 students (competence levels A1–A1+), is a one-minute American rap piece, written and performed by a teenage girl recording herself with her home computer. Despite the amateur quality, the production appealed to the class for two reasons: (1) it was considered to reflect the real-life experiences of many immigrant students in an authentic way; and (2) it features the type of informal, non-standard language encountered everywhere on the internet but never in coursebooks. An extract from the clip and the author's and viewers' comments used in the classroom (with a vocabulary list) are shown in Figure 3.6. Topics and student activities include the following.

- Analysing how immigrants are perceived by themselves and by others.
- Comparing these perceptions with individual perceptions and experiences in Germany.
- Discussing the author's and viewers' statements and finding out about the American Dream.
- Writing and 'posting' their own statement (on the classroom wall).
- Producing their own rap (optional).

Another excellent example of topic-related, student-created YouTube content is the three-minute slam poem *Migration: A Spoken Word Poem* (Naqvi aka Ready2Speak, 2012). Its content offers rich opportunities for the discussion of issues related to the four CEFR domains, such as ethnic and social identity, different concepts of 'home', cultural conflict and bilingualism. As the extract in Figure 3.7 shows, it also features

Figure 3.6 Extract, author's and viewers' comments on Rap for Immigrants! (MinaLinda07, 2009; my transcription)

> ...
> Yes, I'm an immigrant from a long line of immigrants. The feet of my ancestors constantly moved from the dusty desert of Arabia to the mountain ranges of Persia to the spacy heat of India and across the border, trying to heal scars of colonialism, to Pakistan.
>
> My plane ride to Vancouver was just another step. There are too many intricate connections and loyalties and histories and cultures and mixes of languages and colours to pin the hue of my skin to one land. ...

Figure 3.7 Extract from *Migration: A Spoken Word Poem* (Naqvi aka Ready2Speak, 2012; my transcription)

some very poetic and rhythmic language, which can be explored by more advanced students (competence levels B2–C1).

Conclusion

In view of the recent and current political, cultural and economic developments worldwide, it is to be expected that European classrooms will become increasingly diverse in the near future. This needs to be reflected in language teaching materials to address learners' real-world experiences in the sense of the CEFR and accept otherness as an essential topic in the language classroom. Since the standard materials in Germany do not provide many opportunities for teachers to address the issues and chances of super-diversity, other, more authentic materials 'which are designed to be flexible and to offer teachers and students opportunities for localisation, personalisation and choice' (Tomlinson, 2012: 158) can easily be integrated into the curriculum. This chapter has analysed several examples of multilingual film and peer-generated YouTube content for its suitability to supplement standard EFL materials in Germany. However, the underlying rationale may also be applicable within other language teaching contexts and in other countries, especially in Europe, where classrooms are becoming more and more multicultural and standard materials cover the related topics only insufficiently.

The films presented all offer rich opportunities for addressing topics that are specific to super-diverse classrooms, with cultural and linguistic exploitation being closely interrelated. On the one hand, the cultural and emotional aspects of film foster valuable classroom discussion and other authentic and awareness-raising activities; Roell (2010) lists many films that deal with empathy with foreigners, intercultural conflict, racism, stereotypes, etc. On the other hand, multilingual films are suitable for practising and enhancing plurilingual strategies, as suggested by the CEFR. However, to date, few multilingual films are available that are topic related and suitable for classroom use; among the few suitable ones are *Rabbit-Proof Fence* (aka *Long Walk Home*; Noyce, 2002), *Bend It Like Beckham* (Chadha, 2002) and *London River* (Bouchareb, 2009). Therefore, it is hoped that their range will increase quickly and that a special database for them will be established to facilitate the selection of materials.

As the examples presented in this chapter have demonstrated, popular online video platforms, such as YouTube, provide a range of entirely authentic topic-related materials, many of them created by students and some of excellent quality. Therefore, they provide an ideal source of materials that are adapted to students' needs, interests and motives. Their greatest advantage, apart from brevity and accessibility, is that students can be actively involved in the search for suitable materials; thus, they can be motivated to participate in classroom interaction and difficult topics can be discussed on a more impersonal level. In order to address the specific needs and interests of learners in a super-diverse classroom and recognise otherness as an enriching element, it would be desirable to integrate these topics and materials into the curriculum so that learners and teachers may explore cultural and linguistic aspects together. Such a classroom-orientated approach suggests a flexible, modular materials design with optional activities that can be easily adapted for use in a specific classroom and relieve the teacher of the additional workload. However, it would also be desirable for teachers in general to be trained to use (quasi-)authentic materials more and to enable and encourage learner involvement and autonomy with regard to selecting topics, materials and plurilingual learning strategies.

Note

(1) It is impossible to establish numbers for this category, since the multitude of official categories and criteria, such as 'foreign' vs 'immigrant', 'having dual nationality' and other legal statuses, are not represented within a single statistical overview of secondary school students. Students from Turkey and the Russian Federation are indiscriminately counted as Europeans, and German-born students with a different ethnic or cultural family background do not seem to be represented in recent statistics at all. However, even if limited to 'foreign' students, statistics give evidence of over-representation of non-European students at the school types mentioned.

References

BAMF (Bundesamt für Migration und Flüchtlinge [Federal Office of Migration and Refugees]) (ed.) (2016) *Das Bundesamt in Zahlen 2015. Asyl* [*The Federal Office in Numbers in 2015. Asylum*]. Nuremberg: BAMF.

Beckmann, H. and Metz, R. (1997) *Psychosoziale Befindlichkeit und Probleme der Betreuung von minderjährigen Flüchtlingen in Berlin/Projekt am Arbeitsbereich (1995–1997): Vorläufige Ergebnisse* [*Psychosocial State and Issues in the Care of Minor Refugees in Berlin/In-Work Project (1995–1997): Preliminary Results*]. Berlin: Freie Universität Berlin.

Bouchareb, R. (2009) *London River*. Multilingual film: English/French/Arabic. France: 3B Productions et al.

Burwitz-Melzer, E. (2003) *Allmähliche Annäherungen: fiktionale Texte im interkulturellen Fremdsprachenunterricht in der Sekundarstufe I* [*Gradual Approaches: Fictional Texts in the Intercultural Secondary Language Classroom*]. Tübingen: Narr.

Canagarajah, S. (2009) The plurilingual tradition and the English language in South Asia. *AILA Review* 22, 5–22.

Chadha, G. (2002) *Bend It Like Beckham*. Multilingual film: English/Punjabi/Hindi/German. United Kingdom: Kintop Pictures.

Council of Europe (2001) *Common European Framework of Reference for Languages: Learning, Teaching, Assessment*. Cambridge: Cambridge University Press.

Deniz, C. (2004) Interkulturelle Kompetenz in der Schulsozialarbeit [Intercultural competence in social work at schools]. In H. Bassarak, B. Eibeck and G. Schedel-Gschwendter (eds) *Schulsozialarbeit: Impulse für die Bildungsreform?[Social Work in Schools: Impulses for the Education Reform?*] (pp. 151–159). Frankfurt/Main: Gewerkschaft für Erziehung und Wissenschaft.

Gatbonton, E. and Trofimovich, P. (2008) The ethnic group affiliation and L2 proficiency link: Empirical evidence. *Language Awareness* 17 (3), 229–248.

Janmaat, J.G. (2010) *Classroom Diversity and its Relation to Tolerance, Trust and Participation in England, Sweden and Germany*. LLAKES Research Paper 4. London: Centre for Learning and Life Chances in Knowledge Economies and Societies.

King, J. (2002) Using DVD feature films in the EFL classroom. *Computer Assisted Language Learning* 15 (5), 509–523.

Lennon, P. (2008) Learner autonomy and teaching methodology. In S. Gramley and V. Gramley (eds) *Bielefeld Introduction to Applied Linguistics* (pp. 39–50). Bielefeld: Aisthesis.

Lévy, L. (2012) *The Other Son/Le Fils de l'autre*. Multilingual film: French/English/Hebrew/Arabic. France: Rapsodie Production.

Lioret, P. (2009) *Welcome*. Multilingual film: French/English/Kurdish. France: Mars Distribution.

Mansel, J. and Hurrelmann, K. (1993) Psychosoziale Befindlichkeit junger Ausländer in der Bundesrepublik Deutschland [The psychosocial state of young foreigners in the Federal Republic of Germany]. *Soziale Probleme* 3 (1), 167–192.

MinaLinda07 (2009) Rap for Immigrants!. YouTube video, added by MinaLinda07 [online]. See http://www.youtube.com/watch?v=q8sfvdcN0g8 (accessed 23 December 2015).

Mishan, F. (2005) *Designing Authenticity into Language Learning Materials*. Bristol: Intellect Books.

MSW (Ministerium für Schule und Wissenschaft des Landes Nordrhein-Westfalen [Department of Education and Science of the Federal State of North Rhine-Westphalia]) (ed.) (2015) *Das Schulwesen in NRW aus quantitativer Sicht 2014/15 [A Quantitative View of the School System in NRW 2014/15]*. Düsseldorf: MSW.

Naqvi aka Ready2Speak (2012) *Migration: A Spoken Word Poem*. YouTube video, added by Naqvi, Z., aka Ready2Speak [online]. See http://www.youtube.com/watch?v=airL cjPIizk (accessed 23 December 2015).

Noyce, P. (2002) *Rabbit-Proof Fence (aka Long Walk Home)*. Bilingual film: English/Aboriginal. Australia: Rumbalara Films, Rumbalara Films, Olsen Levy and Showtime Australia.

Reynolds, G. (2008) *The Impacts and Experiences of Migrant Children in UK Secondary Schools*. Working Paper No. 47. Brighton: University of Sussex/Sussex Centre for Migration Research.

Riggen, P. (2007) *Under the Same Moon/La misma luna*. Bilingual film: Spanish/English. USA: Fox Searchlight Pictures; Creando Films; Fidecine; Potomac Pictures; Weinstein Company.

Roell, C. (2010) Intercultural training with films. *English Teaching Forum* 2 (2010), 2–15.

Rotter, C. (2012) Lehrkräfte mit Migrationshintergrund. Individuelle Umgangsweisen mit bildungspolitischen Erwartungen [Teachers with a background of migration. Individual attitudes towards expectations in education policy]. *Zeitschrift für Pädagogik* 58 (2), 204–222.

Seeger, I. (2016) Migration in the curriculum and classroom diversity. In M. Hartner and M. Schulte (eds) *Migration in Context: Literature, Culture and Language* (pp. 101–120). Bielefeld: Aisthesis.

Sherman, J. (2003) *Using Authentic Video in the Language Classroom.* Cambridge: Cambridge University Press.

Statistisches Bundesamt [Federal Office of Statistics] (ed.) (2015) *Bildung und Kultur: Allgemeinbildende Schulen Schuljahr 2014/2015 [Education and Culture: Primary and Secondary Schools in the School Year 2014/2015].* Wiesbaden: Statistisches Bundesamt.

Thaler, E. (2014) *Teaching English with Films.* Paderborn: Schöningh.

Tomlinson, B. (2012) Materials development for language learning and teaching. *Language Teaching* 45 (2), 143–179.

Vertovec, S. (2007) *New Complexities of Cohesion in Britain: Super-Diversity, Transnationalism and Civil-Integration.* Wetherby: Communities and Local Government.

4 Playing the Part: Media Re-Enactments as Tools for Learning Second Languages

Anne-Laure Dubrac

Despite the fact that language is a manifestation of the moving body, the body is traditionally overlooked as an educational tool. How, then, can we introduce movement and rhythm into a field where students are (often actively) discouraged from linking body and mind? French anthropologist Marcel Jousse considered film to be a compelling pedagogical medium, because it demonstrates the constant interaction between speech and gestures. Taking inspiration from Jousse, I present a research study conducted with a group of French university students. After screening a clip from an English language film, participants were asked to re-enact and reinterpret it. The objective was to study the links between gestural action and language learning in order to measure the efficiency of re-enactment and task-based mimicry as academic tools.

Introduction

The research I wish to present in this chapter stems from two paradoxes within the French education system. First, despite the growing importance of the moving image in modern Western culture, it has yet to be fully incorporated into language acquisition curricula in France.

Outside the language classroom, the moving image is employed freely and diversely in online clips, film excerpts and television series. Cable television has made it possible to watch hundreds of channels in as many languages in the comfort of one's home. Furthermore, with the increased use of online resources in language teaching, students now have direct access to large numbers of films and television series in the foreign language they are studying. The development of streaming has increased the volume of original visual content that is created for the web. In short, the moving image has never been more ubiquitous. However, in French schools and universities, the belief that knowledge comes uniformly from the written word remains deeply ingrained (Lapaire, 2005). This paradox can be attributed to several factors. First, the lack of time devoted to oral skills can be attributed to the difficulty of implementing the necessary processes in large groups of students. Furthermore, the existing tools used to develop oral skills are woefully limited in scope and substance.[1] They often rely on listening and responding exercises, which require very little by way of significant comprehension.

The second paradox is related to the very nature of language. The French academic model teaches language as cold theory, ignoring its physical and corporeal aspects. In his book, *The Anthropology of Gesture*, Marcel Jousse ([1974] 2008) defines the human being as 'an inter-actional mimic'.[2] We make ourselves a mirror of the world around us and echo it in gestural interaction (Jousse, [1974] 2008: 66–67). For the anthropologist, human beings are, above all, re-enactors who catalogue the gestures and interactions that they see and then reuse them, combining them in original ways when communicating with others. In Jousse's view, mimicry is necessarily linked with rhythm, since the re-enacted gestures must obey the rhythm of the original movement being parroted. Hence, it is this act of playing out in a rhythmic fashion – this performance – that is the origin of all knowledge. As human beings, we need to reproduce what we observe; we can but play out. The act of playing (and replaying) has two significant effects: first, it facilitates the development of our own abilities, since, for Jousse ([1974] 2008: 62–63), to memorise consists of reproducing observed actions and gestures; second, it allows us to better understand the other,[3] and, as a result, to develop empathy. Therefore, it is perplexing that, even though gestures are part of social communication, bodily codes are traditionally overlooked at the expense of the mind. In Western education, as Bräuer (2002: x) underlines in *Body and Language*, '[w]hen seen as a phenomenon of the mind alone, learning is stripped of half of its medium and educational potential'.

Based on these findings, I propose that using film – because it inter-twines image, sound and movement – could better take into account an everyday, rather practical use of language. Because film dramatises the importance of body language in communication, it shows that conversation is a 'multimedia' process, since 'gestures used by speaker-hearers often play an important role in making what is being said more specific or providing additional features of meaning' (Kendon, 1997: 115). Jousse ([1974] 2008: 72) himself considers film to be a powerful medium, since it carries 'an interactional reality'. For Jousse, the dramatic mimodramas played out by actors on-screen offer viewers no choice but to re-enact them. However, he adds that because replaying is never a simple repetition but a personal and dynamic reaction, the re-enactment will always be different from the original filmic scene.

While Jousse's theories are compelling, it is useful to test his overall hypothesis in a real-life setting. Thus, during the first semester of the

2014–2015 academic year, I set up a research study in the Law Faculty of the University Paris-Est Créteil (UPEC). Twenty-six second-year law students took part in the study, which sought to incorporate film and 'verbal-gestural replaying' (Kendon, 2004) into the development of oral English. In other words, the participants were students who did not choose a linguistic discipline and whose levels of English were heterogeneous (from A2 to B2, Common European Framework of Reference for Languages) at the project's outset. To use Jousse's terms, I considered that the analysis of filmic interactions – especially interactions that everyone can relate to (e.g. situations of injustice, embarrassment or conflict) – may help students to develop their own gestural and verbal communication in English.

Screening an excerpt from Alfred Hitchcock's *The Wrong Man* (Hitchcock *et al.*, (1956 [2002])) and then asking the students to re-enact it, I considered the following questions:

(1) Did the students spontaneously engage in gestural and verbal mimicry of the characters on-screen, as Jousse would predict?
(2) Did the students feel more connected with the characters on-screen once they had 'played' them themselves?

In order to answer these questions, I used a theoretical framework that gave importance to the links between body, thought, action and learning. This aimed to establish whether Jousse's anthropological model could be corroborated with scientific research, specifically in the field of neuroscience.

Theoretical Framework

Although Jousse's ideas were developed in the first half of the 20th century, they are by no means obsolete. Indeed, several scientific researchers have recently endorsed his model. In their book, *The Embodied Mind: Cognitive Science and Human Experience*, Varela *et al.* (1991) show that cognition cannot transcend human embodiment. Varela *et al.* (1991: 149) assert: '[the expression of cognition and knowledge] depends on being in a world that is inseparable from our bodies, and our social history – in short, from our *embodiment*'. From this perspective, cognition is not considered to be solely a result of a series of cerebral functions; instead, it can be seen as the outcome of constant activity between the body and the environment. In other words, cognition depends on our body and emerges, or 'is enacted', as we interact with the living world. It is embedded in a biological, psychological and cultural context. Following Jousse, who believes that we know things only as we play them out, Varela *et al.* (1991: 71–72) highlight that the body constitutes and generates knowledge: '[t]he mind is not in the head'.

The neuroscientific work of Rizzolatti corroborates Jousse's model, especially his assertion that film is a compelling pedagogical medium. Rizzolatti's theory of mirror neurons stresses that when we watch someone perform an action, the very same neurons are activated in our brains, as if we were performing the said action. Our cells are designed in such a way that they can interact with those of our partner. For example, when we see somebody on-screen or onstage experiencing powerful emotions – notably, anger or despair – we feel those very stirrings rise in us. As Rizzolatti and Sinigaglia (2008: xii) suggest, 'the perception of pain or grief, or disgust experienced by others, activates the same areas of the cerebral cortex that are involved when we experience these emotions ourselves'.

Rizzolatti and Sinigaglia, like Jousse, stress that the act of mimicry constitutes a very powerful mechanism of communication, since our neurons instinctively imitate those of the person we are observing. In other words, viewing is never completely passive. Furthermore, they show that human beings are not made to learn, feel or act in a vacuum, since 'the bond that ties us to others ... is strong and deeply rooted' (Rizzolatti & Sinigaglia, 2008: xii). In sum, all the scientists cited further the belief that we are organically 'built' to place ourselves into the feeling and thinking of others. This ability to experience someone else's vantage point while consciously remaining ourselves is what researchers define as empathy, whether they are in the field of neuroscience (Decety & Sommerville, 2003; Thirioux & Berthoz, 2010), education (Aden, 2010) or theatre (Blair, 2008).

Thus, the ability to speak is not what comes first. Another neuroscientist, Berthoz (1997: 7), expresses a similar idea by replacing the well-known biblical quotation 'in the beginning was the word' with the statement 'in the beginning was action'. For him, action generates thought and speech (and not the other way around) because 'the origin of thought springs from the need to move', with the act of movement being 'the principal faculty of life' (Berthoz, 2009: 24). In keeping with Jousse, Berthoz believes that a person is by nature a 'situational being' who never stops interacting with the exterior world. Indeed, the human understanding of self and recognition of the outside world are far from dialectical poles: by mapping the world in terms of obstacles and objectives, the two are very much the same.

As a result, the field of neuroscience offers us an original approach that confirms Jousse's anthropological theory. Neuroscience stresses that knowledge is not just a nebulous reflection of the external world; instead, it is the continuing resonance of internal sensation, shaped by our bodies and brains. Applying that to a practical pedagogical model, the drive to downplay gestures and action seems to be all the more misguided. Bodies, and the students who are in command of them, do not need to be idle in order to learn. Furthermore, in keeping with the theory of mirror neurons (Rizzolatti & Sinigaglia, 2008), film seems to be a relevant medium to prompt this kind of understanding, since it requires students to change their point of view and see themselves as another.

Practical Implementation in the Law Faculty

The study ran over a period of 10 weeks, with one 90-minute session per week. Since it lasted for 15 hours only, it was a qualitative study. The task and its aims were announced at the beginning of the semester: students were to analyse a three-minute excerpt from *The Wrong Man* and then create their own interpretation of the scene. It was hoped that they would put themselves in the characters' shoes and adopt an empathetic attitude.

The choice of extract was driven by two objectives. First, I needed an extract that highlighted the physical nature of communication. Then, based on the neuroscientific belief that imitation is a powerful mechanism for communication, I sought a scene in which gestures and emotions were ostentatious rather than subtle. The thinking behind this was that it would be easier for students to (re)interpret such a passage. The excerpt I selected meets these two requirements: it stresses the importance of non-verbal communication, since only a few lines are uttered; and it shows the deep connections that exist between body, feelings, thoughts and language. Indeed, the scene depicts a misunderstanding that is fuelled by fear, which leads three insurance clerks to mistake an innocent man, Manny Balestrero, for a robber. In the excerpt, we see Manny from the clerks' viewpoint only. He is seen behind the bars of a counter, dressed in black, with his face hidden by a hat and his hand reaching into his coat. The clerks think that he is about to pull out a gun and immediately perceive him as a criminal; however, Manny is simply reaching for his insurance policy. The clerks are so afraid of Manny that either they do not dare to look at him or they are unable to see him objectively. They breathe loudly and hold on to each other, as if to give each other strength.

After the clip was screened, the students were given several weeks to form groups and conduct the preparation work. The performances took place during the fifth session. Students video-recorded their own interpretations of the scene. Afterwards, they were given the video of their performance and asked to analyse their speech and poise. The students were encouraged to identify specific areas where they could improve upon specific language points. Once those needs were identified, two constructive methods were suggested to help them better master various phonological and grammatical concepts:

- The use of new media technology. For instance, participants could check the meaning or pronunciation of words using websites, such as The Free Dictionary (http://www.thefreedictionary.com) or Cambridge Dictionary (http://dictionary.cambridge.org). They could

also record their speech using Audacity software to make sure their delivery was fluid and intelligible. Finally, they were encouraged to use Eprel-Langues to tackle grammatical and lexical problems. Eprel-Langues is a self-training platform that offers pedagogical activities (newspaper articles, film clips, conversation simulations and practical/real-life tasks) to students who wish to deal with specific language difficulties.
- The use of the physical form.

Physicality as Communication

Lapaire (2002), following Jousse, argues that body postures can express an infinite number of grammatical principles:

> Yes, English syntax could be understood imaginatively, through metaphor, image schemata and narrative. Yes, abstract – and often elusive – grammatical meaning could be grasped through the senses. ... As the central organizing principle in verbal communication, it had an experiential and interactional grounding. I would [thus] allow young learners to 'grasp', 'feel' or 'see' the syntax of English and refer to sociocultural frames in the presentation of highly technical aspects of English grammar (e.g., auxiliaries as 'helpers'; 'verbal affixes' as 'garments' donned by the base, etc.). (Lapaire, 2002: 624)

For example, to illustrate and visualise the uncertainty that is usually associated with the modal forms *might* and *may*, Lapaire encourages students to transfer the balance of their whole body from one side to the other, while wearing an inquisitive expression. To signify past tense use, often implying a moment of retrospection, he suggests a stance where the chest faces forward and the head cranes backward as if looking at something behind them. In the same way, to explore the use of the superlative form (which students often confuse with the comparative form), learners can extend their body to its limit, with their hands rising as high as possible and their heels as elevated as can be, so as to occupy every available unit of space.

The students used Lapaire's physio-gestural model to address their language needs, and they came back with very imaginative ideas. For instance, to understand the use of the zero article (Ø *happiness*, Ø *you liar*), they stood with their hands open in front of them, as if gazing upon the notion mentioned. In addition, to perceive the pressure implied by the use of *must*, a participant placed his hand on his partner's shoulder and shook it, exerting force on him. A similar approach was used to deal with phonological needs. For example, most of the students tended to omit the pronunciation of [h] and [s]. One of them had the idea of blowing into the palm of his hand when he was uttering [h] and exaggeratedly smiling from ear to ear (a Cheshire Cat grin) when using the sound [s] at the end

> I **think** the **man** at the **window** (the student points towards Manny) is the **man** (his voice starts trembling) who was here **before**.
>
> Could you **wait** a **minute** (lowering his index finger parallel to his thumb, he illustrates a small quantity) while I **check** on **something**? (He pretends to check something on an imaginary piece of paper.)

Figure 4.1 Spatial activity imagined to improve fluency

of a noun or verb. Finally, to improve the fluency of their speech, some participants decided to take sentences that they had previously found difficult and repeat them while including movements and related gestures. In the example shown in Figure 4.1, a student associated sections of his speech with specific gestures and tones of voice. He indicated in bold the words that he wanted to stress.

Finally, students were asked to perform their work again. The comparison between the two video-recorded performances was intended to help us assess whether or not there was some improvement.

Post-implementation Analysis

The aim of the study was to assess how film can be used as a tool to stimulate and develop language learning. Confirming Jousse's predictions, the students seem to have spontaneously engaged in gestural and verbal mimicry of the characters on-screen. In their performances, some groups chose to imitate the film clip while adding bits and pieces of their own. While appropriating certain items, they also made their own imprint. In Figure 4.2, the elements in bold have been added by the participants.

Each student made a unique gestural and verbal contribution when giving his or her re-enactment. The participants showed the employees' bias in different ways. For example, they spatially isolated Manny, putting a chair or table between him and them, as in Figure 4.2. They made a point never to look at him, hiding themselves behind their colleagues' shoulders, as if catching a glimpse of him represented danger. In most of the performances, the students decided to emphasise the clerks' sense

> S1 is dressed in a black coat and hat. We can hardly see his face. S2 is sitting at a desk behind a laptop. When S1 enters the room, S2 is filling in a document.
>
> S1: **Good morning, Madam.** I wonder if you'd look at this policy and tell me how much money we can borrow on it. *S1 slowly pulls out an insurance policy from his coat. S2 stares at him worried, wondering what S1 is reaching for.*
>
> S2: Rose Balestrero?
>
> S1: Yes. That's my wife.
>
> S2: **I need to check something.** Could you wait a minute **while I ask a question to one of my co-workers?**
>
> S1: Yes, but hurry up. **I have an appointment with my wife.**

Figure 4.2 Example from one group's second performance

of fear via gestures, facial mimicry and added dialogue (e.g. 'Oh, my God', 'Peggy', 'Can I hold on to you? I don't want to faint', 'How could he come back to the exact place where he committed a robbery?'). In the re-enactments, Manny becomes a more assertive character than in Hitchcock's film. He hails the clerks because he wants to get his insurance policy back and meet up with his wife. Other groups used the excerpt as a springboard and invented a follow-up scene. In one performance, Manny comes back the following day and asks for a loan again; in another, the clerks go to the police station to inform the officers that they have identified their robber.

The participants reused specific gestures and expressions from The Wrong Man, especially the most suggestive ones. They exaggerated the clerk's look of worry when she thinks that Manny is about to pull out a gun. They also gave significance to the spatial contrast between Manny (isolated on one side of the bars) and the clerks (huddled close together on the other side). Hence, the students did behave as mimics, since they all engaged in the playing and replaying of the scene. No single re-enactment was a mere repetition of the original scene; each was an original answer to the mimodramas they had watched on-screen. To paraphrase the philosopher Guérin (2011: 21), their gestures were an 'invention, an illumination of their bodies', even though they relied on a similar base: the film excerpt.

It is worth noting that for many of the students, engaging in gestural and verbal mimicry was not initially a spontaneous activity. Four students were even strongly reluctant to play a role in front of an audience. In their first video-recorded work, half of the participants were uncomfortable performing in English; several stood in a stiff and unnatural manner, looking at the ceiling instead of interacting with their group, while others fidgeted. They had learned their lines by heart, which, of course, did not follow Jousse's law of rhythmo-mimicry: their speech was not rhythmic at all but choppy, toneless and flat. It was only during the rehearsal sessions between the two filmed sequences that students became aware that using the body could help them convey their message and explore the rhythm of the English language. Subsequently, the few reluctant students relaxed and embraced the spirit of the activity. They were not used to being active and to using physicality in class.

As far as the development of empathy is concerned, the participants stated in a survey conducted at the end of the project that putting themselves in somebody else's shoes had required them to adapt to their character's way of thinking. The task had triggered questions and reactions; for example, why did the clerks think Manny was about to pull out a gun? How did they feel when they thought the man in front of them was the one who had robbed them before? Did they re-experience their trauma? Why did none of the clerks realise that they were being misled by fear? One participant commented that when he watched the scene for the first time, he found it neither believable nor realistic. How could the clerks be terrified of a man who seemed so sweet and polite, especially since they were separated by the protective bars of the counter? However, when he re-enacted the scene, the student found that he experienced the ordeal through the eyes of his character.

Therefore, according to the students' comments, imitation is one of the paths to empathy (Iacoboni, 2009). Even if some of the participants asserted that they did not spontaneously relate to the characters they observed on-screen, they all acknowledged that acting helped them to bond with the characters. The conscious imaginative placing of themselves into the other's perception led them to recognise their intentions and, consequently, to develop their empathetic ability.

The empathy activity allowed students to improve their understanding of specific plot elements in order to appreciate the film better. However, how can a more finely tuned sense of empathy, when engaging with a text in a different language, allow viewers to make a real improvement to their language skills? As emphasised earlier, to understand, communicate with and act with a partner means adapting to what that partner thinks and feels, while remaining self-possessed.[4] To engage with someone inherently other, a level of distance and control needs to be maintained, curbing emotional extremes at both ends and avoiding contempt and blind fascination. If we wish to divorce the 'strange' from the stranger, any language curriculum should emphasise the development of empathy.

Conclusion

The experiment conducted with language students confirmed the research hypothesis presented in the introduction: the analysis and re-enactment of filmic interactions can help learners improve their own gestural and verbal communication in English. Indeed, all the participants incorporated vocabulary and gestures from the film clip into their performances. Like the characters, they used short sentences and suggestive gestures to convey emotions and make an impression on the audience. Using their physicality also enabled them to study various grammatical and phonological concepts. However, this study offers only hints about the method's full potential. Learning is a long and complex process, and 15 hours is not enough time to draw definitive conclusions.

Going forward, and with the desire to conduct further studies, I have established a few guidelines for bringing film into the classroom. First, it is important to choose a film excerpt in which the vocabulary and context are not too far removed from the students' areas of interest so that they can more quickly project themselves and envision their performance. Second, screening a scene that contains ambiguous perceptions and contrasting emotions may trigger reactions and help students to understand that culture is not fixed but 'continually recreated' (Bruner, 1986: 130). It may also enable students to understand the importance of non-verbal cues in communication and perhaps use these cues to grasp cultural and linguistic notions. Finally, working with small groups of students is essential. Indeed, participants, especially when they are not used to this kind of classroom activity, need to be constantly reassured. Some are afraid of being videoed in front of their peers and some find it very difficult to assess their language needs; as a result, the teacher or tutor plays a crucial role in guiding them in their learning process. This activity requires an initial investment of time and energy from students and teacher, but it may yield highly positive results once that hurdle has been overcome. If the group is kept intact, it is likely that the activity will become more efficient with each subsequent implementation.

Notes

(1) Very often, French universities only provide old television sets, which teachers have to book in advance and are difficult to move from one classroom to another.
(2) All translations are mine unless indicated.
(3) By 'other', I mean someone who is different from oneself (culturally, linguistically, geographically or professionally) and, thus, with whom communication and understanding may be problematic.
(4) Berthoz and Jorland (2004: 266) call this displacement 'a change in point of feeling', since it requires a shift in perspective that is not geared towards oneself but towards another. Thus, it would seem relevant to consider empathy as an active skill in itself.

References

Aden, J. (2010) *An Intercultural Meeting through Applied Theatre*. Berlin: Schibri-Verlag.
Berthoz, A. (1997) *Le sens du mouvement*. Paris: Odile Jacob.
Berthoz, A. (2009) *La simplexité*. Paris: Odile Jacob.
Berthoz, A. and Jorland, G. (2004) *L'empathie*. Paris: Odile Jacob.
Blair, R. (2008) *The Actor, Image, and Action: Acting and Cognitive Meuroscince*. New York: Routledge.
Bräuer, G. (2002) *Body and Language, Intercultural Learning through Drama*. Westport, CT: Ablex Publishing.
Bruner, J. (1986) *Actual Minds, Possible Worlds*. Cambridge, MA: Harvard University Press.
Decety, J and Sommerville, A. (2003) Shared representations between self and other: A social cognitive neuroscience view. *Trend in Cognitive Sciences* 7 (12), 527–533.
Guérin, M. (2011) *Philosophie du geste*. Paris: Actes Sud.
Hitchcock, A., Anderson, M.L. and MacPhail, A. (1956 [2002]) *The Wrong Man* (PAL, DVD). USA: Warner Home Video.
Iacoboni, M. (2009) Imitation, empathy and mirror neurons. *Annual Review of Psychology* 60, 653–670.
Jousse, M. ([1974] 2008) *L'Anthropologie du geste*. Paris: Gallimard (original work published 1974).
Kendon, A. (1997) Gestures. *Annual Review of Anthropology* 26, 109–128.
Kendon, A. (2004) *Gesture: Visible Action as Utterance*. Cambridge: Cambridge University Press.
Lapaire, J.R. (2002) Imaginative grammar. *Cognitive Linguistics Today* 6, 623–642.

Lapaire, J.R. (2005) *La grammaire en mouvement*. Paris: Hachette Education.
Rizzolatti, G. and Sinigaglia, C. (2008) *Mirrors in the Brain: How Our Minds Share Actions, Emotions and Experience*. New York: Oxford University Press.
Thirioux, B. and Berthoz, A. (2010) Phenomenology and physiology of empathy and sympathy: How intersubjectivity is the correlate of objectivity. In J. Aden, T. Grimshaw and H. Penz (eds) *Teaching, Language and Culture in an Era of Complexity: Interdisciplinary Approaches for an Interrelated World* (pp. 45–60). Brussels: Peter Lang.
Varela, F., Thompson, E. and Rosch, E. (1991) *The Embodied Mind. Cognitive Science and Human Experience*. Cambridge, MA: MIT Press.

Part 3
Audiovisual Translation and Subtitling

5 Captioned Video, Vocabulary and Visual Prompts: An Exploratory Study

Melissa Cokely and Carmen Muñoz

This chapter presents an exploratory study that aimed to investigate whether viewing captioned videos promotes vocabulary learning. It evaluates the potential of two types of post-viewing interactive tasks (i.e. with and without visual prompts). In addition, it provides some insight into learners' progression from exposure to new language through video to productive language use. Learners of English at the B1/B2 proficiency level according to the Common European Framework of Reference for Languages (Council of Europe, 2001) carried out a speaking task in which they summarised the plot of an episode of the television series *I Love Lucy* (1951). The results show that participants learned the target words that appeared in the episode and maintained their learning over time. Qualitative analysis of the oral data shows that participants were able to use previously unknown target words in the post-viewing tasks with varying degrees of success.

Introduction

Watching films and television series with audio in their original language (rather than dubbed into the local language) was once only possible by going to specialised cinemas or purchasing DVDs. However, as media, particularly in the English language, has become more widely available on the internet through streaming and downloading, more and more people are being exposed to English content in this way. This fairly recent phenomenon is likely to have some positive effects on language proficiency in countries where mainstream media is usually dubbed rather than subtitled, as is the case in Spain at the time of writing. However, the question remains as to how best to exploit this type of input in the classroom in order to maximise learners' opportunities to notice gaps in their knowledge and learn new language.

The general aim of the exploratory study presented in this chapter is to investigate whether viewing captioned videos in the foreign language classroom promotes vocabulary learning. A second, more specific aim of the study is to evaluate the potential of two types of post-viewing interactive tasks: with visual prompts and without visual prompts. The study also aims to gain insight into how learners progress from exposure to new language through video to productive language use. Finally, the study has a pedagogical aim, which is concerned with the exploitation of captioned video in the foreign language classroom.

Background

The effectiveness of captioned video as a tool for vocabulary acquisition has been well researched and has been shown to have advantages over several other input modalities (for an overview, see Montero Perez *et al.*'s [2013] meta-analysis of 18 studies). For example, Neuman and Koskinen (1992) found that seventh and eighth graders who watched a science programme with captions outperformed those who watched the video without captions, read the textbook with audio or read the textbook only (control) in terms of word knowledge and information recall. Montero Perez *et al.* (2014) concluded that groups of Flemish undergraduates watching short clips of French videos with captions performed better than the control group on measures of form recognition. Sydorenko (2010) looked at learners of Russian and found that the group watching videos with captions and audio outperformed the other groups on translation, although the group that watched videos without captions did better than the other groups on aural recognition of form.

Thus far, the majority of the research on vocabulary acquisition and video has focused mainly on incidental learning (e.g. Baltova, 1999; Rodgers, 2013; Winke *et al.*, 2010). Nonetheless, as it has been asserted that conscientiousness does appear to be helpful for acquiring language while viewing videos (Vanderplank, 2013), it would follow that intentional learning should be researched further in order to examine the effects that a more cognisant language focus may have on acquisition. Two examples of research on intentional vocabulary learning through video are the following case studies of individual learners who were asked to use reverse subtitles in an attempt to intentionally increase their target language vocabulary. Milton (2008) reported on a participant who watched videos of an English language television series subtitled in Greek, while Garnier (2013) analysed the vocabulary uptake of an English native speaker learning French who watched the animated film *Toy Story 3* in English with French subtitles every week for two months. Testing revealed that participants in both studies showed substantial increases in vocabulary after doing these activities. Montero Perez *et al.*'s (2015) recent eye-tracking study also compared incidental and intentional language learning through watching videos. The group that was informed that target words would be tested (intentional) outperformed the group that was not informed (incidental). However, as Montero Perez *et al.* (2015: 322) point out, learners must infer the meaning of the target words while viewing, a process that the authors describe as 'slow and often unsuccessful'. To the best of our knowledge, the combination of intentional learning and pre-viewing tasks that provide participants with the meaning of the target words has not been explored to date.

According to the comprehensible input hypothesis (Krashen, 1981), viewing videos with captions is a valid method of providing input to learners of a second language (L2). The comprehensible input hypothesis states that language learners require comprehensible input that is slightly more advanced than their present level in order to progress in the acquisition process (Krashen, 1981). To benefit from such input, learners need to be adequately prepared and in the case of auditory input, the level of input needs to be appropriate to the learners' level of proficiency in order to help them to visualise it (Danan, 2004). Furthermore, captioned videos provide a valuable learning experience, as learners receive verbal input from the audio and written input from the captions at the same time. Bimodal input, with sound and text reinforcing each other, has been shown to result in better recall (Bird & Williams, 2002; Holobow *et al.*, 1984). This confirms the dual coding principle (Paivio, 1986), which explains that the activation of visual images and verbal information enhances L2 learning.

While videos with captions may act as a rich source of input, it is also worth considering the role of productive language use in a teaching intervention based on captioned videos. In fact, current teaching approaches place strong emphasis on output and interaction (Savignon, 2003). The comprehensible output hypothesis (Swain, 1985; Swain & Lapkin, 1995) states that when learners produce output they sometimes become aware of gaps in their linguistic knowledge and take the necessary steps to fill those gaps. Doughty and Williams (1998) also affirm that learners' noticing a 'hole' in their linguistic knowledge is what leads to language learning. De la Fuente (2002) found that learners of Spanish who had to produce target words ('pushed output') in an interaction performed better than learners who received input only in terms of receptive and productive acquisition and productive word retention.

Finally, a key component in acquiring new vocabulary through video is reported by learners to be the association of words with visual images (Sydorenko, 2010). However, further research is necessary to determine what effect visual prompts from videos may have on the recall and production of vocabulary. Likewise, it is generally accepted that using visual prompts makes speaking tasks easier (Iwashita *et al.*, 2001). However, there is a scarcity of research on the role that visual prompts may play in helping participants to recall specific vocabulary from the video input and subsequently produce it.

Research on vocabulary acquisition through captioned video has mainly focused on incidental learning and almost exclusively on contexts in which learners are expected to infer word meaning from input. Exceptions are studies involving smart subtitles, where learners have access to word translations on demand (e.g. Kovacs & Miller, 2014). In contrast, outcomes of intentional learning situations, in which participants are explicitly taught the meanings of the target words before viewing the video, are under-researched. In such situations, the burden of inferring meaning is reduced for learners and the video input, in the case of the target words, serves as reinforcement and contextualisation.

The present study attempts to make a contribution in this area by (1) engaging learners in intentional learning, in which participants are explicitly taught the meaning of the target words before viewing the videos; (2) examining the potential relationship between visual aids in video and vocabulary recall; and (3) exploring opportunities for using video in the language classroom to encourage oral production.

Consequently, the first research question of this study is concerned with whether viewing captioned videos, accompanied by a pre-viewing preparatory task and a post-viewing interactive task, promotes vocabulary learning. The issue of whether those gains are maintained over time is also analysed. The second research question inquires whether post-viewing speaking tasks with and without visual prompts yield different results in vocabulary uptake. The final question asks about the extent to which participants use target words that were previously unknown in a post-viewing speaking task.

The Study

Participants

The participants ($n = 20$) were undergraduate students studying design in Barcelona, Spain. This chapter reports only on participants who completed all measures (pre-test, delayed post-test 1 and delayed post-test 2) for both sessions. This left 14 participants (12 female and 2 male) with a median age of 22 and a mean age of 23.5. The participants were all Spanish-Catalan natives who were enrolled on courses in English as a foreign language to fulfil the language proficiency requirement of their degree. Students' level of proficiency in English was B1/B2 according to the Common European Framework of References for Languages (Council of Europe, 2001).

Materials

The television show chosen for this study was *I Love Lucy* (1951), an American situation comedy from the 1950s. This series was chosen for several reasons. First, the pace and diction of the actors are slow and clear, particularly in comparison with current television programmes, and the use of colloquialisms is fairly limited. As this study is focused on vocabulary uptake and oral production rather than comprehension, the ease with which participants could understand the videos was of great importance so as not to impede their ability to perform the tasks. Additionally, none of the participants had seen any episodes of *I Love Lucy* outside class; this was an advantage because there were no effects due to previous exposure. Finally, as part of the piloting process before data collection, participants were shown several different television programmes and asked for feedback on how much they enjoyed and understood each one. *I Love Lucy* was consistently rated higher than other shows in both areas by most students. The four episodes used ('The Freezer', 'Lucy's Schedule', 'The Lease' and 'Lucy Fakes an Illness') were approximately 23 minutes long, contained between 2629 and 3144 words and had lexical densities of between 21.09 and 24.19, as measured by the text analyser function available from www.online-utility.org.

For each episode screened, 13 target words and phrases were selected (Table 5.1). The target words were selected according to how useful they were believed to be in recounting the plot of the episode, how frequently they appeared and how salient and/or memorable they were in the episode. The objective was to select vocabulary with varying degrees of each of these characteristics in order to explore the relationship between the characteristics and participant uptake. For example, in one episode the target word *freezer* is crucial (because the plot centred around a large freezer) and frequently used (20 occurrences). Conversely, in the same episode, the word *crowbar* occurs only once and is only somewhat salient (because a crowbar appears on the screen for a short time only).

A pre-teaching worksheet was developed for use after the pre-test and before participants viewed the video. The participants were given a list of 13 target words in context along with 13 definitions and were asked to match the definitions with the correct words (see Appendix 1).

Table 5.1 Target word use

Group A: Video 1	Group B: Video 2	Group A: Video 3	Group B: Video 4
cut down	**landlord**	dear (person)	acts (noun)
furnace	tenants	**trained seal**	make it up
butcher	**complain**	put on	keep from being
wholesale	lousy	**on time**	humour (verb)
crowbar	**dripping**	schedule	**faking**
locked in	can't stand	**to run** (a business)	ad
bargain	**pipe**	attaboy	play a trick
side of beef	hold to	**defrosting**	no such thing
pounds (lbs.)	**lease (noun)**	**biscuits (USA)**	**light bulb**
freezer	**kick out**	backwards	**show business**
a cut (of meat)	noise	how do you do?	**pretend**
stand still	pack (verb)	left over	**a complex**
stall (verb)	**month's rent**	stick to	childlike

In accordance with the pedagogic aim of this study, an oral narrative activity was chosen based on an observation of a spontaneous conversation that took place between students earlier in the year. One student was absent from class on the day of a video viewing. As the class was continuing with a discussion about the video during the next lesson, the rest of the class spontaneously provided an oral summary for the student who had been absent so that she could participate in the discussion. During this summary, several students made an effort to use specific vocabulary that had been covered in class for the purpose of watching the video. Thus, it was noted that oral summaries of videos may be a rich source of data for determining the extent and nature of learning that takes place during video viewing. The post-viewing task consisted of each participant working in a pair with another participant who had seen a different video. The participants took turns to summarise the plots of the videos they had watched. This task was repeated twice – first using stills from the videos as visual support for the narrative (see Appendix 2), and second with no visual aids.

Procedure

As the post-viewing task consisted of participants giving their partner an oral summary of the episode of I Love Lucy that they had just watched, the participants were divided into two groups.

In the month prior to the intervention, the entire class viewed two episodes of I Love Lucy on two different occasions so that they would be familiar with the style of the series and the characters who appear in it. The participants also did vocabulary quizzes in the same format as the pre- and post-tests. In addition, they completed one pilot session in which they recorded a speaking activity in pairs on their smartphones and emailed the audio file to the instructor for review. As the quality of the audio was sufficient to understand and analyse the content, it was determined that it was more efficient and practical for learners to use their own mobile phones than to obtain specialised digital recorders.

On the first day of the intervention, each group did a vocabulary pre-test (see Appendix 1) to determine their familiarity with the target words. The pre-test was then collected and the target words were taught by the instructor through a matching exercise that participants completed in pairs and then corrected as a whole group. The teaching of target words lasted approximately 15 minutes. Following this, each group watched a different episode of I Love Lucy with the audio and captions in English. Immediately after watching the episode, each participant was paired with someone from the other group, who had watched a different episode. The participants were given visual aids in the form of stills from the episode that they had just viewed (see Appendix 2). They were then asked to explain the plot of the episode to their partner. These interactions were recorded on participants' smartphones and sent to the researcher immediately after the task. One week later, participants were given a post-test (delayed post-test 1) on the target words from their episode. This procedure was repeated in two sessions; however, in the second session participants were not given visual aids when retelling the plot of the episodes they had viewed. Participants took an additional delayed post-test (post-test 2) two and a half months after the experiment.

Measures

The vocabulary pre-test and the delayed post-test 1 were identical and closely based on the vocabulary knowledge scale (Wesche & Paribakht, 1996). The participants were provided with sentences containing the target words in bold but devoid of clues to their explicit meaning; for example, *I'll go and get a crowbar*. Participants chose between three options:

(1) No. (I don't know.)
(2) It's familiar. I think it means … [translation/synonym].
(3) Yes, and I can use it. It means _____ [translation]. For example: [sentence in English].

Participants were graded for each item from 0 to 4 as follows: 0 for answering 'No' or providing an incorrect translation; 1 for a partially correct translation; 2 for a correct translation but no (or an incomprehensible) example of use in a sentence; 3 for a correct translation and partially correct or non-standard usage; and 4 for a correct translation and correct usage. The delayed post-test 2 was simplified due to time constraints. The participants were provided with the same example sentences and asked only to provide a translation. They were scored for each item as follows: 0 points for an incorrect translation or a blank answer; 1 for a partially correct translation; and 2 for a correct translation.

Results

The mean scores, as measured by percentages on the pre-tests and two delayed post-tests, were analysed to determine whether the participants had learned and retained the target vocabulary over time. After reviewing the data to confirm that the samples were normally distributed and that the assumptions for the test were met, two repeated measure tests were used. The results showed that in both groups the difference between the pre-test and post-test 1 was significant at an alpha level of 0.01 ($p = 0.000$). The differences between post-test 1 and post-test 2 were not significant in either group, although the value almost reached significance for Group B (Group A: $p = 0.565$; Group B: $p = 0.068$). Finally, the differences between the pre-test and post-test 2 were significant at an alpha level of 0.01 for Group A ($p = 0.003^{**}$) and 0.05 for Group B ($p = 0.013$).

In the second session, when participants were not given visual prompts during the retelling of the episode, the differences between the pre-test and post-test 1 remained significant at an alpha level of 0.01 for Group A ($p = 0.003^{**}$) and Group B ($p = 0.000^*$). In contrast, while the results for Group A were similar to the results for the first session, with the differences between delayed post-test 1 and delayed post-test 2 not being significant ($p = 0.681$) and the differences between the pre-test and delayed post-test 2 remaining significant at an alpha level of 0.01 ($p = 0.004^{**}$), Group B did not follow this pattern. Rather, Group B's decrease in gains was significant. The difference between post-tests 1 and 2 (with means of 64.4% and 42.8%, respectively) was $p = 0.021^*$, and the long-term gains, as measured by the difference between the pre-test (mean = 32.7%) and delayed post-test 2, showed no significant differences ($p = 0.182$). The results are shown in Table 5.2 [Note: * = p <.05; ** = p <.005; *** = p <.001].

The audio files were coded for each student by counting the number of target words used or attempted during the speaking task. For this preliminary analysis of target word uptake in production, the list of target words used was compared with the list of target words previously unknown, as shown in the pre-test for each participant.

The participants showed a general tendency to use the target words in the oral task, which consisted of recounting the plot of the episode. The target words previously unknown to the participants (as measured by the pre-test) were counted and coded. In the first session with visual aids, all participants in Group A used at least one previously unknown target word during the retelling, with a range of one to three previously unknown target words used. In Group B, most (75%) of the participants used previously unknown target words, with a range of zero to four words used per participant. Both groups utilised the previously unknown target words slightly less frequently in Session 2 without the visuals: 83% of participants in Group A used previously unknown target words (with a range of zero to three words per participant) and 63% of participants

Table 5.2 Vocabulary test results

	Pre-test		Delayed post-test 1		Delayed post-test 2	
	Mean	SD	Mean	SD	Mean	SD
Group A (*n* = 6)						
Video 1	29.5	7.6	57.7	14.4	54.5	17.1
Video 2	42.2	6.3	71.2	19.0	71.2	14.3
Group B (*n* = 8)						
Video 3	34.6	17.1	74.0	21.3	55.3	25.1
Video 4	32.7	16.8	64.4	22.4	42.8	25.5

in Group B used previously unknown target words (with a range of zero to two words per participant). Table 5.1 shows the complete list of target words for all four videos. The target words that were previously unknown to the participants and were successfully used in the post-viewing oral task are shown in bold.

The preliminary results of the oral data analysis from the post-viewing task show that the task works well as a prompt for learners to spot gaps in their vocabulary knowledge, when retelling the story both with and without visuals. There appears to be some evidence that the number of times a target word occurs in the episode influences partici-pants' success in using the word, although their awareness of gaps in their vocabulary seems to depend on how crucial a word is to retelling the story. One target word, *butcher*, was used by five out of six participants in Group A, despite the fact that four out of six participants could not translate this word correctly on the pre-test.

This task led to several instances of participants translating the target words into the shared first language (L1) for their partner, indicating that the participants assumed that the target word would be unfamiliar.

Participant 1: … goes to the butcher, the *carnicero* … shop of meat.

Participants also showed signs of making a conscious effort to use the target words, even when they initially described the concept in other, simpler terms.

Participant 5: The man that work in the meat, no no, the butcher.

Finally, the only participant who did not successfully use *butcher* in the speaking task explicitly stated that she was aware of the word but did not recall it.

Participant 3: In a … shop where you can buy meat. I don't remember the name. [*butcher*]

In contrast, one target word with no successful productive use was *furnace*, which was also an unknown word in the pre-test for all six learners in Group A. All the participants in this group did, however, show awareness of the need to use the word, whether through resorting to their L1, paraphrasing in English or explicitly stating that they did not know the appropriate word.

Participant 3: Puts in a … I don't know.

Participant 2 (L1): *No sé como se dice, donde puso la carne, en el horno pero no es un horno* [I don't know how you say it, where she put the meat, in the oven, but it's not an oven] … a *fower*, something like that, to make warm the house. [*furnace*]

Participant 4: goes to the ... main machine of the heating system.

Participant 5: ... and put in the ... other place ... the *chimenea*. [*fireplace/furnace*].

It is difficult to pinpoint exactly why one word is successfully learned and employed and another is not. For example, although participants were unable to produce a correct translation on the pre-test, they may have had some previous exposure to the word *butcher* and no exposure whatsoever to *furnace*. However, when looking at the nature of input through video, there are some differences that may have influenced uptake and production. While the frequency of occurrence of the two words was similar, with *butcher* being spoken four times and *furnace* three, the word *butcher* was more salient. One scene in the episode takes place at a butcher's shop, and two different men acting as butchers appear in another scene. The furnace is visible in the episode, but only in the last few minutes. Furthermore, the concept of a furnace is perhaps not as easy to grasp, as it is a somewhat old-fashioned method of heating and it is unlikely that most participants have ever seen a furnace. In contrast, butchers remain fairly common.

In cases where the target words had 'easier' or better known synonyms (for example, *timetable* for *schedule*), participants often used the synonym rather than the target word, whereas words with less apparent synonyms (such as *butcher*) appeared to be produced more frequently. Likewise, target words with synonyms that were cognates appeared to be difficult to reproduce. One clear example is the target phrase *to make something up*, which in Spanish is *inventar*. Several participants used the English word *invent* without appearing to notice that one of the target items was a more appropriate word choice.

The speaking task also yielded a rich source of data that shed light on how participants express awareness of gaps in their vocabulary knowledge. Participants very often articulated this awareness when retelling the story, either by explicitly stating that they did not recall a particular word (*¿cómo se dice para quejarse?* – 'How do you say *to complain?*'), or translating a previously unknown word that they used for the benefit of their partner: 'She is *faking, cómo que lo está fingiendo*'. This would imply that the participants were using words that they did not expect their partner to understand in English and demonstrates an awareness of potential gaps in their fellow learners' knowledge as well.

Discussion

The first research question of this study asked whether viewing captioned videos with a pre-viewing preparatory task and followed by a post-viewing interactive task promoted vocabulary learning. It also examined whether any learning was maintained over a longer time frame. This study has shown that the learning of target vocabulary through video input with captions occurs successfully. In three out of four of the interventions evaluated, these gains were maintained over time, as evidenced by the delayed post-tests.

The second research question focused on visual aids, which were intended as a stimulus and a facilitator for a post-viewing productive task, and their possible effects on vocabulary uptake. Thus far, visual aids have not been shown to have a significant effect on either target item meaning retention or the productive use of new words, although further research is necessary to separate the characteristics of the videos used from the task effects. In fact, the preliminary results show that not only is there no discernible difference in vocabulary gains with the presence or absence of visual aids but also other factors (such as use of target items or length of time speaking) were unaffected. However, after the second intervention many participants in both groups reported informally to the instructor that the speaking activity with visuals was 'easier' and less stressful. This is consistent with previous research stating that visual aids lessen the difficulty of productive tasks (Iwashita *et al.*, 2001). Participants reported greater difficulty in the second retelling (without visuals) despite the fact that they had previous experience of this type of task.

The third research question concerned the extent to which participants would use previously unknown target words in a post-viewing speaking task. Indeed, vocabulary uptake did occur, as participants successfully used target items when recounting the narrative of the video they had watched. Regarding which target words were successfully employed in production, the preliminary analysis indicates that saliency and level of difficulty may each play a role. First, there appears to be some evidence that the increased uptake and productive use of more salient words – those that stand out in the storyline and/or are visually represented (e.g. *butcher, pipe, backwards*) – are more frequent than they are for less salient words. Nevertheless, further research is required to evaluate how to efficiently define and quantify the saliency and necessity of individual target items. Additional study on the role of cognates (such as *invent* and *inventar*) and previously known synonyms (such as *schedule* and *time-table*) would also prove interesting to explore the relationships between these factors and the acquisition of new words. The speaking task also provided the opportunity to examine interactions in order to gain more information on how participants express the realisation that there is a gap in their vocabulary knowledge, as illustrated above.

In terms of the pedagogical aim of designing a meaningful and authentic task for use following video viewing, this was successful, as all the participants produced extended narratives in the target language and spoke for between 3.25 and 11.25 minutes. In addition, the speaking output is based on and mimics authentic language use by giving students the opportunity to have realistic conversations and information exchanges.

Limitations and Further Research

While the results concerning vocabulary acquisition and retention are promising, the sample size of this study is too small to enable full conclusions. In addition, while at this stage of the research visual aids appear to have little or no effect on vocabulary uptake and retention and limited effect on productive vocabulary use, these results may be attributed to the specific language in the videos selected.

The next step is to repeat the process using the same videos but changing the visual/no visual condition to see if the preliminary results are supported. In the future, a control group following the same format but with either no input or a different form of input (e.g. a combination of text and/or audio) to reinforce and contextualise the target items would be beneficial to identify the distinguishing characteristics of captioned video input from general vocabulary teaching and other forms of input.

The analysis of the oral data is still in progress. While it is clear that this type of information gap activity provides rich data in terms of provoking the productive use of target words and language-related episodes between students, the effects of video viewing need to be analysed further. For example, there appears to be a relationship between how salient a target item is and the participants' use (or attempted use) of the target item. In addition, the relationship between the uptake and productive use of target words is still being explored, as is the role of expressed gaps of knowledge in productive vocabulary.

Conclusion

The results of this study support the published literature that points to the effectiveness of using captioned videos as a language learning tool in the classroom. There are several pedagogical implications of this study. With a fairly minimal length of time spent on teaching explicit vocabulary meaning (approximately 15 minutes), it is possible for learners to acquire a significant number of new words, to use these words productively (albeit in the context of a somewhat structured classroom activity) and to retain these vocabulary gains over time.

The productive component of the intervention also proved fruitful in that participants spoke virtually uninterrupted, and at length, and became more aware of the gaps in their vocabulary knowledge. With the rising popularity and accessibility of English language television and film, there are numerous possibilities for exploiting this form of media – both as an in-class viewing activity and as an independent activity for learners to do outside the classroom – as a starting point for productive practice.

References

Baltova, I. (1999) The effect of subtitled and staged video input on the learning and retention of content and vocabulary. Doctoral dissertation, University of Toronto. See https://tspace.library.utoronto.ca/bitstream/1807/13234/1/nq41096.pdf (accessed 7 March 2016).

Bird, S.A. and Williams, J.N. (2002) The effect of bimodal input on implicit and explicit memory: An investigation into the benefits of within-language subtitling. *Applied Psycholinguistics* 23 (4), 509–533.

Council of Europe (2001) *Common European Framework of Reference for Languages: Learning, Teaching, Assessment.* Cambridge: Cambridge University Press.

Danan, M. (2004) Captioning and subtitling: Undervalued language learning strategies. *Meta: Journal des traducteurs [Meta: Translators' Journal]* 49 (1), 67–77.

Daniels, M. (dir.) (1952) *Lucy Fakes Illness.* Series 1, Episode 16. *I Love Lucy,* TV programme. Hollywood, CA: Desilu Productions.

Daniels, M. (dir.) (1952) *Breaking the Lease.* Series 1, Episode 18. *I Love Lucy,* TV programme. Hollywood, CA: Desilu Productions.

Daniels, M. (dir.) (1952) *The Freezer.* Series 1, Episode 29. *I Love Lucy,* TV programme. Hollywood, CA: Desilu Productions.

Daniels, M. (dir.) (1952) *Lucy's Schedule.* Series 1, Episode 33. *I Love Lucy,* TV programme. Hollywood, CA: Desilu Productions.

de la Fuente, M. (2002) The roles of input and output in the receptive and productive acquisition of words. *Studies in Second Language Acquisition* 24 (1), 81–112.

Doughty, C. and Williams, J. (1998) Issues and terminology. In C. Doughty and J. Williams (eds) *Focus on Form in Classroom Second Language Acquisition* (pp. 197–262). New York: Cambridge University Press.

Garnier, M. (2013) Intentional vocabulary learning from watching DVDs with subtitles: A case study of an 'average' learner of French. *International Journal of Research Studies in Language Learning* 3 (1), 21–32.

Holobow, N., Lambert, W.E. and Sayegh, L. (1984) Pairing script and dialogue: Combinations that show promise for second or foreign language acquisition. *Language Learning* 34 (4), 59–74.

I Love Lucy (1951) TV series. Produced by D. Arnaz and J. Oppenheimer. Hollywood, CA: Desilu Productions.

Iwashita, N., McNamara, T. and Elder, C. (2001) Can we predict task difficulty in an oral proficiency test? Exploring the potential of an information-processing approach to task design. *Language Learning* 51 (3), 401–436.

Kovacs, G. and Miller, R.C. (2014) Smart subtitles for vocabulary learning. In *Proceedings of the SIGCHI Conference on Human Factors in Computing Systems* (pp. 853–862). Toronto: ACM.

Krashen, S.D. (1981) *Second Language Acquisition and Second Language Learning.* Oxford: Pergamon Press.

Milton, J. (2008) Vocabulary uptake from informal learning tasks. *Language Learning Journal* 36 (2), 227–237.

Montero Perez, M., Van Den Noortgate, W. and Desmet, P. (2013) Captioned video for L2 listening and vocabulary learning: A meta-analysis. *System* 41 (3), 720–739.

Montero Perez, M., Peters, E., Clarebout, G. and Desmet, P. (2014) Effects of captioning on video comprehension and incidental vocabulary learning. *Language Learning and Technology* 18 (1), 118–141.

Montero Perez, M., Peters, E. and Desmet, P. (2015) Enhancing vocabulary learning through captioned video: An eye-tracking study. *The Modern Language Journal* 99 (2), 308–328.

Neuman, S.B. and Koskinen, P. (1992) Captioned television as comprehensible input: Effects of incidental word learning from context for language minority students. *Reading Research Quarterly* 27 (1), 95–106.

Paivio, A. (1986) *Mental Representations*. New York: Oxford University Press.

Rodgers, M. (2013) English language learning through viewing television: An investigation of comprehension, incidental vocabulary acquisition, lexical coverage, attitudes, and captions. Unpublished doctoral dissertation, Victoria University of Wellington.

Savignon, S.J. (2003) Teaching English as communication: A global perspective. *World Englishes* 22 (1), 55–66.

Swain, M. (1985) Communicative competence: Some roles of comprehensible input and comprehensible output in its development. In S. Gass and C. Madden (eds) *Input in Second Language Acquisition* (pp. 235–253). Rowley, MA: Newbury House.

Swain, M. and Lapkin, S. (1995) Problems in output and the cognitive processes they generate: A step towards second language learning. *Applied Linguistics* 16 (3), 371–391.

Sydorenko, T. (2010) Modality of input and vocabulary acquisition. *Language Learning and Technology* 14 (2), 50–73.

Vanderplank, R. (2013) 'Effects of' and 'effects with' captions: How exactly does watching a TV programme with same-language subtitles make a difference to language learners? *Language Teaching* 49 (2), 1–16.

Wesche, M. and Paribakht, T.S. (1996) Assessing second language vocabulary knowledge: Depth versus breadth. *Canadian Modern Language Review* 53 (1), 13–40.

Winke, P., Gass, S. and Sydorenko, T. (2010) The effects of captioning videos used for foreign language listening activities. *Language Learning and Technology* 14 (1), 65–86.

Appendices

Appendix 1

PRE_POST LUFR DATE:_____   NAME:_____

Vocabulary	No	Me suena. Creo que significa....(traducción /sinónimo)	Sí, y lo puedo usar. Significa.....(traducción) Por ejemplo.... (frase en inglés)
There's just no other place to **cut down.**			Traducción: Frase:
We can't use the **furnace.**			Traducción: Frase:
We could go to a **butcher.**			Traducción: Frase:
Get your meat **wholesale.**			Traducción: Frase:
I'll go and get a **crowbar.**			Traducción: Frase:
She's **locked in!**			Traducción: Frase:
Do you want a **bargain?**			Traducción: Frase:
How big is **a side** of beef?			Traducción: Frase:
Oh, 20, 25 **pounds** of beef.			Traducción: Frase:
I asked Fred to buy us **a freezer.**			Traducción: Frase:
You can buy any **cut** you want.			Traducción: Frase:
Just **stand still!**			Traducción: Frase:
How can I **stall** them?			Traducción Frase:

Appendix 2

For copyright reasons the stills used could not be included. Please find them at https://drive.google.com/drivefolders/0B0DE81qqHfZVZDItM3 1qaGhJcXM

6 The Effects of Bimodal L2 Input on the Processing of Function Words by Spanish EFL Learners: An Eye-Tracking Study

Joan C. Mora and Eva Cerviño-Povedano

The reduced phonetic form of English function words poses pronunciation problems for learners of syllable-timed languages, such as Spanish. Research investigating input modality in language learning has shown the benefits of watching subtitled videos for vocabulary acquisition and listening comprehension, but little is known about the effect of subtitling on the processing of second language (L2) function words and on L2 pronunciation in general. This chapter reports on an eye-tracking experiment that was conducted to investigate the effects of bimodal input (audio + text) on Spanish English as a foreign language (EFL) learners' processing of English function words while watching subtitled videos. In addition, we explored the role of individual differences in L2 proficiency and executive function control (working memory, attention and inhibition) in learners' reading behaviour. Participants watched film clips in English with intralingual subtitles under three conditions: (a) on-screen images + audio + text; (b) audio + text; and (c) text only. The analysis of the eye-gaze data showed fewer and shorter looks at function words in bimodal input conditions and among more proficient learners, which indicates more target-like processing of function words. No clear pattern emerged regarding the role of cognitive control. These findings suggest that exposure to bimodal input may enhance the processing of subtitled text according to the rhythmic structure of the presentation language. This highlights the potential of intralingual subtitling for L2 pronunciation development.

Introduction

The pronunciation of English function words (e.g. articles, prepositions, conjunctions and pronouns, which primarily serve a grammatical function), when compared with that of content words (which carry the main semantic content of the language) presents considerable difficulty for Spanish learners of English as a foreign language (EFL). This is because Spanish learners are likely to transfer the syllabic rhythm of their first language (L1) when speaking English and this prevents them from reducing vowels in unstressed syllables (Flege & Bohn, 1989; Gómez Lacabex et al., 2007). In addition, the stress-timed rhythm of English leads to generalised vowel and consonant cluster reduction processes in unstressed syllables, which results in function words being relatively low in perceptual prominence. Spanish is a typical syllable-timed language, which lacks stress-based syllable reduction processes. Therefore, Spanish learners' production of English speech often lacks, especially at lower levels of proficiency, the characteristic vowel reduction processes of stress-timed languages like English, where stressed syllables have been reported to be almost double the length of unstressed syllables (Lee et al., 2006).

Previous research on the acquisition of English rhythm by Spanish learners has shown that Spanish learners fail to reduce syllables in their second language (L2) speech to the extent that English speakers do (White & Mattys, 2007). However, several studies have shown that specific training in L2 English vowel reduction (Gómez Lacabex et al., 2007; Gómez Lacabex & Gallardo del Puerto, 2014) and intensive input exposure through immersion in the form of study abroad (Valls-Ferrer, 2011) lead to positive gains in Spanish learners' production of English stress-timed speech. In instructed L2 acquisition settings, exposure to oral input is limited to a few hours a week in the classroom environment. The limited amount of input makes the acquisition of segmental (vowels and consonants) and supra-segmental (stress, rhythm and intonation) features of pronunciation a learning challenge: a situation that is often aggravated by at least two other factors commonly affecting the teaching of pronunciation. First, several surveys have shown that teachers tend to devote very little class time, if any, to teaching pronunciation (Darcy et al., 2012). Secondly, teachers, especially in foreign language instruction in school contexts, are often non-native and speak the L2 with some degree of foreign accent.

Given these limited input conditions, it is not surprising that teachers resort to strategies in order to provide learners with as much comprehensible authentic input as the available class time allows; for example, using a variety of multimedia materials. The increased use of audiovisual materials in the language classroom has motivated researchers to investigate the impact of input modality on language learning (Vanderplank, 2010). More specifically, a substantial body of research has examined the potential benefits of providing learners with exposure to various types of bimodal input through different types of subtitled video: standard (L2 video and soundtrack with L1 subtitles), reversed (L1 video and soundtrack with L2 subtitles), intralingual (L2 video and soundtrack with L2 subtitles) and keyword captioning (L2 video and soundtrack with L2 keywords). This research, using eye-tracking measures that capture on-screen reading behaviour, has revealed an overall positive effect of subtitled text on listening comprehension in any presentation modality (see Montero Perez *et al.* [2013] for an overview). Besides the benefits of listening comprehension (e.g. Kruger & Steyn, 2013; Markham, 2001; Montero Perez *et al.*, 2014), previous research has reported positive effects of subtitling on the incidental acquisition of L2 vocabulary (Bird & Williams, 2002; Bisson *et al.*, 2014; d'Ydewalle & Van de Poel, 1999; Montero Perez *et al.*, 2015). However, very little research to date has examined the potential benefits of subtitling for the development of L2 learners' perceptual phonological competence and pronunciation skills (but see Borrás & Lafayette, 1994; Mitterer & McQueen, 2009).

This chapter outlines a study that is part of a larger project investigating the effects of extensive exposure to intralingual subtitling on the perception and production of the stress-timed rhythmic parameters of English. The current study responds to the well-attested difficulty of Spanish learners in correctly producing and perceiving the reduced forms of English function words (skills that are essential to the acquisition of English stress-timed rhythm) and investigates the effects of bimodal input presentation on Spanish EFL learners' processing of function words. More specifically, we explore the extent to which the constraints imposed on learners' attentional resources during subtitled video exposure result in a more target-like processing of function words, as indexed through eye-gaze measures.

Eye-tracking reading research shows that in normal reading not all words are fixated on, and words that are not fixated on tend to be function words. According to some studies, only about 35% of function words are fixated on, as opposed to content words, which are fixated on about 85% of the time (Carpenter & Just, 1983; Rayner & Duffy, 1988). In subtitled videos, words are skipped more often than in the reading of printed text (Krejtz *et al.*, 2016); this is because subtitled text is only available to read for a few seconds and because a certain proportion of the reader's attention is allocated to the action on the screen. The differential processing of content and function words follows the same tendency as in printed text: function words are fixated on less often and, when they are fixated on, they are fixated on for shorter durations (Krejtz *et al.*, 2016). Spanish learners' failure to reduce function words when reading English text suggests that they process English function words differently from how L1 English readers process these words. This is not only because the transparent phonetic spelling of Spanish is likely to induce spelling-based misreading but also because of the rhythmic structure of Spanish, which lacks the kind of reduction processes that affect English function words. For example, whereas the English phrase *I should have thought so* is likely to be rendered as /aɪʃdvˈθɔːtsəʊ/ by native English speakers, Spanish learners are likely to pronounce it as /ˈaɪ ˈʃʊd ˈhæv ˈθɔːt ˈsəʊ/ with unreduced function words. However, it remains an empirical question as to whether Spanish learners fixate on function and content words in a similar way when reading subtitled text in L2 English. In addition, there is the question of whether processing differences between Spanish learners and native English speakers may be due to differences in the rhythmic structure of the two languages, besides other reader-dependent factors known to affect the frequency and duration of fixations on words, such as individual reading skills (Rayner, 1998) or vocabulary size and overall proficiency in the L2 (Webb & Rodgers, 2009).

It is also possible that learners vary in how efficiently they manage to distribute their attentional resources so as to simultaneously process the three sources of information present in subtitled video (the on-screen action, the soundtrack and the subtitle text), which may also be related to individual differences in executive functioning. Executive functions are a set of mental processes that allow individuals to concentrate and pay attention, and they include working memory, inhibition and cognitive flexibility (Diamond, 2013). Working memory involves holding information in the mind and manipulating it, which is essential for understanding language as it unfolds in time (Baddeley & Hitch, 1994). Inhibitory control allows individuals to automatically or voluntarily control their behaviour and attention by selectively attending to target stimuli while suppressing attention to, or avoiding interference from, other stimuli. Cognitive flexibility, also called attention control, allows individuals to flexibly switch their attentional focus, as when switching between tasks (Miyake *et al.*, 2000). Working memory (Baddeley *et al.*, 1998), inhibition (Darcy *et al.*, 2016; Pivneva *et al.*, 2012) and attention (Segalowitz & Frenkiel-Fishman, 2005) are important cognitive skills in language processing and learning and have been found to correlate significantly with L2 proficiency attainment.

In the study that we are considering in this chapter, we hypothesised that Spanish learners' eye fixations on function and content words would vary according to how much attention they devoted to reading the subtitled text, their proficiency level and inter-learner differences in phonological short-term memory (PSTM) and inhibitory control. The less attention paid to the subtitled text (due to presentation conditions), the less often function words would be fixated on and the shorter the fixation on function words would be; that is, the more English-like the reading behaviour would be. Similarly, the higher the L2 learners' proficiency, the less attention they would pay to function as opposed to content words. PSTM allows listeners to hold acoustic verbal information momentarily in working memory for further processing, and it has been shown to be implicated in L1 and L2 vocabulary acquisition and language learning (French & O'Brien, 2008; O'Brien et al., 2006). Therefore, learners with better PSTM capacity may be more efficient at processing auditory verbal information under the constraints imposed by the simultaneous processing of various sources of information in subtitled video. We also predicted that learners with stronger inhibitory control would show more efficient behaviour in reading subtitled text, so that they might be better able to process content words under high attentional demands.

Study Overview

The study discussed in this chapter investigates the effects of bimodal input through subtitled video presented under various input conditions. We assessed how Spanish EFL learners' processing of English function words, as indexed by fixation durations, was affected by these presentation conditions. We also explored inter-learner differences in reading behaviour (eye fixations on function and content words) as a function of L2 proficiency and executive function control. The following research questions were addressed:

RQ1. What is the effect of bimodal input exposure on the processing of English function words by Spanish learners of English?

RQ2. To what extent is this effect related to learners' individual differences in L2 proficiency and executive function?

The participants were 32 Spanish EFL learners taking a degree in English at a university in Catalonia (age: mean = 22.5, SD = 5.6).[1] The bimodal input was presented in the form of video clips with intralingual subtitles in the learners' L2 (English), as this is a common way to provide learners with L2 exposure in foreign language teaching. It has been shown to be more beneficial for vocabulary acquisition (Bird & Williams, 2002) and L2 speech perception and production than subtitles in the listeners' native language (Borrás & Lafayette, 1994; Lambert et al., 1981; Mitterer & McQueen, 2009). We used eye-tracking to monitor learners' reading behaviour in relation to the subtitled text. The subtitled text was presented under three conditions that differed in terms of the amount of information processing required: (a) on-screen images + audio + text; (b) audio + text; and (c) text only. We obtained a measure of the total duration of participants' fixation on the same set of selected function and content words presented under the three conditions described above, while keeping the subtitle presentation time identical across all three conditions.[2]

The learners were asked to engage in a language comprehension task in English. They were told that they would watch several short clips from one episode of the British television series *Sherlock* (McGuigan & Moffat, 2012) containing short conversations and that they would be asked to answer a True/False question after each clip to test whether they had understood the conversation. The questions were based on the content of the subtitles in order to motivate learners to process as much dialogue in the soundtrack and as much subtitled text as possible. The task started with two presentation slides: one containing the written task instructions and one presenting a description of the four characters appearing in the clips (Sherlock, John, Mycroft and Irene). These presentation slides were followed by three initial sample clips to familiarise participants with the task of reading subtitled text in the three conditions (no eye fixations were recorded). Six experimental subtitled video clips were then presented in counterbalanced order and learners' eye fixations were recorded using Tobii Studio eye-tracking software and a Tobii T120 eye-tracker. The participants' eye movements were registered at a 120 Hz sampling rate through infrared diodes capturing 120 gaze data points per second. The eye-tracker was installed at a distance of 60 cm from the participants' eyes. Two clips were presented in each condition, so that each learner watched six different clips and every clip appearing in the three different conditions was watched by at least 10 subjects, as Table 6.1 illustrates. The task took 10–15 minutes to complete.

The original subtitles consisted of short conversational excerpts between two characters without on-screen action other than showing the faces of the characters who were speaking. For Condition C, these were modified to include the speaker's name to facilitate speaker identification. We selected 16 function and 16 content words to control for word frequency (F (2, 29) = 0.298, p = 0.744) and word length (F (2, 29) = 1.96, p = 0.159) across the conditions (Table 6.1) using the SUBTLEX$_{US}$ corpus (Brysbaert & New, 2009) and lightly highlighted them in soft yellow to increase the likelihood of sufficient subject hit counts. We obtained the total duration of fixation on these words, which were presented identically (same size, colour, duration and on-screen location) across all three conditions.[3]

The participants also completed a vocabulary breadth test (X/Y_Lex: Meara, 2005; Miralpeix, 2012)[4] as a proxy for L2 proficiency, which provided an estimate of their vocabulary size in English (0–10,000 words). They performed a PSTM task (serial non-word recognition: Cerviño-Povedano & Mora, 2011), which required participants to hold sequences of non-words of increasing length in their short-term memory and provided a measure of their PSTM capacity. The participants carried out two tasks that measured their visual-spatial inhibitory control: first, a Simon task (Simon, 1969), which required participants to associate a coloured square (blue or red) with a response key (right or left) while ignoring the stimulus location on the screen; and secondly, a version of a Flanker task (Costa *et al.*, 2009), which provided a measure of their

Table 6.1 Characteristics of video clips

Presentation conditions		A Image + audio + text		B Audio + text		C Text	
		1	**2**	**3**	**4**	**5**	**6**
Duration (sec)		28	28	30	40	41	41
Subtitles (n)		11	9	12	13	12	12
Words	Total (n)	79	55	81	87	95	82
Selection	Function (n)	3	2	2	3	3	3
	Content (n)	3	2	2	3	3	3
Frequency	Function	7035		4389		4900	
	Content	249		656		340	
Length	Function	2.60		4.00		3.67	
	Content	4.80		5.60		5.67	
Presentation	n = 10	1	2	3	4	5	6
	n = 12	3	4	5	6	1	2
	n = 10	5	6	1	2	3	4

ability to selectively attend to a stimulus (arrow) while ignoring interfering stimuli (surrounding arrows) in the background.[5] The vocabulary and cognitive tasks took 30 minutes to complete.

In the X/Y_Lex tasks, participants had to decide whether they knew the meaning of an English word appearing on the computer screen; that is, they had to decide whether or not they could translate it into Spanish. The list of lexical items included English words from all frequency ranges and a set of English non-words used as controls and consisting of strings of letters that conformed to pronounceable sequences of sounds in English (e.g. *gurley*). This test estimated learners' vocabulary size by computing a score between 0 and 10,000 words, based on the number of words known within each one of the 10 frequency bands (1–10,000) and adjusted according to the number of non-words identified as known words.

The PSTM task used in this study was a serial non-word recognition task employing Danish non-words developed by Cerviño-Povedano and Mora (2011), see also Isaacs and Trofimovich (2011). The use of non-words in an unfamiliar language (Danish) forced participants to map phonetically unfamiliar sound sequences to their own phonology during non-word sequence recall. This more closely resembles what learners do when decoding L2 speech and still provides a valid phonological memory capacity measure unbiased by inter-subject differences in proficiency (French & O'Brien, 2008). In addition, since our participants were Spanish–Catalan bilinguals differing in how much they used Spanish on a daily basis, the use of non-words in Danish was also meant to neutralize the likely effect of inter-subject differences in degree of L1 dominance on the phonological memory measure. Participants were presented with 24 trials for same–different discrimination, each consisting of a pair of sequences of Danish consonant-vowel-consonant (CVC) non-words. Half the pairs (12) consisted of two identical sequences of non-words ('same pairs'); the other half (12) consisted of two sequences of non-words that were identical except for a change in the serial position of one of the non-words in the second sequence ('different pairs'). The sequences differed in item length (sequences of five, six and seven non-words) with four same and four different pairs of sequences at each item length. For example, on any given trial, participants would hear a pair of sequences of non-words and they would need to decide whether the two sequences were the same; that is, whether the same items appeared in the same order (e.g. /tys, dam, rød, mild, fup/ vs /tys, dam, rød, mild, fup/) or in a different order (e.g. /tys, dam, rød, mild, fup/ vs /tys, dam, mild, rød, fup/). Different sequence pairs were created by changing the position of one non-word only in the second non-word sequence of each trial. Each sequence was built in such a way that no vowel appeared more than once in the sequence and the non-words varied maximally in their initial and final consonants. The sequences appeared with a 500-millisecond silence interval.

The 24 pairs of sequences were presented to participants in three blocks of five-, six- and seven-item lengths. Participants were instructed to decide whether the non-words were presented in the same or a different order in the two sequences by pressing one of two designated keys. The task required participants to keep the first sequence of non-words and their serial order in their short-term memory to be able to compare it with the second, which was increasingly difficult as the item length increased. A PSTM score was computed by assigning one correct point to every correct response up to a maximum score of 24. This task provides a measure of participants' PSTM capacity by testing their ability to retain sequences of phonological units (speech sounds and their serial order) in their short-term memory; therefore, it is a task that taps into the phonological sound processing required, for example, in the segmentation of strings of sounds into word-sized units in an L2.

In the version of the Simon task that we used,[6] participants were instructed to press a key to the left of the space bar on the computer keyboard (left hand, *Alt*) as quickly as possible when they saw a blue square on the screen, and to press a key to the right of the space bar (right hand, *Alt Gr*) when they saw a red square. Blue and red squares appeared randomly on the left or right side of the screen, creating congruent or incongruent spatial overlap trials. An inhibition score was obtained by subtracting the mean faster response latencies of the congruent condition from the mean slower response latencies of the incongruent condition, with higher scores representing poorer inhibitory control.

In the Flanker task, participants decided as quickly as possible whether an arrow appearing in the centre of a sequence of five arrows on the computer screen was pointing left or right on a set of congruent (←— ←— ←— ←— ←— or —→ —→ —→ —→ —→) and incongruent (←— ←— —→ ←— ←— or —→ —→ ←— —→ —→) trials by pressing a left-hand or a right-hand key (*Alt* or *Alt Gr*).[7] In the incongruent condition, subjects tend to be slower because they need to inhibit the conflicting arrows in the background. As with the Simon task, an inhibition score was obtained by subtracting the mean faster response latencies of the congruent condition from the mean slower response latencies of the incongruent condition, with higher scores representing poorer inhibitory control. The Simon and Flanker tasks both provide a measure of learners' ability to supress processing interference caused by conflicting information; therefore, they may index their ability to deal with the simultaneous processing of visual and auditory information sources when watching a subtitled video.

Results

The fixation durations were submitted to a mixed analysis of variance (ANOVA) analysis with condition (A, B, C) and word type (function, content) as independent factors. The main effects of condition ($F_{(2, 30)} = 5.09$, $p = 0.012$) and word type (function, content; $F_{(1, 31)} = 37.48$, $p < 0.001$) were significant, as was the interaction between the two factors ($F_{(2, 30)} = 21.66$, $p < 0.001$). The interaction arose because although the overall effect of the presentation condition was significant for function words ($F_{(2, 30)} = 5.93$, $p = 0.007$) and content words ($F_{(2, 30)} = 22.3$, $p < 0.001$), the total fixation duration that function words received in Condition A (M = 1.15 sec, SD = 0.63) and Condition B (M = 1.49 sec, SD = 1.03) was not significantly different ($p = 0.301$). The interaction also arose because content words received fixation durations in Condition A (M = 2.16 sec, SD = 1.18) that were not statistically different from those in Condition C (M = 1.45 sec, SD = 1.01; $p = 0.175$). However, in general, clear differences as a function of presentation condition (see Figure 6.1) in learners' total fixation duration on function and content words could be observed. Total fixation durations, as expected, were shorter in Condition A than they were in Condition B, where the subtitled text was presented without the on-screen image, for function words (A: M = 1.15 sec, SD = 0.63; B: M = 1.49 sec, SD = 1.03) and content words (A: M = 2.16 sec, SD = 1.81; B: M = 4.05 sec, SD = 3.45). In both conditions the total fixation duration was significantly shorter on function words than it was on content words (A: M = 1.15 sec vs 2.16 sec, $t_{(31)} = -3.97$, $p < 0.001$; B: M = 1.49 sec vs 4.05 sec, $t_{(31)} = -3.97$, $p < 0.001$). However, the difference was greater in Condition B; this was driven by learners' increase in fixation duration on content words. Thus, in Condition B, where subtitled text was presented with audio but without on-screen action, learners fixated more

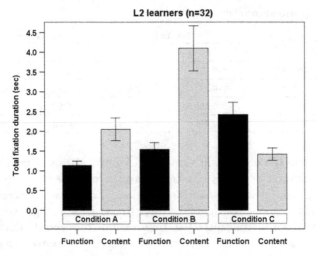

Figure 6.1 Total fixation durations (sec) by condition and word type (error bars indicate ±1 standard error from mean)

frequently and for longer on content words, increasing their fixation duration on function words only slightly.

The relatively large standard deviations in these data suggest considerable inter-learner variation in fixation duration. However, Pearson-r correlation coefficients suggest that learners were internally consistent in how much attention they paid to function and content words. That is, those learners who fixated for longer on function words also fixated for longer on content words, and this pattern was consistent across the three presentation conditions: A ($r = 0.750, p < 0.001$), B ($r = 0.665, p < 0.001$) and C ($r = 0.613, p < 0.001$). We then explored whether inter-learner differences in fixation duration on function and content words across the conditions might be explained by differences in L2 proficiency and executive function control (Table 6.2).

We computed Pearson-r correlation coefficients between fixation duration on function and content words and learners' scores in the X/Y_Lex, PSTM, Simon and Flanker tasks (Table 6.3). We did this for

Table 6.2 Descriptives for L2 proficiency (vocabulary size) and executive control measures

	n	Mean	SD	Min	Max
Vocabulary (X/Y_Lex) in words	29	6268	1603	3550	9050
PSTM (out of 24)	17	16.06	3.19	11	21
Simon (milliseconds)	28	28.08	31.59	−42.84	82.64
Flanker (milliseconds)	30	44.56	23.85	8.12	95.22

Note: Not all participants completed all tests.

Table 6.3   Pearson-*r* correlation coefficients

	Function		Content	
	r	*p*	*r*	*p*
Vocabulary (X/Y_Lex)	−0.455	0.013	−0.212	0.270
PSTM	−0.232	0.388	−0.223	0.406
Simon	−0.048	0.811	−0.262	0.187
Flanker	0.051	0.797	−0.388	0.041

the gaze data obtained from Condition A only, as this is the condition where we expected cognitive control measures to play a role in explaining inter-learner differences in fixation durations. These results revealed that, as expected, higher-proficiency learners (those with a larger vocabulary size) fixated for significantly less time on function words than lower-proficiency learners did. In general, the executive control task scores appeared to be unrelated to fixation duration, except for a relatively weak negative correlation between the Flanker score and fixation duration on content words, suggesting that good inhibitors tended to fixate for longer on content words.

Discussion and Conclusion

The study outlined in this chapter has investigated Spanish EFL learners' processing of function words as they performed a language comprehension task based on a series of captioned video clips, which they watched as their eye movements were recorded by an eye-tracker. Fixation durations on function and content words provided by the eye-tracker indexed the processing of function and content words. Fixation durations were used to determine the extent to which manipulating the conditions under which the clips were presented yielded a more target-like reading behaviour, reflecting the stress-timed rhythmic structure of English as opposed to the syllable-timed rhythm of Spanish. The presentation conditions were manipulated to include two bimodal input (audio + text) conditions, with and without on-screen action, and one condition that involved reading identical subtitled text on the screen without either on-screen action or audio. The results show, in line with previous research, that function words were fixated on less time than content words and that the total fixation duration varied according to the presentation condition. An important finding of the present study with regard to learners of English who speak such syllable-timed languages as Spanish is that a more target-like, stress-timed reading pattern, where function words get very low total fixation durations compared with content words, occurred only under presentation conditions of bimodal input. In the reading-only condition, where competition for attentional resources from various sources of information was not a processing issue, learners appeared to rely on a native-like syllable-timing pattern, as suggested by the large increase in fixation duration on function words in this condition. This finding highlights the potential of bimodal input and intralingual subtitled video for assisting learners to acquire the rhythmic structure of languages.

A second objective was to explore inter-learner differences in L2 proficiency and executive function control on their processing of function and content words under different presentation conditions. As expected, learners with higher L2 proficiency levels were more native-like in their processing of function and content words in subtitles; that is, more advanced learners tended to fixate less time on function words than learners at lower proficiency levels did. PSTM and inhibitory control were not found to have a consistent role in facilitating processing under conditions of bimodal input exposure with on-screen images (Condition A). In particular, we could not explain why the Flanker inhibition score was negatively correlated with fixation durations on content words. A smaller difference in response latencies between the congruent and the incongruent conditions in the task, resulting in lower inhibition scores, reflects learners' stronger ability to inhibit interference from the conflicting surrounding information and indicates better selective attention skills. Although the negative correlations we obtained indicated that good inhibitors (those with lower inhibition scores) fixated for longer on content words, they did not indicate that they fixated less time on function words, as we had expected. Thus, it appears that better inhibitory control capacity, as measured through a Flanker task involving the use of selective attention, is not associated with a more target-like processing of function words. This may be because learners' selective attention skills are not directly involved in the integration of different information sources, and it is the integration of the auditory input produced on a stressed-timed rhythm with the text in the caption that leads to a target-like processing of function words. The executive control function tasks chosen may not be sensitive enough to reflect individual differences in the integration of multiple sources of information. Further research should examine the role of executive functions other than inhibitory control that are involved in processing multimodal input, such as working memory and attention switching. For example, an attention-switching task, such as that used by Segalowitz and Frenkiel-Fishman (2005), might prove to be more effective at capturing effectiveness in attention switching between auditory and visual dimensions during exposure to video with intralingual subtitles, which may facilitate the integration of different sources of information. Further research could explore individual differences in attention in a task-switching paradigm (Monsell, 2003) designed to reflect the kind of processing that is required as speakers attend simultaneously to auditory and visual sources of linguistic information.

The interpretation of the results in the present study must be placed within the perspective of its limitations. First, the learners' eye movements were measured through a single broad measure of total duration of fixation. Further analyses with the same data should be carried out to include additional measures, such as fixation counts and first fixation duration, which may help to explain individual differences in the processing of function and content words (Krejtz et al., 2016; Kruger & Steyn, 2013). In order to be able to offer a full account of inter-language differences in the processing of function and content words based on differences in rhythmic structure (syllable vs stress timing), a follow-up of the present study should include data from the learners' L1 and L2. Finally, longitudinal approaches to the study of the processing of intralingual subtitles under bimodal input conditions could be very useful in determining to what extent this type of exposure can enhance the acquisition of L2 pronunciation skills. Captioned video may help Spanish learners of English process function words in a more target-like manner, which may lead them to improve and acquire the stress-timed rhythmic structure of English.

Notes

(1) Data from a control group of native speakers of English are currently under analysis.
(2) Eye-tracking metrics used to measure word processing in subtitled video include such measures as the number of subjects who fixate on a word, the number of fixations that a word recieves, the duration of the first fixation on a word and the overall fixation duration (e.g. Krejtz et al., 2016), among others (see Kruger & Steyn, 2013).
(3) Fixation duration data from non-highlighted words are currently under analysis.
(4) The X_Lex and Y_Lex vocabulary tests can be downloaded from http://www.lognostics.co.uk/.
(5) Participants also completed a verbal colour Stroop task (Stirling, 1979; Stroop, 1935), the data of which are under analysis.
(6) The Simon task and the Simon effect (Simon & Wolf, 1963) are named after J.R. Simon. The Simon effect shows that people respond faster and more accurately if there is a match between stimulus and response features, such as the location of a stimulus on a computer screen (left or right) and the hand (left or right) that the participant needs to use to provide a response when pressing a response key.
(7) In the Flanker task (Eriksen & Eriksen, 1974) a target (e.g. a left-pointing arrow) is flanked by non-target stimuli (e.g. other arrows) that correspond either to the same directional response (left-pointing arrows) as the target (congruent trials) or to the opposite directional response (right-pointing arrows) as the target (incongruent trials). Participants are slower at determining the direction of the target arrow in incongruent trials.

References

Baddeley, A.D. and Hitch, G.J. (1994) Developments in the concept of working memory. *Neuropsychology* 8 (4), 485–493.
Baddeley, A., Gathercole, S. and Papagno, C. (1998) The phonological loop as a language learning device. *Psychological Review* 105 (1), 158–173.

Bird, S.A. and Williams, J.N. (2002) The effect of bimodal input on implicit and explicit memory: An investigation into the benefits of within-language subtitling. *Applied Psycholinguistics* 23 (4), 509–533.

Bisson, M.J., Van Heuven, W.J., Conklin, K. and Tunney, R.J. (2014) Processing of native and foreign language subtitles in films: An eye tracking study. *Applied Psycholinguistics* 35 (2), 399–418.

Borrás, I. and Lafayette, R.C. (1994) Effects of multimedia courseware subtitling on the speaking performance of college students of French. *The Modern Language Journal* 78 (1), 61–75.

Brysbaert, M. and New, B. (2009) Moving beyond Kucera and Francis: A critical evaluation of current word frequency norms and the introduction of a new and improved word frequency measure for American English. *Behavior Research Methods* 41 (4), 977–990.

Carpenter, P. and Just, M. (1983) What your eyes do while your mind is reading. In K. Rayner (ed.) *Perceptual and Language Processes* (pp. 275–307). New York: Academic Press.

Cerviño-Povedano, E. and Mora, J.C. (2011) Investigating Catalan learners of English over-reliance on duration: Vowel cue weighting and phonological short-term memory. In K. Dziubalska-Kołaczyk, M. Wrembeland and M. Kul (eds) *Achievements and Perspectives in the Acquisition of Second Language Speech: New Sounds 2010* (Vol. 1; pp. 56–64). Frankfurt am Main: Peter Lang.

Costa, A., Hernández, M., Costa-Faidella, J. and Sebastián-Gallés, N. (2009) On the bilingual advantage in conflict processing: Now you see it, now you don't. *Cognition* 113 (2), 135–149.

d'Ydewalle, G. and Van de Poel, M. (1999) Incidental foreign-language acquisition by children watching subtitled television programs. *Journal of Psycholinguistic Research* 28 (3), 227–244.

Darcy, I., Ewert, D. and Lidster, R. (2012) Bringing pronunciation instruction back into the classroom: An ESL teachers' pronunciation 'toolbox'. In J. Levis and K. LeVelle (eds) *Social Factors in Pronunciation Acquisition. Proceedings of the 3rd Annual Pronunciation in Second Language Learning and Teaching Conference* (pp. 93–108). Iowa State University, Ames, IA, 16–17 September 2011.

Darcy, I., Mora, J.C. and Daidone, D. (2016) The role of inhibitory control in acquiring a new phonological system. *Language Learning* 66 (3), 741–773.

Diamond, A. (2013) Executive functions. *Annual Review of Psychology* 64, 135–168.

Eriksen, B.A. and Eriksen, C.W. (1974) Effects of noise letters upon identification of a target letter in a non-search task. *Perception and Psychophysics* 16 (1), 143–149.

Flege, J.E. and Bohn, O.S. (1989) An instrumental study of vowel reduction and stress placement in Spanish-accented English. *Studies in Second Language Acquisition* 11 (1), 35–62.

French, L. and O'Brien, I. (2008) Phonological memory and children's second language grammar learning. *Applied Psycholinguistics* 29, 463–487.

Gómez Lacabex, M.L., Garcia Lecumberri, M.P. and Cooke, M. (2007) Perception of English vowel reduction by trained Spanish learners. In A.S. Rauber, M.A. Watkins and B.O. Baptista (eds) *New Sounds 2007: Proceedings of the Fifth International Symposium on the Acquisition of Second Language Speech* (pp. 294–299). Florianópolis, Brazil, 25–28 November 2007. Florianópolis: Federal University of Santa Catarina.

Gómez Lacabex, E. and Gallardo del Puerto, F. (2014) Two phonetic training procedures for young learners: Investigating instructional effects on perceptual awareness. *Canadian Modern Language Review* 70 (4), 500–531.

Isaacs, T. and Trofimovich, P. (2011) Phonological memory, attention control, and musical ability: Effects of individual differences on rater judgments of second language speech. *Applied Psycholinguistics* 32 (1), 113–140.

Krejtz, I., Szarkowska, A. and Łogińska, M. (2016) Reading function and content words in subtitled videos. *Journal of Deaf Studies and Deaf Education* 21 (2), 222–232.

Kruger, J.L. and Steyn, F. (2013) Subtitles and eye tracking: Reading and performance. *Reading Research Quarterly* 49 (1), 105–120.

Lambert, W.E., Boehler, I. and Sidoti, N. (1981) Choosing the languages of subtitles and spoken dialogues for media presentations: Implications for second language education. *Applied Psycholinguistics* 2 (2), 133–148.

Lee, B., Guion, S.G. and Harada, T. (2006) Acoustic analysis of the production of unstressed English vowels by early and late Korean and Japanese bilinguals. *Studies in Second Language Acquisition* 28 (3), 487–513.

Markham, P. (2001) The influence of culture-specific background knowledge and captions on second language comprehension. *Journal of Educational Technology Systems* 29 (4), 331–343.

Meara, P.M. (2005) X_Lex: *The Swansea Vocabulary Levels Test* (Version 2.05). Computer software. Swansea: Lognostics.

McGuigan, P. and Moffat, S. (2012) *Sherlock*. Series 2, Episode 1: *A Scandal in Belgravia*. TV programme. UK: BBC.

Miralpeix, I. (2012) X_Lex and Y_Lex: A validation study. In VARG (Vocabulary Acquisition Research Group), *22nd VARG Conference*. Newtown, 16–19 March 2012. Newtown: VARG.

Mitterer, H. and McQueen, J.M. (2009) Foreign subtitles help but native-language subtitles harm foreign speech perception. *PloS ONE* 4 (11), e7785.

Miyake, A., Friedman, N.P., Emerson, M.J., Witzki, A.H., Howerter, A. and Wager, T.D. (2000) The unity and diversity of executive functions and their contributions to complex 'frontal lobe' tasks: A latent variable analysis. *Cognitive Psychology* 41, 49–100.

Monsell, S. (2003) Task switching. *Trends in Cognitive Sciences* 7 (3), 134–140.

Montero Perez, M., Van Den Noortgate, W. and Desmet, P. (2013) Captioned video for L2 listening and vocabulary learning: A meta-analysis. *System* 41 (3), 720–739.

Montero Perez, M., Peters, E. and Desmet, P. (2014) Is less more? Effectiveness and perceived usefulness of keyword and full captioned video for L2 listening comprehension. *ReCALL* 26 (1), 21–43.

Montero Perez, M., Peters, E. and Desmet, P. (2015) Enhancing vocabulary learning through captioned video: An eye-tracking study. *The Modern Language Journal* 99 (2), 308–328.

O'Brien, I., Segalowitz, N., Collentine, J. and Freed, B. (2006) Phonological memory and lexical, narrative, and grammatical skills in second language oral production by adult learners. *Applied Psycholinguistics* 27 (3), 377–402.

Pivneva, I., Palmer, C. and Titone, D. (2012) Inhibitory control and L2 proficiency modulate bilingual language production: Evidence from spontaneous monologue and dialogue speech. *Frontiers in Psychology* 3, 1–18.

Rayner, K. (1998) Eye movements in reading and information processing: 20 years of research. *Psychological Bulletin* 124 (3), 372–422.

Rayner, K. and Duffy, S.A. (1988) On line comprehension processes and eye movements in reading. In M. Daneman, G.E. MacKinnon and T.G. Waller (eds) *Reading Research: Advances in Theory and Practice* (pp. 13–66). New York: Academic Press.

Segalowitz, N. and Frenkiel-Fishman, S. (2005) Attention control and ability level in a complex cognitive skill: Attention shifting and second-language proficiency. *Memory and Cognition* 33 (4), 644–653.

Simon, J.R. (1969) Reactions towards the source of stimulation. *Journal of Experimental Psychology* 81 (1), 174–176.

Simon, J.R. and Wolf, J.D. (1963) Choice reaction times as a function of angular stimulus-response correspondence and age. *Ergonomics* 6 (1), 99–105.

Stirling, N. (1979) Stroop interference: An input and an output phenomenon. *Quarterly Journal of Experimental Psychology* 31 (1), 121–132.

Stroop, J.R. (1935) Studies of interference in serial verbal reactions. *Journal of Experimental Psychology* 18 (6), 643–662.

Valls-Ferrer, M. (2011) The development of oral fluency and rhythm during a study abroad period. Unpublished doctoral dissertation, Universitat Pompeu Fabra, Barcelona.

Vanderplank, R. (2010) Déjà vu? A decade of research on language laboratories, television and video in language learning. *Language Teaching* 43 (1), 1–37.

Webb, S. and Rodgers, M.P. (2009) Vocabulary demands of television programs. *Language Learning* 59 (2), 335–366.

White, L. and Mattys, S.L. (2007) Calibrating rhythm: First language and second language studies. *Journal of Phonetics* 35 (4), 501–522.

7 'A Friend in Need Is a *Film* Indeed': Teaching Colloquial Expressions with Subtitled Television Series

Anca Daniela Frumuselu

Teaching and learning informal language in the form of single-word lexis and multi-word expressions (idioms, collocations, phrasal verbs and slang) has always been a challenge in the English as a foreign language (EFL) classroom. Foreign language teaching theoreticians perceive that the acquisition of vocabulary – individual words and phrases – is the key to attaining a high level of proficiency. According to these premises, the use of subtitled films and television series in the EFL setting becomes a meaningful tool for developing and enhancing foreign language skills. Various elements, such as the authenticity of the video materials, the quality of the audiovisual input in television series and sitcoms and the facility with which learners process subtitled materials, support the argument in favour of the use of subtitled series in the EFL classroom. This chapter critically presents two longitudinal studies carried out by the researcher/author to highlight the acquisition by EFL learners of informal and colloquial language following exposure over a period of seven weeks to authentic audiovisual sources containing intralingual and interlingual subtitles. It evaluates learners' long- and short-term retention, and their recall of colloquial expressions, using pre-post and immediate tests. Analysis of the data reveals some statistically significant results in favour of the use of subtitled and captioned television series in the EFL classroom.

Introduction

The importance of acquiring informal vocabulary began to be more greatly acknowledged in the mid-1980s. However, the impact of providing students with strategies to remember target vocabulary in the long term has scarcely been addressed. Several theories have been discussed in relation to vocabulary learning, such as the depth or level of processing theory (Craik & Lockhart, 1972), which claims that the level of processing has a significant effect on word memory. The involvement load hypothesis (Laufer & Hulstijn, 2001) stresses the effect of the level of involvement in the task on the retention of words and lexical phrases. Vocabulary acquisition is considered to be an essential element in the process of learning a foreign language (Milton, 2008: 228); however, there are mixed opinions about promoting it efficiently either in an explicit or an implicit way. For instance, Boers and Lindstromberg (2008: 3) claim that foreign language learners are able to learn new words and expressions incidentally, similar to the way in which children learn their first language (L1); they argue that the best way for teachers to promote vocabulary learning is to encourage learners 'to deploy their pre-existing ability to infer word meanings from context'.

Adding subtitles to audiovisual material, in the form of either interlingual titles (in learners' L1) or intralingual titles (in learners' second language [L2]), enhances language acquisition because of the activity's beneficial function as a bridge between reading and listening skills (Borrás & Lafayette, 1994). Learners benefit from the above-mentioned aids because the powerful assets of authentic video are merged with the reinforcing and facilitating effects of using subtitles inside the EFL classroom. Although it is considered to be a laborious and demanding task in language learning, providing EFL learners with access to subtitled audiovisual materials could also enhance and develop their informal and colloquial vocabulary.

In the literature, few empirical studies have investigated the issue of informality and conversational speech in connection to subtitles and audiovisual aids, and very few longitudinal studies have been carried out in this specific area (Araújo, 2008; Bravo, 2008; Ghia, 2007, 2011; Vanderplank, 1990). This chapter presents two research projects that investigate informal and colloquial language learning by EFL learners in their second year of study for a bachelor's degree in English at Rovira i Virgili University, Tarragona, Spain. Students were exposed to authentic audiovisuals with intralingual and interlingual subtitles over a period of seven weeks. The chapter also addresses additional elements (such as the implication of using authentic materials in the foreign language classroom), considers how learners process subtitled materials, assesses the effectiveness of the audiovisual input and discusses how informal and colloquial language learning is approached in EFL settings.

The Authenticity of Subtitled Videos

Defining the manifold and complex notion of authenticity in language teaching is a bold undertaking. Authenticity is a rather heterogeneous concept among language theoreticians and practitioners. This section of the chapter aims to provide a framework for the term 'authenticity' in the literature and its relevance to foreign and L2 teaching and learning. The prime concern is that classroom language is often perceived as artificial and unnatural (Van Lier, 1996). This implies that language use in the classroom is different from language use in 'real life'. Thus, people in the classroom are expected to speak and write as if they were not in the classroom and use 'street language' in order to sound 'authentic'. In other words, 'the classroom must become inauthentic as a classroom' (Van Lier, 1996: 123).

However, the issue of authenticity in the classroom cannot be so easily standardised. The concept of authenticity is still perceived as a central benchmark for the selection and evaluation of language teaching materials (MacDonald *et al.*, 2000; Taylor, 1994; Widdowson, 1979). In addition, a pedagogical value is assigned to the similarity between the input received in the classroom and the language and social context of everyday life (MacDonald *et al.*, 2000). Therefore, it is inferred that the reality that resides outside the classroom should be reflected in the instructional materials and practices inside the classroom.

According to Breen (1985), authenticity is a complex notion; it encompasses several types of authenticity, which are not easily distinguishable, as many scholars do not make clear references to the type of authenticity to which they are referring. Breen (1985: 61) identifies four types of authenticity: (1) text authenticity, which is related to the way we use the input for learners; (2) the authenticity of learners' own interpretations of such texts; (3) task authenticity, which may lead to language learning; and (4) the authenticity of the actual social situation of the classroom as a language learning environment.

Although each classroom has its own reality and authentic language, which is created by its participants (the teacher and students), there is a basic need to further analyse the characteristics of ready-made educational resources for foreign or L2 learning. Porter and Roberts (1981) call authentic texts the ones that are created by native speakers and aimed at native speakers. The use of an authentic resource would not only benefit foreign language acquisition and retention but also successfully complement the explicit pedagogical materials that are already present in textbooks.

Most of the researchers in the EFL field agree on the fact that the language presented to students in textbooks is a poor representation of the real language used in ordinary speaking interactions in life, which highlights the lack of informal language structures taught (Buendgens-Kosten, 2014: 458). The main advantage of using genuine texts and authentic activities in language teaching is that they provide better linguistic models than those in non-genuine texts, which, in spite of including language that is grammatically correct, lack the genuineness and informality of non-textbook language use (Gilmore, 2004).

Videos, CDs and DVDs have been successfully brought into the classroom since the 1980s. However, nowadays the presence of the internet and the possibility of adding captions to any visual material counterbalance the limitations of traditional audiovisual materials. One of the advantages of video is that it permits students to witness authentic linguistic and cultural interactions between native speakers (Herron, 1994). Hence, video enables learners to use visual information to enhance comprehension and to observe the gestures, facial expressions and other aspects of body language alongside authentic language and cultural information about speakers of English. However, educational videos, created for the classroom, are far more present in the lesson routine than are authentic videos (e.g. news, films, adverts and television series) aimed at native speakers.

The benefits of authentic videos when compared with English as a second language (ESL)/EFL videos were first stated in the early 1990s. Although teachers need to spend more time previewing and selecting authentic videos, Stempleski (1991) advocates for the use of authentic videos with language learners from beginner to advanced. First, they present real language: although it is not real in the sense of being unscripted, it is real because it is aimed at native speakers. Thus, it is ungraded and not simplified, it is spoken at a normal pace and it is current, as it makes use of idioms and expressions that are common in contemporary English-speaking environments. Authentic video materials can also lead to follow-up activities, such as cross-cultural discussions and writing activities. Moreover, if video-based media is implemented into teaching, students may become more effective and more critical viewers: they can become aware of how to transform their daily practice of watching television into a learning experience. Finally, authentic videos can be a motivating source for language learners, as they feel they have achieved their goal when they comprehend material – especially spoken material – that is intended for native speakers. They can extend this classroom practice in their free time, so they can look for authentic material to watch independently (Stempleski, 1991: 9–10).

Subtitle Processing

Two questions are essential when learners engage in the task of watching subtitled videos. Is processing a subtitled programme an effortless procedure? Are learners achieving good levels of performance when engaged in subtitle processing, without causing concession between image and text processing? In this case, one might wonder if subtitling could have a negative influence upon learners' understanding and perception of audiovisual materials, such as films and television programmes.

Perego *et al.* (2010: 262–263) conducted an experimental study in which the researchers analysed the cognitive processing of a subtitled film excerpt. They adopted a methodological approach based on the integration of a variety of measures: eye-movement data, word recognition and visual scene recognition. The results indicated that participants who had a good understanding of the film content, regardless of the line segmentation, reached good levels of performance in both subtitle recognition and scene recognition and there was no trade-off between subtitle recognition and scene recognition. The results of the study are in line with previous research (d'Ydewalle & Gielen, 1992; d'Ydewalle & Pavakanun, 1992), which highlights individuals' ability to process, integrate and remember information coming from various sources. A possible conclusion is, therefore, that individuals do not usually encounter serious difficulties in processing information from multiple sources.

Nonetheless, this contradicts an experiment carried out by Lavaur and Bairstow (2011), who investigated the correlation between different subtitle conditions (intralingual, interlingual and without subtitles) and the English language fluency of beginner, intermediate and advanced French native speakers. The results indicated that, for beginners, the visual information is best processed in the version of the film without subtitles; however, dialogue comprehension was best processed in the versions with interlingual and intralingual subtitles. Intermediate learners were not affected by any version of the film, but they did score higher in the dialogue questions, which may lead to the assumption that they relied on the subtitled versions of the films; hence, they performed better at the comprehension level. On the other hand, the advanced learners achieved higher comprehension scores for both visual and dialogue information with the version without subtitles, and their dialogue information processing was better than their visual information processing. The authors claim that overall, subtitles appear to be detrimental to visual information processing but have a facilitating effect on linguistic information processing (Lavaur & Bairstow, 2011: 457).

Criticisms still arise concerning the use of interlingual subtitles, as one may believe that learners stop listening to the original soundtrack while reading their native language. The reading of the subtitles tends to be automatic behaviour, as mentioned in previous eye-movement studies (d'Ydewalle & Gielen, 1992; d'Ydewalle & Pavakanun, 1992). Reading subtitles and processing visual information are considered to be highly efficient and partly automatised cognitive activities by other researchers, too (Lang, 1995, 2000; Lang *et al.*, 1999; Logan, 1997; Zhou, 2004). However, this does not imply that viewers stop processing the soundtrack. To demonstrate this point, a series of cognitive experiments carried out by d'Ydewalle and Pavakanun (1997: 146–147) relied on a double-task technique involving measuring reaction times to a flashing light during a television programme. The slower reactions in the presence of both sound and subtitles suggested that more complex, simultaneous processing of the soundtrack and the subtitles was occurring. Another experiment confirmed that participants processed sound when it was available, since slightly more time was devoted to the subtitles in the absence of sound (d'Ydewalle & Gielen, 1992: 417–418). Another study, however, reported that using interlingual subtitles leads to a global deterioration in visual information processing when compared with using a soundless film or a version dubbed in the viewer's own language (Lavaur & Nava, 2008).

Another group of researchers, De Bot *et al.* (1986), set up a news programme with subtitles that occasionally deviated from the speech on the phonological, grammatical, lexical or informational level. Two groups of participants – 50 secondary school pupils learning English at school and 20 advanced university students, who were no longer studying English – watched the programme in English with subtitles in their native Dutch. The participants responded to a multiple-choice test about each news item; the questions were equally divided between deviations and non-deviations. The results disproved the notion of exclusive subtitle orientation and showed that all viewers made use of the audio input, although this particular experiment was unable to quantify the extent of learning that directly resulted from the spoken text (De Bot *et al.*, 1986: 78–80).

When considering audiovisual dialogue in relation to L2 acquisition, Pavesi (2012: 159) states that the first aspect to evaluate is the degree of its adjustment to spontaneous speech, or its naturalness. Thus, the crucial issue is whether the language of film and television fiction is realistic enough to provide valuable input for language learning or adequate data for the L2 learning of spontaneous spoken language. Accordingly, several independent corpus-based investigations (Forchini, 2009, 2012; Quaglio, 2009; Rodríguez Martín, 2010; Rodríguez Martín & Jaén, 2009) have addressed the issue of naturalness, or genuineness, by comparing the language of film and television fiction with large corpora of spontaneous conversion.

Starting from the same emphasis on conversational language, the researchers sought to delve into the degree of spontaneity and naturalness of screen dialogue. In this context, naturalness is defined by the degree to which audiovisual dialogue mirrors the use of language in reality. However, the aim was not to prove that screen dialogue is a representation of spontaneous conversation and can be a direct substitute for face-to-face conversation; rather, the study sought to identify the degree of similarity to spontaneous conversation and the number of characteristics and features that the two registers have in common (Pavesi, 2012: 159).

Forchini (2009, 2012) carried out an empirical investigation of the linguistic features of American face-to-face and film conversation: two areas that differ in terms of spontaneity. The method of describing the linguistic characteristics of texts was based on Biber's (1988) multidimensional analysis approach and aimed at investigating to what extent conversations that happen face-to-face and in films differ from or resemble each other. In addition, a lexical element (i.e. *you know*), which is very frequent in spoken language and conversation, was researched. Therefore, the study investigated the frequency of *you know* in film language by making use of empirical data from the Longman Spoken American Corpus and the American Movie Corpus. The decision to use an American film conversation corpus was that no other available American film corpus provided appropriate material for the analysis of language in American films, and the transcriptions of speech in films available and downloadable from the web differ considerably from what is actually said in the films; therefore, those corpora were not suitable for this type of investigation. The results indicate that the two conversational domains do not differ to a great extent and that, according to the multidimensional analyses, both are informal, non-narrative and situation dependent and the features characterising them are present in the same quantities (Forchini, 2009: 23).

Quaglio (2009) also carried out a corpus-based investigation that is relevant to the scope of this chapter. His multidimensional analysis of the American sitcom *Friends* is the most comprehensive book-length lexico-grammatical study of fictional dialogue to date (Pavesi, 2012). On the grounds of the analysis of more than 100 morphosyntactic and lexical features, Quaglio (2009) compared the language of *Friends* with a sub-corpus of American English conversation contained in the Longman Grammar Corpus. He reaches the conclusion that the series *Friends* presents high frequencies of the vast majority of features that are typically used in natural conversation. He also reveals that the language of *Friends* is 'involved, interactive, and affective like face-to-face conversation' because it exhibits a 'high frequency of key correlated features such as first and second person pronouns, demonstrative pronouns, present tenses, private verbs (e.g., think, feel), contractions, emphatics, and that-deletions'. Overall, conversation in *Friends* is predominantly characterised by discourse immediacy, focusing on immediate concerns and making use of first- and second-person pronouns, greetings and leave-takings (Quaglio, 2009: 146).

Another series of publications (Rodríguez Martín, 2010; Rodríguez Martín & Jaén, 2009) compares the language of another corpus of 10 American films with the conversational section of the British National Corpus. Their findings are in line with previous research, in the sense that several features that are usually present in spontaneous conversation are also found in audiovisual dialogue, although not to the same extent. The findings revealed that the language of Anglophone films is closer to spontaneous face-to-face spoken English than to written English, and that the presence of spoken language in film dialogue has deeper implications than providing information on individual frequency counts (Rodríguez Martín, 2010). Similar to spontaneous conversation, the frequency of personal pronouns indicates the significance of personal deixis and anaphora in film language, whereas the widespread distribution of the response signal *yes* highlights the activation of turn-taking adjacency pairs, which are considered to be two basic organisational structures of dialogue and co-construction of meaning in spontaneous interaction.

Informal and Colloquial Language Learning

Colloquial speech seems to be one of the most difficult areas for achieving native-like language competence in the acquisition of a foreign language, and very few studies have been conducted on this topic. In fact, acquiring the colloquial speech of a discourse community is crucial for foreign language learners who wish to achieve native-like proficiency in the target language of such a community; failing 'to acquire colloquial-isms, or even slang, could result in the failure of mastering the language' (Bradford, 2010).

Research on the acquisition of L2 colloquial speech is limited, as the materials available in this field are mainly dictionaries and thesauruses. Although these present examples of colloquial speech and slang from the target language, they neither define the specific terms of colloquial speech and slang nor give insight into the acquisition of this type of speech. Other pedagogical materials related to informal language include self-study coursebooks that present lists of idioms, collocations or phrasal verbs for independent language learners. Some studies have examined attitudes towards the teaching of colloquialisms in language classroom settings or the opinions of native speakers on non-native speakers' use of colloquial speech and slang (Bradford, 2010: 1), but few have focused on the process of learning and acquiring this type of vocabulary.

The lack of acquisition of L2 colloquial speech comes from the difficulty that learners encounter, as outsiders, in achieving group membership (Bradford, 2010). Moreover, physiological and sociological factors, such as race, sex, age and religion, contribute to the type of language that people use (Fishman, 1979). A speaker who is not part of a given group will not be able to use the language that is specifically associated with that group. A general tendency among L2 learners is to stay away from colloquial speech and slang, because they may not feel that they belong to a specific group or culture that uses a culturally specific vocabulary (Xu & McAlpine, 2008).

Although belonging to a culturally specific group is an important factor to consider, when looking into learners' production of informal and colloquial speech other aspects need to be acknowledged, such as time spent in an English-speaking country, interaction with the target language and culturally specific communities, the learner's proficiency and the formal instruction of colloquial speech and slang in the classroom. However, in order to have access to considerable levels of input, extensive exposure to authentic communities in which the culturally specific language is spoken is required. In fact, some researchers claim that 'the benefits of residence in an L2 context only begin to appear after about two years' (Laufer & Paribakht, 1998: 366). Colloquial speech is a rich part of any language's vocabulary and its acquisition can be meaningful for L2 language learners, their social integration into a community, their comprehension of various forms of media, such as films, television and radio, and their conversations with peers (Bradford, 2010).

Case Studies

Despite the bulk of theoretical and empirical studies that have already been carried out on the issue of subtitled audiovisual materials, there is a scarcity of investigations on the aspect of informality and conversational speech in connection with the use of subtitles and audiovisual aids. Bravo (2008) is among the few who have approached a specific element of informal language and shed some light on the issue of idiomaticity in language learning. The findings from three experiments indicate that both interlingual and intralingual subtitles enhance viewers' comprehension of the content, even in culture-specific areas, such as idioms (Bravo, 2008).

In order to investigate which of the two subtitle conditions are more beneficial for foreign language learning, two research studies, carried out at Rovira i Virgili University (Spain) with second-year students, considered several types of informal and colloquial expressions, including slang, phrasal verbs, spoken and informal nouns and expressions, in connection with the effect of interlingual and intralingual subtitles upon the acquisition of informal and colloquial vocabulary.

The participants ($n = 49$) were second-year university students (A2–C1 level of English according to the Common European Framework of Reference for Languages) between 19 and 25 years old (M = 20.2, SD = 1.82). Of these, 24% were male and 76% were female. A questionnaire was distributed before starting the data collection in order to gain an insight into participants' backgrounds and viewing habits and eliminate students who were not suitable for the study. The questionnaire contained several questions related to participants' background in terms of their nationality, mother tongue, contact with the target language and English-speaking people, and viewing habits. The majority (90%) were Catalan and Spanish speakers and the other 10% mentioned that they had another mother tongue, including German, Russian, Romanian, Dutch and Moldavian. However, they had moved to the area long before the study took place, so they were fully integrated into the Catalan/Spanish educational system and were fluent speakers of Catalan and Spanish. The participants were studying a bachelor's degree in English studies in the Department of English and German Studies at Rovira i Virgili University in Spain.

A set of authentic audiovisual materials (episodes from season one of the American television series *Friends*) were selected and exploited by the teacher/researcher in the classroom for use as pedagogical support for the two studies. The sitcom *Friends* was chosen as a didactic material due to its rich informal and lexical content and because it reveals authentic cultural aspects of an English-speaking country. It also presents communicative, real-life situations that are highly relevant to the age group of our participants.

This first quasi-experimental study aimed to evaluate the effectiveness of subtitles (interlingual and intralingual) as language learning tools among EFL learners in higher education for informal and colloquial language acquisition in classroom settings.

The data for the first case study (Study 1) were collected from only 40 participants ($n = 40$) out of the group of 49, due to some students missing the pre- or post-test. The participants were randomly assigned to one of the two groups formed: either Group 1 (English sound + Spanish subtitles) or Group 2 (English sound + English subtitles). Both groups contained students from level A2 to C1 in English as follows: one student = A2, eight students = B1, seven students = B2 and two students = C1 in Group 1 (Spanish subtitles); and two students = A2, eight students = B1, eight students = B2 and four students = C1 in Group 2 (English subtitles). In total, there were 18 participants in Group 1 and 22 participants in Group 2. See Table 7.1 for student distribution in the two subtitling conditions according to their proficiency level.

The participants in both groups watched 13 episodes from the television series *Friends* over a period of seven weeks.

A 30-item pre- and post-test was administered to participants in Study 1 at the beginning and end of the viewing sessions in order to trace any differences in their achievement scores before and after the intervention took place. The scoring scale was from 1 to 30, one point being awarded for each correct answer in the case of multiple-choice questions and one point being awarded for each correct explanation of the meaning of a word (or words) in answer to the open questions.

The second case study (Study 2) involved the same participants and testing material and sought to approach the added value of subtitled

Table 7.1 Student distribution in the two subtitling groups according to their proficiency level

G1 Interlingual subtitles		G2 Intralingual subtitles	
Level	No. students	Level	No. students
A2	1	A2	2
B1	8	B1	8
B2	7	B2	8
C1	2	C1	4
Total	18	Total	22

video materials in relation to the immediate acquisition of colloquial and informal language among EFL students in higher education. Therefore, a 20-item immediate test (10 open questions and 10 multiple-choice questions) was administered after each viewing session in order to assess learners' immediate retention of colloquial and informal vocabulary. The scoring scale was from 1 to 20, one point being awarded for each correct answer in the case of multiple-choice questions and one point being awarded for each correct explanation of the meaning of word (or words) in answer to the open questions.

Findings

Based on the data analysis carried out in Study 1, it was found that the intralingual condition (Group 2 – English sound + English subtitles) had a significant effect on participants' post-test scores after they were exposed to authentic episodes of the American sitcom *Friends*. Therefore, students were able to rely on the visual, audio and written elements of the videos to identify the correct meaning of the informal expressions and words in the provided context. A detailed explanation of the findings and the procedure employed for the first case study can be found in Frumuselu *et al.* (2015).

Students' immediate scores, tested after each session in Study 2, revealed that neither of the two conditions (with English or with Spanish subtitles) was significant in changing the proficiency acquired by learners in terms of informal and colloquial vocabulary. However, individual growth was observed independently of the type of subtitles to which the students were exposed. The findings of Study 2 contradict the results of Study 1, carried out with pre- and post-tests over the same period of seven weeks, in which the intralingual condition (with English subtitles) was shown to be more beneficial than the interlingual one.

These results could be explained by the length of time allocated to learners in order to internalise and further recall the vocabulary concepts to which they were exposed. Thus, participants in Study 2 faced more difficulty than those in Study 1, mainly because the testing procedure was different. In Study 2, the participants were encountering most of the idiomatic and colloquial expressions for the first time and they had to answer the test immediately after they had watched the episode. Consequently, they had to remember the target vocabulary from the episodes in an ad hoc way. Furthermore, the tests in Study 2 were not comparable, containing colloquial and informal expressions related only to the episode in question. This could constitute the primary explanation for the differences between the results of the two studies. Students in Study 1 were already familiar with the target vocabulary when tested and they had had time to internalise the target language over seven weeks. Students in Study 2 had their vocabulary recall tested immediately after watching each new episode each week, which did not allow them to base their answers on previously acquired knowledge.

Conclusions

The two longitudinal studies show that subtitled and captioned series bring considerable benefits for developing and enhancing colloquial speech in EFL settings. In the first study, learners who were exposed to authentic audiovisual materials for a period of seven weeks with intralingual (English) subtitles benefited more than those who watched the episodes with interlingual (Spanish) subtitles. The findings of the two case studies presented in this chapter contradict those of previous research studies, which claim that interlingual subtitles are more beneficial than intralingual subtitles for language learning (Bianchi & Ciabattoni, 2008; Bravo, 2010; d'Ydewalle & Van de Poel, 1999; Koolstra & Beentjes, 1999). However, they support several investigations that account for the benefits of L2 subtitles (Araújo, 2008; Bird & Williams, 2002; Borrás & Lafayette, 1994; Caimi, 2006; Garza, 1991; Vanderplank, 1988).

The conclusions of Study 2 contradict previous findings in published experiments, which either reveal the benefits of intralingual subtitles (Vanderplank, 1990) or are in favour of interlingual subtitles (Ghia, 2007, 2011). However, the results of Study 2 support Bravo's (2008) findings, which show that both conditions (interlingual and intralingual subtitles), with no major significant differences, lead to better comprehension of dialogue – even in culture-specific items, such as idioms.

Considering the two longitudinal case studies, it can be concluded that subtitled and captioned series bring considerable benefits for developing and enhancing colloquial speech in EFL settings. Moreover, the experimental evidence encourages further investigation into the topic and assures foreign language instructors and researchers that authentic subtitled videos are profitable didactic tools and resources that can be used in the classroom to enhance foreign learners' language skills and target language acquisition, even for low-level students. However, further investigation should focus on the importance of the use of subtitled audiovisual materials not only in formal teaching but also in informal contexts, referring to individual language learning for adult learners and autonomous language learners, as advocated by Vanderplank (2015: 30). Evidence of adult learning in informal contexts is investigated by d'Ydewalle and Pavakanun (1992, 1996, 1997) and by Van Lommel *et al.* (2006), who claim that viewers can pick up language, mainly vocabulary items, from watching foreign language films.

Notwithstanding the above, the current advances in technology are compelling foreign language teachers and researchers to deal with not only the 'effects of' but also the 'effects with' technology (Vanderplank, 2015: 31–32). In other words, it is not enough to measure what exposure to subtitles or captions does in terms of language learner behaviour; it is also necessary to investigate what learners and viewers do with captions or subtitles. The effects of captions show increased comprehension, increased vocabulary acquisition and enhanced speaking and listening skills, whereas the effects with technology refer to how a particular task can be performed better once we become experienced and skilled users of a tool or a piece of technology, such as a personal computer, tablet, smartphone or DVD with captions or subtitles.

References

Araújo, V. (2008) The educational use of subtitled films in EFL teaching. In J. Díaz Cintas (ed.) *The Didactics of Audiovisual Translation* (pp. 227–238). Amsterdam: John Benjamins.

Bianchi, F. and Ciabattoni, T. (2008) Captions and subtitles in EFL learning: An investigative study in a comprehensive computer environment. In A. Baldry, M. Pavesi, C. Taylor Torsello and C. Taylor (eds) *From Didactas to Ecolingua* (pp. 69–90). Trieste: Edizioni Università di Trieste.

Biber, D. (1988) *Variation Across Speech and Writing*. Cambridge: Cambridge University Press.

Bird, S.A. and Williams, J.N. (2002) The effect of bimodal input on implicit and explicit memory: An investigation into the benefits of within-language subtitling. *Applied Psycholinguistics* 23 (4), 509–533.

Boers, F. and Lindstromberg, S. (2008) How cognitive linguistics can foster effective vocabulary teaching. In F. Boers and S. Lindstromberg (eds) *Cognitive Linguistic Approaches to Teaching Vocabulary and Phraseology* (pp. 1–61). Berlin: Mouton De Gruyter.

Borrás, I. and Lafayette, R.C. (1994) Effects of multimedia courseware subtitling on the speaking performance of college students of French. *The Modern Language Journal* 78 (1), 61–75. http://doi.org/10.2307/329253

Bradford, P.B. (2010) The acquisition of colloquial speech and slang in second language learners of English in El Paso, Texas. Master thesis, The University of Texas at El Paso. See http://digitalcommons.utep.edu/dissertations/AAI1484150/ (accessed 9 February 2014).

Bravo, C. (2008) Putting the reader in the picture. Screen translation and foreign-language learning. Doctoral thesis, Rovira i Virgili University. See http://tdx.cat/bitstream/handle/10803/8771/Condhino.pdf?sequence=1 (accessed 25 June 2013).

Bravo, C. (2010) Text on screen and text on air: A useful tool for foreign language teachers and learners. In J. Díaz-Cintas, A. Matamala and J. Neves (eds) *New Insights into Audiovisual Translation and Media* (pp. 269–283). Amsterdam: Rodopi.

Breen, M.P. (1985) Authenticity in the language classroom. *Applied Linguistics* 6 (1), 60–70.

Buendgens-Kosten, J. (2014) Authenticity. *ELT Journal* 68 (4), 457–459. http://doi.org/10.1093/elt/ccu034

Caimi, A. (2006) Audiovisual translation and language learning: The promotion of intralingual subtitles. *The Journal of Specialised Translation* 6, 85–98.

Craik, F.I.M. and Lockhart, R.S. (1972) Levels of processing: A framework for memory research 1. *Journal of Verbal Learning and Verbal Behavior* 11, 671–684.

De Bot, K., Jagt, J., Janssen, H., Kessels, E. and Schils, E. (1986) Foreign television and language maintenance. *Second Language Research* 2 (1), 72–82. http://doi.org/10.1177/026765838600200105

d'Ydewalle, G. and Gielen, I. (1992) Attention allocation with overlapping sound, image, and text. In K. Rayner (ed.) *Eye Movements and Visual Cognition* (pp. 415–427). New York: Springer. http://doi.org/10.1007/978-1-4612-2852-3

d'Ydewalle, G. and Pavakanun, U. (1992) Watching foreign television programs and language learning. In F.L.D. Engel, G. Bouwhuis, T. Bosser and G. d'Ydewalle (eds) *Cognitive Modelling and Interactive Environments in Language Learning* (pp. 193–198). Berlin: Springer.

d'Ydewalle, G. and Pavakanun, U. (1996) Le sous-titrage à la télévision facilite-t-il l'apprentissage des langues. In Y. Gambier (ed.) *Les transferts linguistiques dans les médias audiovisuels* (pp. 217–223). Paris: Presses universitaires du Septentrion.

d'Ydewalle, G. and Pavakanun, U. (1997) Could enjoying a movie lead to language acquisition? In P. Winterhoff-Spurk and T.H.A. van der Voort (eds) *New Horizons in Media Psychology: Research Cooperation and Projects in Europe* (pp. 145–155). Opladen: Westdeutcher Verlag.

d'Ydewalle, G. and Van de Poel, M. (1999) Incidental foreign-language acquisition by children watching subtitled television programs. *Journal of Psycholinguistic Research* 28 (3), 227–244.

Fishman, J.A. (1979) *Sociología del lenguaje*. Madrid: Cátedra.

Friends: Season 1 (1994) TV series. CA, USA: Warner Bros NBC.

Forchini, P. (2009) Spontaneity reloaded: American face-to-face and movie conversation compared. In C. Mahlberg, C. González-Díaz and C. Smith (eds) *Proceedings of the Corpus Linguistics Conference 2009* (pp. 1–27). Liverpool, 20–23 July. Liverpool: University of Liverpool. See http://ucrel.lancs.ac.uk/publications/cl2009/ (accessed 5 January 2015).

Forchini, P. (2012) *Movie Language Revisited: Evidence from Multi-Dimensional Analysis and Corpora*. New York: Peter Lang.

Frumuselu, A.D., De Maeyer, S., Donche, V. and Colon Plana, M. (2015) Television series inside the EFL classroom: Bridging the gap between teaching and learning informal language through subtitles. *Linguistics and Education* 32, 107–117. http://doi.org/10.1016/j.linged.2015.10.001

Garza, T.J. (1991) Evaluating the use of captioned video materials in advanced foreign language learning. *Foreign Language Annals* 24 (3), 239–258.

Ghia, E. (2007) A case study on the role of interlingual subtitles on the acquisition of L2 syntax: Initial results. *Voices on Translation, Linguistic, Multimedia, and Cognitive Perspectives, RILA*, 39 (special issue), 167–177.

Ghia, E. (2011) The acquisition of L2 syntax through audiovisual translation. In A. Şerban, A. Matamala and J.-M. Lavaur (eds) *Audiovisual Translation in Close-up: Practical and Theoretical Approaches* (pp. 95–112). Bern: Peter Lang.

Gilmore, A. (2004) A comparison of textbook and authentic interactions. *ELT Journal* 58 (4), 363–374. http://doi.org/10.1093/elt/58.4.363

Herron, C. (1994) Investigation of the effectiveness of using an advance organizer to introduce video in the foreign language classroom. *The Modern Language Journal* 78 (2), 190–198. http://www.jstor.org/stable/329009

Koolstra, C.M. and Beentjes, J. (1999) Children's vocabulary acquisition in a foreign language through watching subtitled television programs at home. *Educational Technology Research and Development* 47 (1), 51–60.

Lang, A. (1995) Defining audio/video redundancy from a limited-capacity information processing perspective. *Communication Research* 22 (2), 86–115. http://doi.org/10.1177/009365095022001004

Lang, A. (2000) The limited capacity model of mediated message processing. *Journal of Communication* 50 (1), 46–70. http://doi.org/10.1111/j.1460-2466.2000.tb02833.x

Lang, A., Potter, R. and Bolls, P. (1999) Something for nothing: Is visual encoding automatic? *Media Psychology* 1 (2), 145–163.

Laufer, B. and Paribakht, T.S. (1998) The relationship between passive and active vocabularies: Effects of language learning context. *Language Learning* 48 (3), 365–391. http://doi.org/10.1111/0023-8333.00046

Laufer, B. and Hulstijn, J. (2001) Incidental vocabulary acquisition in a second language: The construct of task-induced involvement. *Applied Linguistics* 22 (1), 1–26. http://doi.org/10.1093/applin/22.1.1

Lavaur, J.-M. and Nava, S. (2008) Interférences liées au sous-titrage intralangue sur le traitement des images d'une séquence filmée [Interferences of intralingual subtitling on image processing in a filmed sequence]. In J-H. Hoc and Y. Corson (eds) *Proceedings of the French Society of Psychology Congress* 2007 (pp. 59–64). Nantes.

Lavaur, J.-M. and Bairstow, D. (2011) Languages on the screen: Is film comprehension related to the viewers' fluency level and to the language in the subtitles? *International Journal of Psychology* 46 (6), 455–462. http://doi.org/10.1080/00207594.2011.565343

Logan, G.D. (1997) Automaticity and reading: Perspectives from the instance theory of automatization. *Reading and Writing Quarterly* 13 (2), 123–146.

MacDonald, M., Badger, R. and White, G. (2000) The real thing? Authenticity and academic listening. *English for Specific Purposes* 19 (3), 253–267. http://doi.org/10.1016/S0889-4906(98)00028-3

Milton, J. (2008) Vocabulary uptake from informal learning tasks. *Language Learning Journal* 36 (2), 227–237. http://doi.org/10.1080/09571730802390742

Pavesi, M. (2012) The potentials of audiovisual dialogue for second language acquisition. In P. Alderete-Díez, L. Incalaterra McLoughlin, L. Ní Dhonnchadha and D. Ní Uigín (eds) *Translation, Technology and Autonomy in Language Teaching and Learning* (pp. 155–174). Bern: Peter Lang.

Perego, E., Del Missier, F., Porta, M. and Mosconi, M. (2010) The cognitive effectiveness of subtitle processing. *Media Psychology* 13 (3), 243–272. http://doi.org/10.1080/15213269.2010.502873

Porter, D. and Roberts, J. (1981) Authentic listening activities 1. *ELT Journal* 36 (1), 37–47. http://doi.org/10.1093/elt/36.1.37

Quaglio, P. (2009) *Television Dialogue. The Sitcom Friends vs. Natural Conversation.* Amsterdam: John Benjamins.

Rodríguez Martín, M. (2010) Comparing conversational processes in the BNC and a micro-corpus of movies: Is film language the 'real thing'? *Language Forum* 36 (1), 1–15.

Rodríguez Martín, M. and Jaén, M. (2009) Teaching conversation through films: A comparison of conversational features and collocations in the BNC and a micro-corpus of movies. *International Journal of Learning* 16 (7), 445–458. See http://ijh.cgpublisher.com/product/pub.30/prod.2296 (accessed 1 May 2015).

Stempleski, S. (1991) Teaching communication skills with authentic video. In S. Stempleski and P. Arcario (eds) *Video in Second Language Teaching: Using, Selecting, and Producing Video for the Classroom* (pp. 7–24). Washington, DC: Teachers of English to Speakers of Other Languages.

Taylor, D. (1994) Inauthentic authenticity or authentic inauthenticity? The pseudo-problem of authenticity in the language classroom. *TESL-EJ*, 1 (2), 1–11.

Van Lier, L. (1996) *Interaction in the Language Curriculum: Awareness, Autonomy and Authenticity.* New York: Longman.

Van Lommel, S., Laenen, A. and d'Ydewalle, G. (2006) Foreign-grammar acquisition while watching subtitled television programmes. *The British Journal of Educational Psychology* 76 (2), 243–258. http://doi.org/10.1348/000709905X38946

Vanderplank, R. (1988) The value of teletext sub-titles in language learning. *ELT Journal* 42 (2), 272–281. http://doi.org/10.1093/elt/42.4.272

Vanderplank, R. (1990) Paying attention to the words: Practical and theoretical problems in watching television programmes with uni-lingual (CEEFAX) sub-titles. *System* 18 (2), 221–234. http://doi.org/10.1016/0346-251X(90)90056-B

Vanderplank, R. (2015) Thirty years of research into captions/same language subtitles and second/foreign language learning: Distinguishing between 'effects of' subtitles and 'effects with' subtitles for future research. In Y. Gambier, A. Caimi and C. Mariotti (eds) *Subtitles and Language Learning. Principles, Strategies and Practical Experiences* (pp. 19–40). New York: Peter Lang.

Widdowson, H.G. (1979) *Teaching Language as Communication*. Oxford: Oxford University Press.

Xu, H. and McAlpine, J. (2008) Anglophone, peewee, two-four... are Canadianisms acquired by ESL learners in Canada? *TESL Canada Journal* 26 (1), 11–30. http://www.teslcanadajournal.ca/index.php/tesl/article/view/388

Zhou, S. (2004) Effects of visual intensity and audiovisual redundancy in bad news. *Media Psychology* 6 (3), 237–256.

8 Enhancing Student Motivation in Foreign Language Learning through Film Subtitling Projects

Rosa Alonso-Pérez

Combining learning a foreign language with the use of media and technology is common practice nowadays (Heafner, 2004). This chapter discusses the effects of a subtitling project on motivation. The project was conducted at Sheffield Hallam University among a group of second-year learners with level B1–B2 Spanish according to the Common European Framework of References for Languages (CEFR). It aimed to observe the effect of subtitling and project work on these students, to what extent it enhanced their motivation for self-study and to what degree the use of authentic materials (short films) and the active manipulation of these resources are a motivating factor. The activity lasted for 10 weeks and culminated in a Spanish short-film festival, where students presented their work to a judging panel of final-year students in a competition for the best subtitled short film. Using subtitling software, students had to choose a short film in Spanish and work individually and collaboratively to complete several tasks, such as transcribing the audio in Spanish, translating the script into English, subtitling the clip and synchronising the subtitles with the images. A multi-method approach was employed to collect data through quantitative and qualitative research methods, including initial and final questionnaires, the teacher's observational notes, students' feedback and the students' interlingual subtitles.

Introduction

In recent years, the use of technology and the practice of audiovisual translation (AVT) techniques in the classroom have become a recurrent pedagogic combination in language learning. As Witte *et al.* (2009: 5) suggest, 'new technologies, coupled with flexible and innovative teaching methodologies and didactics, offer very motivating ways of learning through translation exercises'. Consequently, it has become increasingly popular to use AVT techniques (such as subtitling, dubbing, voice-over and audio description) as didactic resources when working on specific learning areas (Baños & Sokoli, 2015; Danan, 2010; Talaván, 2013). For instance, in a recent study, the European Commission (2011: 28) observed that subtitling can be a valuable didactic tool in foreign language learning; hence, it creates motivation to learn languages, 'improve[s] foreign language skills' and can contribute 'to creat[ing] awareness of language and cultural diversity'. Therefore, it is advised that teachers make the most of the various possibilities that this technology offers.

The present study focuses on the evaluation of students' motivation before and after the completion of a project on subtitling short films. The project aimed to stimulate students' interest in and enjoyment of Spanish and Latin American culture and it encouraged them to work in groups as autonomous learners. In other words, learners were invited to take an active role in their learning experience. The project sought to increase their enthusiasm for the subject through the preparation and organisation of a short-film festival.

The first section of this chapter introduces 'language learning motivation' as conceptualised in this study and discusses how subtitling can contribute to its enhancement. In the second section, the teaching case study is described. The results are presented in the third section, and are discussed in the fourth section. Some concluding remarks are made on the implications of this study for future research on the use of subtitling in second language (L2) learning.

Language Learning Motivation and Subtitling

Combining learning a foreign language with the use of media and technology is common practice nowadays, since there is evidence that technology enhances student motivation (Heafner, 2004). Research shows that multimedia is considered to be a valuable resource in the language learning classroom (Brett & Nash, 1999), as a large proportion of the Western population is exposed to audiovisual input on a daily basis (Talaván, 2013); for example, through the use of computers, MP4 players, smartphones, iPods and other devices.

The rationale behind the present study is based on the idea that there are many factors that affect students' motivation. Dörnyei (1998: 118) defines motivation as 'a process whereby a certain amount of instigation force arises, initiates action, and persists as long as no other force comes into play to weaken it and thereby terminate action, or until the planned outcome has been reached'. Moreover, language learners can act according to different motives, which can be derived from internal or external motivational factors. Schaefer (2010: 44–45) refers to intrinsic and extrinsic motivation as two interrelated concepts: 'Intrinsic motivation involves doing something for internal reasons, such as meeting a challenge, because something is enjoyable in itself, or satisfying personal interest and curiosity. Extrinsic motivation involves doing something for external reasons, such as getting good grades or other rewards, avoiding punishments, and pleasing parents and teachers'.

This differentiation does not imply that these two types of motivation are mutually exclusive; on the contrary, they can interact, as it has been pointed out that extrinsic motivation can lead to intrinsic motivation. However, Ryan and Deci (2006) have shown that intrinsically motivated people try harder and for longer, perform more flexibly and creatively, and learn more deeply than extrinsically motivated people do. In other words, students whose motivational purpose is to focus on learning and mastering the subject matter will probably display a more sustained engagement with academic work than those who are motivated merely by completing their assigned work satisfactorily in order to pass (Ames, 1992, in Thomas, 2000).

With regard to the language context, there is a noticeable distinction between learning, which occurs in a complex context, and motivation to learn. In addition, Keblawi (2009) shows that it must not be assumed that students have only one type of motivation. Likewise, students' motivation is not the same at all times: it changes in accordance with the ways in which they perceive the learning context and with their mood. Noels *et al.* (2000: 75) argue that 'foster[ing] sustained learning ... may not be sufficient to convince students that language learning is interesting and enjoyable; they may need to be persuaded that it is also important for them'. Students will need to find a valuable reason for wanting to learn a language in order to feel motivated to learn it.

Within the AVT context, it has been argued that subtitling contributes to language learning to a greater or lesser degree of effectiveness depending on several variables, such as whether the student is 'accustomed to subtitling', 'the learner's level', 'the objectives of the teaching' and 'the proximity between languages' (European Commission, 2011: 16). In addition, in the past decade the following authors have observed some positive effects related to subtitling. For instance, Incalcaterra McLoughlin and Lertola (2014) support the idea of integrating AVT techniques into L2 curricula. They taught a 24-week subtitling module as part of a standard Italian course for undergraduate students, and their results suggest that 'subtitling represents an additional type of activity which students enjoy and which can therefore be profitably employed' (Incalcaterra McLoughlin & Lertola, 2014: 79). Similarly, Talaván (2006: 45) points out that the creative activity of writing subtitles enhances all language areas and 'provides learners with the opportunity to negotiate meaning, to notice language [and] to become motivated'.

In another study, Fernández Costales (2014) discusses the opinions of trainee secondary school teachers on the use of subtitles as a teaching resource. The author suggests further investigation in order to observe whether students' motivation when learning a foreign language increases after the subtitling practice, and whether this affects students' academic performance. He also advises considering the possibility of integrating subtitling techniques into the framework of content and language integrated learning (CLIL) methodology and developing a specific language teaching methodology that includes subtitling (Fernández Costales, 2014).

Furthermore, the present subtitling project shares some of the key characteristics that define the project-based learning model (Diehl *et al.*, 1999; Jones *et al.*, 1997; Moursund, 1999; Thomas *et al.*, 1999). With the exception of centrality, since the subtitling project is not the main teaching, learning and assessment activity in the subject curriculum, the proposed subtitling practice has some similarities with the aforementioned model: it involves student autonomy, collaborative learning, authentic performance, variety, challenge, student choice, technology as a cognitive tool and non-academic-like problems. All these aspects intend to encourage students to learn and become proficient and to promote their interest in the activity and its perceived value (Blumenfeld *et al.*, 1991). At the same time, through the subtitling project students are able to establish a direct connection with the audiovisual material: they are working in an environment that is both motivating and rewarding, and they can share their work and show their immediate results to their peers. Therefore, the present study explores the effectiveness of a subtitling project from the students' point of view by analysing whether it has a positive effect. This is achieved by comparing their motivation levels before and after completing the project.

Subtitling Short Films: A Professional Practice with a Didactic Purpose

Two decades ago, Nunan (1999) suggested that the creation of subtitles should become a proper communicative task, since it is an authentic, functional and active process with a clear target and visible results. It is strongly believed that the benefits of subtitling are not limited to learning about language and culture, as practising this professional AVT technique can help language students develop and acquire many other transferrable skills (Baños & Sokoli, 2015; Chiu, 2012; Clouet, 2005; Ibáñez & Vermeulen, 2015; Navarrete, 2013; Sánchez-Requena, 2016; Talaván & Lertola, 2016).

The chosen audiovisual format for this particular subtitling project has been observed to offer numerous advantages. First, the simplicity and brief duration of short films make them perfect for transmitting information, and aids understanding (Talaván, 2006). From a constructivist point of view, videos are used as visual stimuli, which can help students to activate previous knowledge and generate predictions. In addition, this particular format offers visual support to the oral text, which helps to contextualise the story. According to Cabero (2007), the fact that short films have a logical storyline, have a protagonist or multiple characters and depict a variety of typical everyday situations help to enhance students' motivation and stimulate their interest by directly influencing their emotions. Numerous authors (McGrath, 2002; Nunan, 1999; Underwood, 1990) agree that the use of authentic materials better prepares students to face the real world, as practically any situation can be studied and practised. Learners become aware that this type of resource will help them to improve their communicative and language skills; therefore, this can motivate them to watch foreign films in their own time (Talaván, 2013). Ideally, students engage and work outside the classroom, as they 'feel the extra motivational factor of accomplishing a real outcome with total completion and achievement' (Talaván, 2006: 49). If students start to watch foreign films outside the academic context, they may be able to gradually improve their command of the foreign language while enjoying and appreciating the activity. In other words, the audiovisual language and the appropriate use of videos will awaken interest and enthusiasm in students.

Another justification for this project is that translation works as a bridge between different cultures, allowing them to interact. Currently, translation plays an important role in the language classroom; the Council of Europe (2001) considers it an essential skill by referring to it in the Common European Framework of Reference for Languages as follows:

> In both the receptive and productive modes, the written and/or oral activities of mediation make communication possible between persons who are unable, for whatever reason, to communicate with each other directly. Translation or interpretation … provides for a third party a (re)formulation of a source text to which this third party does not have direct access. Mediating language activities – (re)processing an existing text – occupy an important place in the normal linguistic functioning of our societies. (Council of Europe, 2001: 14)

Learners are encouraged to take responsibility for establishing a relationship between people from different cultures by acting as mediators between cultures (Brissett, 2003). Students worked on this project with a clear objective: to prepare a festival of Spanish short films for a target audience for which it was necessary to subtitle some short films in English, so that these were accessible to the attendees. The previous objective was encouraged by stating that students would be offering linguistic–cultural mediation to increase accessibility for non-Spanish speakers.

Therefore, the interlingual subtitling task required students to reach an awareness of the responsibility they had been assigned, as the audience reading their subtitles would be placing their trust in the students' work.

In a similar study, where students were asked to subtitle several clips into their first language (L1), Borghetti and Lertola (2014) highlight the importance of the concept of responsibility: to not only the target audience but also the film director, the source culture and the source text (Borghetti, 2011). In addition, these authors state that, in the case of subtitling, it is important to assume this responsibility in order to avoid distorting the original content or monopolising the viewer's attention because of the subtitles' 'excessive length, altering the rhythm [or] tone of the dialogues' (Borghetti & Lertola, 2014: 426). Students must be aware that their choices may affect the audience's perception of the target culture and will probably cause some stereotyping (Ramière, 2006), for which Borghetti and Lertola (2014: 426) suggest that students should be forced 'to reflect on their own role as mediators between cultures'.

Finally, it is necessary to mention that professional subtitling demands a proficiency in information technology (IT) skills. In the language learning context, it is necessary to create files of subtitles and synchronise them with the screen images. As discussed by Williams and Thorne (2000: 221), the technological aspect 'can be a motivating experience for those students who have a basic knowledge but for students with limited IT skills, this element of the course can be daunting'. However, Incalcaterra McLoughlin and Lertola (2014: 73) argue that the creation of subtitles as a didactic tool may 'differ considerably from "official" subtitles ... [created by professionals] both in terms of translation choices and in synchronisation'. They explicitly state that the aim of the module offered at their university is 'to teach Italian language through AVT, not to train students to be future subtitlers' (Incalcaterra McLoughlin & Lertola, 2014: 74). They explain that the most important aspect of subtitling in the language learning context is 'to sensitise learners to pragmatic, functional, lexical and other aspects of communication, basic elements of conversation analysis and how and to what extent these can be transferred into another language' (Incalcaterra McLoughlin & Lertola, 2014: 73). The main focus should not be on the technical aspects of the activity. For similar reasons, the aim of this project was not to train students as professional subtitlers, but to teach and present the Spanish language and culture through audiovisual materials.

Context and Methodology

The case study presented in this section is a project that was carried out with a group of second-year undergraduate students with level B1–B2 Spanish. The project saw learners work for one semester on the subtitling of nine short films. These were eventually screened at a festival of Spanish short films, celebrated at faculty level, which worked as a means of showcasing the students' work.

The project offered an original activity, which was expected to enhance students' motivation and participation. One of the main purposes was to engage the students in their Spanish module, for which they had only a two-hour weekly seminar with their tutor. The module aims to enable students to: (1) consolidate and develop their existing linguistic competence, both orally and in writing; (2) develop their ability to operate within their own specialism; (3) develop their awareness of business culture in the country or countries where Spanish is spoken; (4) develop their analytical and research skills; and (5) foster independent language learning and reflection in order to enable students to direct their own learning outside the classroom (ULS Stage 5, Module Guide, 14–15, unpublished classroom materials).

A total of 26 undergraduate students with level B1–B2 Spanish participated in the project. The gender breakdown of the participants was 19 females (73%) and 7 males (27%). Their ages ranged from 19 to 32 and the mean age was 19.8. With regard to their nationalities, the participants came from different backgrounds: there were 22 British students and 1 Romanian, 1 Brazilian, 1 French and 1 Italian student.

Of the 26 students, 22 were in their second year at university (Level 5) and enrolled for only 10 credits in this module (Semester 1), which was aimed at preparing them for their semester abroad (Semester 2). Twenty-four were doing a degree at the Sheffield Business School (comprising international business, marketing, tourism, teaching English as a second or other language) in combination with one or two languages. Six students were studying only one foreign language (Spanish), whereas 20 were also enrolled in a second foreign language. Moreover, only 6 students were planning to go to Spain as part of the Erasmus+ programme, while another 16 were going to study in France, Germany or Italy. The last four students – three studying human geography and computer science – were enrolled on the full 20 credits of the module, studying it for two semesters. In this module, students must pass two summative assessments in order to gain 10 credits during Semester 1. Both assessments consist of an oral presentation (in either pairs or groups) about a Spanish or Latin American city and a translation of a text from Spanish into English (L2 > L1).

Due to the inevitable development of the new media age, which has moved from paper-based to digital translations, it was considered appropriate to provide students with an introduction to AVT through subtitling in order to meet current social needs. Hence, the project was considered to give students valuable practice for their final assessments. However, the students were not formally assessed, as the project did not count towards their final semester grade.

The project lasted for 10 weeks and was presented in Week 11. Learners were given an overview of the subtitling process carried out by those working in the profession, which usually includes the following tasks: transcription, translation, subtitling and synchronisation. Several deadlines were set for each task and the process was divided into four stages (see Figure 8.1).

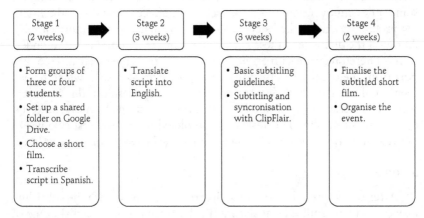

Figure 8.1 Project stages

Stage 1

During the initial phase, students formed groups of three or four according to their personal preferences, choosing the peers with whom they wanted to work. To make it easier for them to share their work within their group, students were asked to create a shared folder on Google Drive. Although it had been planned for learners to work on the project during the final period of every session (equivalent to 30–45 minutes), by sharing a folder on Google Drive the students had the opportunity to work from home and be in contact with other members of their group. This step was considered essential, as it allowed the teacher to provide them with encouraging feedback at every stage throughout the semester. Consequently, applications, such as Google Docs, appear to be useful, as they enable students in the same group to edit a file simultaneously. Amendments appear on the screen automatically, with the collaborator's name next to their cursor so everyone can see who is typing.

In the subtitling industry, when the client contacts the subtitling company or freelance translator/subtitler, they provide details concerning the film, such as the dialogue list. In order to check that no information is missing from the list, such as songs or inserts, the professional subtitler needs to verify it. However, according to research, sometimes 'the dialogue list is missing, [so] the dialogue exchanges need to be transcribed *ab initio* from the soundtrack' (Díaz Cintas & Remael, 2007: 30). For this reason, learners were assigned their first task: to transcribe their chosen short film in the original language.

Apart from simulating a real-life situation, it is believed that students benefited from this task because they were free to pause the clip as many times as necessary, which meant that they were in charge of their own learning process. Rost (2002: 145) provides a definition of 'paused texts'. According to the author, 'by pausing the spoken input … and allowing for some quick intervention and response, we in effect "slow down the listening process" to allow the listeners to monitor their listening more closely'. At times, the dialogue in these authentic resources is complicated to understand. Therefore, once learners had finalised the task, they were offered support from their teacher in the form of appropriate feedback, which helped them to fill the gaps in their transcription. The final result of this first stage consisted of creating a subtitle file (.srt format) with the Spanish transcription of the short film. This task was completed within the first two weeks of the semester, which was necessary in order to be ready for the next stage.

Stage 2

After concluding the first stage, learners continued with the subtitling process, which required translating the dialogue list into English. One of the main differences between traditional translation and AVT is that in AVT other relevant information may be provided by the acoustic and visual elements that should also be translated. These elements, such as 'songs, inserts, newspaper headlines, or voices coming from a radio or television set' (Díaz Cintas & Remael, 2007: 32), might not be included in the actors' dialogue, so learners will have to pay special attention in order to translate them into the L1.

Students were given three weeks to complete this task. In order to be able to watch the clip while translating the dialogue, it was suggested that learners import the subtitling file into ClipFlair (2011) and update it as they worked on their translations. Once they had finished translating for the day, they could easily export the updated file and share it with their group in their Google Drive folder so that another student could continue with the work until the task was complete.

Stage 3

As soon as students had finalised their translation of the script and created a new subtitling file, they were set another three-week deadline to synchronise the image with the text by 'spotting' the subtitles. In other words, students had to split the subtitles on to different lines when they were too long and insert the start and end times for each subtitle, synchronising them with the images.

As discussed previously, the aim of the project was not to train students as professional subtitlers but to engage them in the module by teaching them Spanish language and culture through audiovisual materials. However, it was considered appropriate to encourage students to follow some subtitling guidelines related to basic technical, linguistic and punctuation conventions in order to give them an overview of the professional task, as it was believed that this exercise could help them become aware of the constraints imposed by the medium. Many authors (e.g. Díaz Cintas, 1997; Talaván, 2006) argue that this technique provides students with practice of condensing expression, as they have to focus on transmitting the main ideas of the message by adapting the original discourse to the new limitations of time and space in order to make it fit into the subtitles. Once the students had finished this task, a subtitle file was created in order to embed the subtitles into the image.

Stage 4

Finally, students had to complete the project with the organisation of a festival of short films. The event was part of the semester's programme of social activities run by the Language Society at Sheffield Business School, and it was advertised using posters to make sure that it was well publicised and all language students were invited. The advertisement was also shared on social media, such as Facebook and Twitter, to reach a wider international audience. Each group of students wrote a synopsis of their short film, which included relevant information about the director and main actors. Students presented information about their films before they were screened, defending their work and wishing the audience an enjoyable viewing.

After the short films were screened, two prizes were awarded for the best subtitled film: the judging panel prize and the audience prize. The panel was carefully selected and was composed of four final-year students of Spanish and the department's Spanish language assistant. Each panel member had the opportunity to speak for a few minutes to provide some feedback and praise the students' work. The winner of the audience prize was decided by a mixed international audience, who voted for their preferred subtitled film through a polling system. The winners received a Spanish or Latin American film on DVD; however, all the students who participated in the project were also rewarded for their hard work during the semester and congratulated for completing the project by receiving a certificate of completion.

Research Question and Hypotheses

In order to examine whether the subtitling project is an effective tool for enhancing students' motivation, this study focuses on the following research question: To what degree is the use of authentic materials (short films) and the active manipulation of these resources a motivating factor?

The question raises three hypotheses:

(1) Students will feel more engaged with the module after having actively manipulated authentic resources through the use of specific software.
(2) Students will be aware of the transferable skills developed through this project.
(3) The use of authentic materials will result in enhancing students' intrinsic motivation.

Data Collection Tools

A multi-method approach was employed to collect quantitative and qualitative data. This included initial and final questionnaires, the teacher's observational notes, students' feedback and students' interlingual subtitles.

Questionnaires. Students were asked to complete an initial questionnaire at the beginning of the semester (Week 4) and a post-test in the week after the celebration of the short film festival (Week 11). Learners were grouped into two different classes according to their university timetable. Through this survey, quantitative and qualitative data were collected; however, due to the small sample of students, the analysis relevant to this study is mainly of a qualitative nature, as it is focused on students' feedback.

The questionnaire is an adaptation of a survey previously designed by Bernard (2010), a professor from Carnegie Mellon University who conducted a research study in motivation in foreign language learning and, in particular, compared the relationship between language classroom activities and students' motivation in a university learning context. Bernard's questionnaire proved to be valid for a similar type of research to that discussed in this chapter. According to Dörnyei and Csizér (2012: 77), it is possible to borrow questions from established questionnaires, as 'questions that have been used frequently before must have been through extensive piloting and therefore have a certain "track record"'. The original survey was divided into three categories: a classroom activities inventory, a motivation questionnaire and a demographics and outcomes page. However, only the two first sections were considered relevant to this study, which is why the third category was omitted. In addition, due to the nature of this study, it was appropriate to adapt the questionnaire in order to answer the research question.

The pre- and post-tests were composed of the same close-ended questions relating to classroom activities and motivation. However, the second survey presented an extra section with close-ended questions explicitly related to the subtitling project and two final and optional open-ended questions, which provided space for further comments about the project. By permitting greater freedom of expression to respondents, researchers can be led to identify issues not previously anticipated and can be provided with illustrative quotes and graphic examples, which may enrich the analysis (Dörnyei, 2010).

With regard to the sections containing close-ended questions, the classroom activities inventory asked students about the frequency with which they engaged in 20 different types of activities, either inside or outside the classroom. Students responded using a five-point frequency scale: 5 = Daily, 4 = Weekly, 3 = Monthly, 2 = At least once this semester and 1 = Never. The motivation questionnaire and the questions related to the subtitling project included a Likert rating scale: students were asked to respond to whether they agreed or disagreed with a total of 29 statements using a five-point scale ranging from 'Strongly disagree' to 'Strongly agree'. A neutral option, such as 'Neither agree nor disagree', was also available (see the appendices for a full list of activities and statements).

Results

With regard to motivation to use the language, positive results were obtained. As can be seen in Table 8.1, in Week 4, 95% of respondents strongly agreed with the statement 'I wish to someday be able to communicate with someone who speaks Spanish', whereas 100% strongly agreed with this statement in Week 11. Again, 95% of participants strongly agreed with the affirmation 'I want to be fluent in Spanish someday' in Week 4, a result that had increased to 100% by Week 11. In relation to enjoying learning about other cultures, 91% of respondents strongly agreed in Week 4 – a figure that increased to 96% by Week 11.

At the same time, a comparison of the results regarding how motivating students found the class was established (Table 8.2).

In Week 4, 82% of participants showed a positive attitude towards the statement 'I enjoy coming to class' by strongly agreeing or simply agreeing with the statement; a total of 92% agreed in Week 11. Similar results were observed for the responses provided to the affirmation 'I enjoy working with my classmates': 91% of respondents agreed and strongly agreed with the statement in Week 4, a result that increased by

Table 8.1 Comparison of students' responses regarding motivation to use the language

Motivation to use the language	'Agree' and 'Strongly agree' (Week 4) (%)	'Agree' and 'Strongly agree' (Week 11) (%)
(1) I wish to someday be able to communicate with someone who speaks Spanish.	95	100
(2) I want to be fluent in Spanish someday.	95	100
(3) I enjoy learning about other cultures.	91	96

Table 8.2 Comparison of students' responses regarding how motivating students found the class

Motivation about the class	'Agree' and 'Strongly agree' (Week 4) (%)	'Agree' and 'Strongly agree' (Week 11) (%)
(4) I enjoy coming to class.	82	92
(5) I enjoy working with my classmates.	91	93
(6) I find classroom activities interesting.	81	84
(7) I feel that the teacher wants me to do well in this class.	100	100

2% in Week 11, when 93% of participants chose these positive options. In Week 4, 81% of respondents indicated that they agreed or strongly agreed with the statement 'I find classroom activities interesting'; this percentage appears to be once again higher in Week 11, with 84% agreeing or strongly agreeing with it.

Finally, it was confirmed that students felt supported by their tutor throughout the semester, as 100% of the respondents agreed or strongly agreed with the statement 'I feel that the teacher wants me to do well in this class' in both weeks.

Discussion and Conclusion

The combination of the previous quantitative results and the students' feedback was reflected in their answers to the two open-ended questions, which displayed valuable information and helped to confirm the three research hypotheses and identify the strengths and weaknesses of the project.

With regard to the strengths, the results obtained so far suggest that students' motivation can be increased effectively by the introduction of subtitling in the language learning classroom. According to the responses, students show high levels of motivation and it can be inferred that the subtitling project enhanced their engagement with the module. In general, students have a positive attitude towards the classroom environment and activities. In particular, they feel encouraged to work with, and supported by, their peers and their tutor.

A further hypothesis has been proved: the use of specific software plays an important part in motivating students, and learners show awareness of having acquired new skills. For example, one student mentioned that the project helped them to develop skills in 'meeting deadlines, team work, IT skills' and that it 'helped with written Spanish and listening'.

It was also confirmed by students that working with authentic materials allowed them to learn and understand 'real' Spanish, learning about the culture in a more interesting way. Learners also appreciated being introduced to slang and colloquial Spanish, which, according to another student, they 'would not otherwise be able to learn in class'.

The culmination of the project in the celebration of the film festival provided students with a positive reward for their work on the subtitling activity, and further positive feedback reflecting this fact was collected. In general, students' comments show that the project was 'enjoyable' and 'interesting' and that it was 'fun to watch the result'.

Nevertheless, several areas for improvement were identified. Even though the project was designed with concision in mind, helping learners to work towards their translation assessment, according to some students the project demanded a considerable amount of time in order for them to accomplish the work. The fact that their work on the project was not graded may have considerably affected their motivation, as most students had to prioritise and focus on their final assessed piece of work. Many participants suggested that the project should be part of the summative assessments, which would increase their motivation to work. At the same time, having to meet the various deadlines for each task may have affected their intrinsic motivation (Amabile et al., 1976). These suggestions will be considered for future subtitling projects in order to reduce students' levels of stress.

To sum up, the results confirm that intrinsic and extrinsic motivational factors can affect students' experience and that, in order for them to fully enjoy a similar project, external rewards, such as gaining marks, play an important role. However, it has also been observed that there are other types of motivational factors that could enhance students' motivation in relation to the foreign language and culture, which should be taken into consideration. These include group motivation and teacher motivation in combination with interesting and authentic materials and challenging but encouraging activities, which may require the use of IT and specific and innovative software.

In spite of the limitations, this study contributes ideas for future studies. Based on students' formal and informal feedback, it was observed that, even though this entertaining activity was mainly enjoyed and appreciated, special attention should be paid to the periods when assessments are taking place, as these may considerably affect the students' learning experience. Thanks to the students' comments, the possibility of including similar projects as part of the summative evaluation of the module will be investigated; this may also have a direct impact on students' motivation levels. In addition, it is recommended for both teachers and students to gain some technical knowledge in order to avoid possible technical limitations arising during the project. This final aspect is considered essential, as it will reduce the potential frustration that can affect both student and teacher motivation.

References

Amabile, T.M., Dejong, W. and Lepper, M.R. (1976) Effects of externally imposed deadlines on subsequent intrinsic motivation. *Journal of Personality and Social Psychology* 1 (34), 92–98.

Ames, C. (1992) Classrooms: Goals, structures, and student motivation. *Journal of Educational Psychology* 84 (3), 261–271.

Baños, R. and Sokoli, S. (2015) Learning foreign languages with ClipFlair: Using captioning and revoicing activities to increase students' motivation and engagement. In K. Borthwick, E. Corradini and A. Dickens (eds) *10 Years of the LLAS eLearning Symposium: Case Studies in Good Practice* (pp. 203–213). Dublin: Research-publishing. net. doi:10.14705/rpnet.2015.000280

Bernard, J. (2010) Motivation in foreign language learning: The relationship between classroom activities, motivation, and outcomes in a university language-learning environment. MA thesis, Carnegie Mellon University.

Blumenfeld, P., Soloway, E., Marx, R., Krajcik, J., Guzdial, M. and Palincsar, A. (1991) Motivating project-based learning: Sustaining the doing, supporting the learning. *Educational Psychologist* 26 (3–4), 369–398.

Borghetti, C. (2011) Intercultural learning through subtitling: The cultural studies approach. In L. Incalcaterra McLoughlin, M. Biscio and M.Á. Mhainnín (eds) *Audiovisual Translation Subtitles and Subtitling. Theory and Practice* (pp. 111–137). Bern: Peter Lang.

Borghetti, C. and Lertola, J. (2014) Interlingual subtitling for intercultural language education: A case study. *Language and Intercultural Communication* 14 (4), 423–440.

Brett, P.A. and Nash, M. (1999) Multimedia language learning courseware: A design solution to the production of a series of CD-ROMs. *Computers and Education* 32 (1), 19–33.

Brissett, A. (2003) Alterity in translation: An overview of theories and practices. In S. Petrilli (ed.) *Translation, Translation* (pp. 102–132). Amsterdam: Rodopi.

Cabero, J. (2007) *Nuevas tecnologías aplicadas a la educación.* Madrid: McGraw-Hill.

ClipFlair (2011) ClipFlair. See http://clipflair.net/ (accessed 7 June 2012).

Chiu, Y. (2012) Can film dubbing projects facilitate EFL learners' acquisition of English pronunciation? *British Journal of Educational Technology* 43 (1), 24–27.

Clouet, R. (2005) Estrategia y propuestas para promover y practicar la escritura creativa en una clase de inglés para traductores [Strategy and proposals to promote and practise creative writing in an English class for translators]. In *Actas Del IX Simposio Internacional De La Sociedad Española De Didáctica De La Lengua y La Literatura* (pp. 319–326).

Council of Europe (2001) *Common European Framework of Reference for Languages: Learning, Teaching, Assessment.* Cambridge: Cambridge University Press.

Danan, M. (2010) Dubbing projects for the language learner: A framework for integrating audiovisual translation into task-based instruction. *Computer Assisted Language Learning* 23 (5), 441–456.

Diehl, W., Grobe, T., Lopez, H. and Cabral, C. (1999) *Project-Based Learning: A Strategy for Teaching and Learning.* Boston, MA: Center for Youth Development and Education, Corporation for Business, Work, and Learning.

Díaz Cintas, J. (1997) Un ejemplo de explotación de los medios audiovisuales en la didáctica de lenguas extranjeras [An example of how to use media in foreign language learning]. In M. Cuéllar (ed.) *Las nuevas tecnologías integradas en la programación didáctica de lenguas extranjeras [New Technologies in Foreign Language Teaching]* (pp. 181–191). Valencia: Universitat de Valencia.

Díaz Cintas, J. and Remael, A. (2007) *Audiovisual Translation: Subtitling.* Manchester: St. Jerome Publishing.

Dörnyei, Z. (1998) Motivation in second and foreign language learning. *Language Teaching* 31 (3), 117–135.

Dörnyei, Z. (2010) *Questionnaires in Second Language Research. Construction, Administration, and Processing* (2nd edn). London: Routledge.

Dörnyei, Z. and Csizér, K. (2012) How to design and analyze surveys in SLA research? In A. Mackey and S. Gass (eds) *Research Methods in Second Language Acquisition: A Practical Guide* (pp. 74–94). Shanghai: Shanghai Foreign Language Education Press.

European Commission (2011) *Study on the Use of Subtitling: The Potential of Subtitling to Encourage Foreign Language Learning and Improve the Mastery of Foreign Languages*. Final Report. See http://www.mcu.es/cine/docs/Novedades/Study_on_use _subtitling.pdf (accessed 26 May 2017).

Fernández Costales, A. (2014) Teachers' perception on the use of subtitles as a teaching resource. In Pixel (ed.) *Conference Proceedings. ICT for Language Learning* (pp. 426–433). Padova: libreriauniversitaria.it.

Heafner, T. (2004) Using technology to motivate students to learn social studies. *Contemporary Issues in Technology and Teacher Education* 1 (4), 42–53.

Ibáñez, A. and Vermeulen, A. (2015) Using VISP (VIdeos for SPeaking), a mobile app based on audio description, to promote English language learning among Spanish students: A case study. *Procedia-Social and Behavioral Sciences* 178, 132–138.

Incalcaterra McLoughlin, L. and Lertola, J. (2014) Audiovisual translation in second language acquisition. Integrating subtitling in the foreign-language curriculum. *The Interpreter and Translator Trainer* 8 (1), 70–83. doi:10.1080/1750399X.2014.908558

Jones, B.F., Rasmussen, C.M. and Moffitt, M.C. (1997) *Real-Life Problem Solving: A Collaborative Approach to Interdisciplinary Learning*. Washington, DC: American Psychological Association.

Keblawi, F. (2009) A critical appraisal of language learning motivation theories. *The Fifth International Biennial SELF Research Conference*. 13–16 January 2009, Dubai, United Arab Emirates.

McGrath, I. (2002) *Materials Evaluation and Design for Language Teaching*. Edinburgh: Edinburgh University Press.

Moursund, D. (1999) *Project-Based Learning Using Information Technology*. Eugene, OR: International Society for Technology in Education.

Navarrete, M. (2013) El doblaje como herramienta en el aula de español y desde el entorno ClipFlair [Dubbing as a tool in the Spanish classroom and in the environment of Clip-Flair]. *MarcoELE* 16, 75–87.

Noels, K., Pelletier, L., Clément, R. and Vallerand, R. (2000) Why are you learning a second language? Motivational orientations and self-determination theory. *Language Learning* 50 (1), 57–85.

Nunan, D. (1999) *Second Language Teaching and Learning*. Florence, KY: Heinle & Heinle.

Ramière, N. (2006) Reaching a foreign audience: Cultural transfers in audiovisual translation. *Journal of Specialised Translation* 6, 152–166.

Rost, M. (2002) *Teaching and Researching Listening*. London: Longman.

Ryan, R.M. and Deci, E.L. (2006) Self-regulation and the problem of human autonomy: Does psychology need choice, self-determination, and will? *Journal of Personality* 74, 1557–1586.

Sánchez-Requena, A. (2016) Audiovisual translation in teaching foreign languages: Contributions of dubbing to develop fluency and pronunciation in spontaneous conversations. *Porta Linguarum* 26, 9–21.

Schaefer, E. (2010) Teacher motivation: The missing link in ESL motivational studies. *Journal of the Ochanomizu University English Society* 1, 43–52.

Talaván, N. (2006) Using subtitles to enhance foreign language education. *Porta Linguarum* 6, 41–52.

Talaván, N. (2013) *La subtitulación en el aprendizaje de lenguas extranjeras* [*Subtitling in Foreign Language Learning*]. Barcelona: Octaedro.

Talaván, N. and Lertola, J. (2016) Active audiodescription to promote speaking skills in online environments. *Sintagma* 28, 59–74.

Thomas, J. (2000) *A Review of Research on Project-Based Learning* (report prepared for The Autodesk Foundation). See http://www.bobpearlman.org/BestPractices/PBL_Research.pdf (accessed 26 May 2017).

Thomas, J.W., Mergendoller, J.R. and Michaelson, A. (1999) *Project-Based Learning: A Handbook for Middle and High School Teachers*. Novato, CA: The Buck Institute for Education.

Underwood, M. (1990) *Teaching Listening*. London: Longman.

Williams, H. and Thorne, D. (2000) The value of teletext subtitling as a medium for language learning. *System* 28 (2), 217–228. doi: 10.1016/S0346-251X(00)00008-7

Witte, A., Harden, T. and Ramos de Oliveira, A. (2009) Introduction. In A. Witte, T. Harden and A. Ramos de Oliveira Harden (eds) *Translation in Second Language Learning and Teaching* (pp. 1–14). Bern: Peter Lang.

Appendices

Appendix 1: Classroom activities inventory

1 Never	2 At least once this semester	3 Monthly	4 Weekly	5 Daily

PERSONALISED LANGUAGE USE

1 Speak about your life or interests using Spanish

2 Write about your life or interests using Spanish

EXCLUSIVE USE OF THE LANGUAGE

3 Do translation exercises

4 Read in the language (includes reading directions, simple sentences, questions...)

5 Do worksheets or exercises out of the textbook or workbook

6 Role play or create dialogues in Spanish

DEEP LANGUAGE USE

7 Read longer selections in Spanish (i.e. literature/poetry/stories)

8 Have class discussions using Spanish

9 Do large projects (write stories or reports, make videos, give presentations...)

MECHANICS

10 The teacher gives lectures in Spanish and we participate

11 Take quizzes or tests

12 Repeat things the teacher says, or do call-and-response exercises

13 How much of the time does your teacher speak in Spanish? (e.g. 20%)

FUN AND CULTURAL EXPOSURE

14 Sing or listen to songs in Spanish

15 Play games using Spanish

16 Watch films/television in Spanish

17 Do cultural activities (learn dances, make food, celebrate holidays...)

(*Continued*)

1 Never   2 At least once this semester   3 Monthly   4 Weekly   5 Daily

USE OF THE LANGUAGE BEYOND THE CLASSROOM

18 Use authentic materials (newspapers, magazines, films, etc., which were originally made for people who grew up speaking the language, not students learning the language)

19 Use technology (not including television/films); e.g. language apps, websites and special software

20 Talk with native speakers (people who grew up speaking the language) – not including the teacher

Appendix 2: Motivation questionnaire

1 Strongly disagree   2 Disagree   3 Neither agree nor disagree   4 Agree 5 Strongly agree

MOTIVATION FOR LEARNING THE LANGUAGE

1 I wish to someday be able to communicate with someone who speaks Spanish.

2 I want to be fluent in Spanish someday.

3 I enjoy learning about other cultures.

MOTIVATION FOR CLASS PARTICIPATION

4 I enjoy coming to class.

5 I find classroom activities interesting.

6 The things I am learning in this class are interesting.

7 I feel that the teacher wants me to do well in this class.

8 My teacher expects a lot of me.

9 I enjoy working with my classmates.

CONFIDENCE

10 What I learn in this class will be useful in my life.

11 I am currently capable of effective communication in the language.

12 I am capable of learning the material taught in this class.

13 I will someday be capable of effective communication in Spanish.

14 I will go far in life.

15 By the end of the semester, I will have learned everything I am supposed to for this class.

EXTERNAL MOTIVATION

16 Someone in my family wants me to do well in this class.

17 This class will look good on grad school and/or job applications.

18 I want to get a good grade in this class.

19 I am taking this class because it is required.

Appendix 3: Questions related to the subtitling project (included in post-test only)

1 Strongly disagree   2 Disagree   3 Neither agree nor disagree 4 Agree   5 Strongly agree

INTRINSIC MOTIVATION

1 I enjoyed working on this project.

2 I learned about the culture in a more interesting way.

3 I enjoyed working with my group.

4 I enjoyed working with the new subtitling software.

TEACHER MOTIVATION

5 I felt supported while working on this project.

EXTERNAL MOTIVATION

6 The project is relevant to my studies.

7 I feel I learned new skills thanks to this project.

8 Having worked on this project, I feel better prepared for my exams.

9 I think this project is going to look good on my CV.

OTHER

10 I wish I could have spent more time working on this project.

9 Audiovisual Translation Modes as L2 Learning Pedagogical Tools: Traditional Modes and Linguistic Accessibility

Juan Pedro Rica Peromingo and
Ángela Sáenz Herrero

In recent years there has been considerable growth in research on audio-visual translation (AVT) in the field of teaching and learning foreign languages (Díaz Cintas, 2008, 2012a; Mayoral, 2001; Rica Peromingo, 2014, 2016; Rica Peromingo *et al.*, 2014; Rica Peromingo & Braga Riera, 2015); in the study of subtitling (including subtitling for the deaf and hard of hearing and audio description); and in teaching and learning linguistic aspects of AVT at the university level. AVT training is now offered at several universities at undergraduate and postgraduate levels (Talaván, 2013). This chapter analyses the results of different projects using AVT as a pedagogical tool for language learning that were carried out by students in two university contexts in Madrid, Spain. The first involved students on a master's degree course in English linguistics at Complutense University of Madrid (UCM), and the second involved undergraduate students on a media and cinema degree course at Camilo José Cela University (UCJC). Although the objectives, methodologies and access to resources and working tools differed, both groups received the same linguistic and technical training in AVT and both were asked to carry out similar activities for the different modes of AVT. Students were assessed on their linguistic accuracy and use of different tools in AVT.

Introduction

In recent years, a significant amount of research has been conducted on audiovisual translation (AVT) in the field of teaching and learning foreign languages (Díaz Cintas, 2008, 2012a; Mayoral, 2001; Rica

Peromingo, 2014, 2016; Rica Peromingo *et al.*, 2014); in the study of subtitling, including for the deaf and hard of hearing (SDH) and audio description (AD); and in teaching and learning linguistic aspects in AVT didactics at the university level.

Consequently, AVT training is now offered at several Spanish universities at undergraduate and postgraduate levels and in specialised courses (Talaván, 2013). In Spain, one of the reasons for this interest in teaching AVT for the purpose of learning a second language (L2) is the considerable number of audiovisual products (such as films, television and online series, and learning platforms) consumed by the Spanish public, especially films in the English language. In addition to dubbed materials and subtitling for the hearing population, Spanish institutions have recently become interested in making audiovisual materials available to sections of society (mainly people who are deaf or blind) that were previously unable to access them. Here lies the interest in supplementing traditional modes of AVT (subtitling for the hearing population and dubbing) with new ones (SDH and AD).

One of the main challenges of introducing AVT into university syllabuses is the specialist technology: the students need to be familiarised with the software used, the programs are expensive for most universities and the technology soon becomes obsolete (Rica Peromingo *et al.*, 2014). Online AVT software and other available resources are affordable for some teaching institutions, but their use is usually limited to instructing and training in a professional context.

In this chapter, we present an analysis of students' production of several AVT modes. First, we review the literature on using AVT methods as pedagogical tools for language learning, where technology and software resources play a vital role. Next, we describe the two university contexts in which the projects using AVT modes as pedagogical tools for L2 learning were carried out: with students enrolled in the English linguistics master's degree course at Complutense University of Madrid (UCM) and with a group of undergraduate students enrolled on a media and cinema degree course at Camilo José Cela University (UCJC). We then outline the activities completed by the students and explain the different aims, methodologies and resources and software used (Amara, Aegisub, Audacity, Spot, Subtitle Workshop, etc.) in each case. The two groups of students received similar linguistic and technical training in AVT and were asked to carry out similar activities for the different modes of AVT. The same criteria were followed for correcting and assessing their work, and all students were evaluated based on their linguistic accuracy and their ability to use different AVT tools. After the preliminary results are presented, the students' technical and linguistic accuracy are described.

Overview: AVT as a Pedagogical Tool

AVT is one of the fastest-growing trends within translation studies and, in Spain, these studies are justified by the continuous growth in the production and consumption of translated products (Rica Peromingo, 2016; Rica Peromingo et al., 2014). Initially, AVT studies focused on the different AVT modes and their features. The studies then included a focus on the professional stages of AVT and, most recently, on the pedagogical and didactical aspects. Nowadays, AVT has become an established academic field worldwide.

New educational programmes have been introduced in various language degrees within the university structure, especially modules focusing on AVT, such as those included in the master's degree in English linguistics and the degree syllabus for English studies at UCM (Rica Peromingo, 2016). We can observe similar cases in other areas of Spain, where more specific AVT programmes are offered up to master's level, such as those at the University of Granada, the University of Salamanca, the Autonomous University of Barcelona and the National Distance Education University, among others. This sustained growth in teaching and learning different AVT modes in undergraduate degrees and postgraduate studies at Spanish universities should not be overlooked (Rica Peromingo, 2016).

The integration of AVT into language learning is no longer a new trend, and many scholars promote the pedagogical use of AVT in language learning. Díaz Cintas (2012a) proposes the use of translation in the foreign language classroom and analyses the advantages and disadvantages of creating subtitles as an active way of learning. Sokoli et al. (2011) defend not only the use of AVT modes, such as subtitling and video subtitling, but also the use of information and communication technology. Talaván (2013) supports the integration of AVT into the language learning process as an innovative methodology, highlighting the use of intralingual and interlingual subtitles as effective tools in the process of acquiring a foreign language.

There are also platforms such as ClipFlair (see Chapter 11), a European project managed by several universities and entities around Europe, which promotes learning a foreign language through interactive activities for teachers and students, such as revoicing and captioning clips. Research groups, such as Film, Languages and Media in Education (FLAME) and the Film in Language Teaching Association (FILTA), have formed an online community of practice of language teachers and film educators who provide a forum for the exchange of information, activities and ideas between scholars and professionals. Others, such as the Audiovisual Learning Archive (AVLA) project,[1] include articles and interesting material for researchers and students focused on AVT, in addition to a complete and varied repository of exercises and activities carried out by students in different modes of AVT.

AVT in any linguistic process cannot be understood without considering the limitations of the technical aspects: the use of software and new technology, and the space–time limitations that characterise each of the modes of translation (Díaz Cintas, 2012b; Díaz Cintas *et al.*, 2007; Orero, 2007; Rica Peromingo, 2016). Students in different university-level contexts receive specific training in AVT, its different modes and their technical and linguistic characteristics.

In this chapter, we propose the pedagogical use of traditional AVT modes: not only subtitling for the hearing population and dubbing, but also for accessibility (AD and SDH).

Media Resources and Software

Technology is a requisite for teaching and learning AVT methods. Nowadays, the internet is a basic resource for teachers, researchers and students, especially audiovisual translators and language students (Rica Peromingo *et al.*, 2014). The use of software is essential for the different modes of AVT. Along with the large number of professional programs used in the cinematographic industry, an extensive market of free software is available to teachers and students, which facilitates the learning and teaching of AVT processes (Rica Peromingo, 2016).

The continuous development of technology also applies to teaching and learning AVT at university level. We find two possible options for using software at universities: professional software and freely available software. Professional software is too costly for most universities; furthermore, because of the speed at which technology and software evolve, most programs become obsolete within a few years. Most universities resort to the non-professional software that is available in the market for the purposes of teaching AVT at degree level.

Examples of professional software include Spot, Fab, Wincaps and EZTitles. In addition, we can consider some interesting online free AVT software, which only requires a connection to the internet. Although this software is free and available to students and universities, it is somewhat limited and does not offer all the necessary features for professional AVT training.

Some of the professional and non-professional software used in this study includes Aegisub, Amara, Audacity, Spot, Subtitle Workshop and Windows Movie Maker. The typical characteristics of these programs are shown in Table 9.1.

Table 9.1 Features of AVT software

Software	Feature
Aegisub http://www.aegisub.org	Non-professional subtitling editor.
	One of the few free software applications that includes a version for Windows and another for Mac users.
	Excellent for subtitles for the hearing and for SDH.
	Possible to include different combinations of formats and colours on screen.
Amara https://www.amara.org	Non-professional subtitling editor.
	Very convenient for students with no previous knowledge of AVT software or editing subtitles.
	Only available for Windows users.
Audacity http://audacity.es	Non-professional and free sound editor.
	Very useful for dubbing tasks and AD activities.
	Available for both Mac and Windows users.
Spot http://www.spotsoftware.nl	Professional subtitling software widely used by freelance translators and subtitling companies.
	Includes all professional possibilities for subtitling for hearing and SDH materials.
	Only available for Windows users.
Subtitle Workshop http://www.uruworks.net/index.html	Non-professional subtitling editor.
	Most widely used software in Spanish universities.
	Appropriate for new users and professionals.
	Includes different subtitle formats (subtitling for the hearing population and SDH).
	Includes various features for editing subtitles.
	Lacks the more professional functions needed for subtitling.
	Only available for Windows users.
Windows Movie Maker	Non-professional and free sound editor.
	Included in all Windows systems.
	Allows a new soundtrack to be recorded.
	Excellent for dubbing and AD.

Methodology

The two groups of students involved in this research were studying at different levels (undergraduate and postgraduate) on different degree courses. All participants received clear instructions on how to perform the tasks designed for their linguistic and technical training in AVT.

The undergraduate group was composed of 18 students enrolled in media and film degrees at UCJC (www.ucjc.edu). These students had an average level of B1 in English according to the Common European Framework of Reference for Languages (CEFR). They were taking a compulsory module in their second year titled Specialised English for the Media. This module lasted for the entire semester and was divided into different units focusing on specialised English, one being a section on AVT. The section on AVT included a general overview and focused on two main modes: subtitling for the hearing population and dubbing. The training period was three weeks. The students had no specialisation in or previous knowledge of AVT.

The second group was composed of 25 postgraduate students who had completed a variety of bachelor's degrees, from translation studies to English philology. All the students had opted to take the specialised module titled Linguistic Aspects of Audiovisual Translation as part of their master's degree – English linguistics: New applications and international communication – at UCM (https://www.ucm.es/ma-elnaic). They were required to have a minimum level of C1 in English according to the CEFR, which is also an entry requirement for the master's programme. The module lasted for an entire semester and students received training and knowledge in the specific discipline of AVT modes (subtitling, SDH, dubbing and AD) and their linguistic and technical features. They had to complete several individual and group activities throughout the semester, culminating in a final project at the end of the course. Some of the students had previous knowledge of translation, but most of them had little or no knowledge of AVT.

Evidently, the academic purposes (objectives, methodology and access to software and AVT resources) differed between the two groups. These are described in the following sections.

Academic objectives

The academic objectives were different for each group. For the undergraduate students, the first objective was to familiarise them with the main linguistic issues in audiovisual media translation. The students were also required to distinguish and recognise the different modes of AVT: dubbing, subtitling for the hearing population, SDH and audio description for the blind and partially sighted. Finally, they were taught to identify the benefits of using AVT technology in foreign language classes. For the master's degree students, these previously mentioned objectives were taken for granted and the main objective was to familiarise them with the linguistic and technical issues involved in AVT.

Methodology

The methodology used was also different: for the undergraduate group, foreign language subtitling and dubbing activities were programmed. By contrast, for the postgraduate group, AVT activities that incorporated a variety of modes (subtitling for the hearing population, SDH, AD and dubbing) were used; the postgraduate students also had to work on their final projects using new AVT resources.

Access to software and resources

A third difference was the students' access to software: the undergraduate group used free software (Amara and Audacity) available online. As part of their degree, students have access to a dubbing and sound studio on campus, where they can record their voices and insert the recordings into clips. The postgraduate group was able to use professional (Spot) and non-professional (Aegisub, Audacity, Windows Movie Maker and Subtitle Workshop) software for their subtitling activities (for the hearing population and SDH), dubbing and AD. The software was available in the language lab at UCM.

Activities and Examples

Activities and Examples: Undergraduate group (UCJC)

As previously mentioned, the group at UCJC was made up of second-year students on a cinema and media degree course (Specialised English for the Media). They had no previous specialisation in or knowledge of AVT, and they were working with a B1 level in English. The unit on AVT was one of the sections included in their module on specialised English for the media.

The initial objectives were, first, to integrate English language sources with innovative trends, and to enhance students' foreign language learning, and secondly, to identify the benefit of subtitling and dubbing in the language learning process. Apart from these objectives, the students were also encouraged to improve their listening comprehension while enhancing their vocabulary acquisition (deduction of meaning from context), to identify structures and to produce coherent syntactical units while summarising information.

The methodology included a seminar on AVT modes delivered by an academic working in the field. This was followed by two weeks of learning about and practising using the key features of traditional AVT modes – dubbing and subtitling – using Amara and Audacity. The students needed to complete both tasks on subtitling and dubbing using this free online software. Students were assessed on their linguistic accuracy and on their use and understanding of different tools in AVT.

The students were instructed to select a scene with a maximum duration of five minutes from a film or television series. After listening to the scene in the original language (English) without a dialogue list, they had to write and complete the dialogue. Finally, they had to subtitle the scene (English into English) using Amara and reduce the information provided according to the restrictions and limits of the subtitling process they had learned about in class. They were also required to include the time code in and out. Some of the subtitling features used (e.g. intralingual subtitles) included the reduction of contextual information and the production of language conditioned by space–time restrictions.

In the section on dubbing activities, the objectives focused on oral and written production. Students were assessed on the creation of new dialogue for clips from different films, trying as often as possible to produce natural spoken language with an emphasis on pronunciation and intonation. For these activities, the participants watched the footage without a soundtrack. The groups of students had to create the dialogue while bearing in mind the film genre, the types of characters, gestures, lip movement, pauses, timing, etc. (dubbing features). Once they had created the dialogue, they read it aloud and rehearsed the voices, pronunciation and intonation in English. The final step was to record the scene with Windows Movie Maker or Audacity. Once the activity was finished, they were able to record it again in the studio on campus. The characteristics emphasised in these tasks were lip synchrony and the speakers' rhythm.

Activities and Examples: Postgraduates group (UCM)

As previously detailed, the postgraduate students had selected the optional module, 'Linguistic Aspects of Audiovisual Translation', as part of their master's degree in English linguistics at UCM. The module lasted for a full semester. Some of the students had previous knowledge of translation but very little or no experience of AVT. Their English level was advanced (C1) according to the CEFR.

During the course the students received training in and learned about specific disciplines of AVT: subtitling for the hearing population, SDH, dubbing, voice-over and AD. The initial objective was to familiarise students with the AVT process and its linguistic and technical aspects. Another important objective of this postgraduate course is to allow students to work on different AVT strategies that are normally used in the process of translating audiovisual material (Rica Peromingo, 2016: 43). The students have direct access to professional and non-professional software. Moreover, the linguistic aspects of translation in different modalities of AVT (accessibility) are also considered in the programme.

The course syllabus includes the following sections: an introduction to AVT, dubbing, subtitling for the hearing population, SDH and AD for the blind and partially sighted. The students are required to carry out a combination of compulsory and optional tasks (in groups and individually) throughout the semester in each of the AVT modes described.

Cultural and linguistic peculiarities are part of the course, in addition to the technical use of professional and non-professional software: Spot, Subtitle Workshop, Aegisub and Windows Movie Maker. Students are assessed on their linguistic accuracy and on their use of different tools in AVT.

For the subtitling for the hearing population and SDH activities, the main objectives were to make students aware of the AVT problems that may arise from the linguistic and technical points of view when subtitling for both the hearing and non-hearing population. In addition, translation problems and contextual information (in the case of SDH) were emphasised. The students selected a scene from a film to be translated as part of their final project, considering the linguistic and technical aspects of subtitling for the hearing population and of SDH. First, they translated the text and subtitled the scene (English into Spanish) using Subtitle Workshop, Spot or Aegisub. In the case of the SDH, the main techniques used were the reduction of contextual information, the production of language conditioned by space–time restrictions, identifying subtitles in the scene and the correct positioning and colour of the subtitles.

For the AD activities, the main objectives were to be able to recognise AVT complexities when audio-describing a scene, to be able to use the appropriate translation strategies (linguistic and cultural traits) and to consolidate the technical skills of this AVT method. As part of their final project, students had to select a scene from a film they had previously worked on using different AVT modes. They needed to consider the linguistic and technical aspects of AD, write the narration to be audio-described and include the audio heard in the original soundtrack. They audio-described the scene (both from Spanish into Spanish and from Spanish into English) using Audacity or Windows Movie Maker.

As mentioned previously, all students (UCJC and UCM) were assessed using similar criteria with respect to their accuracy in English and their technical knowledge of the AVT modes used. The results, which are described in the following section, differ with respect to the technical knowledge acquired by the students in the two contexts.

Results and Conclusions

The results of the analysis of the students' production indicate that there was no significant difference in their linguistic accuracy, despite the fact that the two groups received different training in the technical aspects, production and use of different tools for learning AVT.

Both groups used different software to learn AVT: the use of professional tools allowed the postgraduate students to concentrate more on the linguistic aspects of AVT. There was a successful progression in their work and results: in both groups of students, their linguistic accuracy and their technical knowledge improved.

In the case of the students at UCJC, non-explicit AVT training resulted in increased linguistic accuracy in English and allowed the students to use all of their language learning skills: writing, reading, listening and speaking. It also enabled them to be aware of the development in their linguistic accuracy. In the case of the students at UCM, their level of English did not significantly improve; however, it is clear that their technical knowledge and use of translation strategies improved.

The use of audiovisual material and specific professional and non-professional software opens up possibilities for new, active and dynamic classes (Díaz Cintas, 2012a). Both groups of students felt highly motivated by the possibility of using different software and resources. As a result, their participation levels and time spent on the activities increased.

We are certain that the use of AVT modes as a pedagogical tool for L2 learning opens up a wide range of activities for teachers and students, not only for language learners for linguistics and translation degrees but also in other academic contexts and with other students.

Our intention for future research (within the research project) is to include more activities related to linguistic accessibility and to use the experiences of participants who are deaf or blind in order to test the production of the students participating in this project. It is hoped that this will enable students to produce better SDH and AD for audiovisual products.

Note

(1) The AVLA project (Audiovisual Learning Archive), funded by the UCM, has been carried out in the English Department at the UCM with the collaboration of various Spanish universities and institutions (UCM, UAB, UNED, UCJC, CSIM at the UCM) since 2015, under the direction of Juan Pedro Rica Peromingo. The members of this research project are university teachers (Pilar Orero Clavero, UAB; Ángela Sáenz Herrero, UCJC, Ana Laura Rodríguez Redondo and Arsenio Andrades Moreno, UCM; Gloria Fernández Lijó from the CSIM at the UCM) and university students (Blanca Puchol Vázquez and Alejandro Rodríguez de Jesús, UCM). More information is available at https://avlearningarchive.wordpress.com.

References

Audiovisual Translation and Audiovisual Accessibility. See https://avlearningarchive.wordpress.com (accessed 12 June 2017).

ClipFlair. See http://clipflair.net (accessed 2 February 2017).

Díaz Cintas, J. (2008) *The Didactics of Audiovisual Translation*. Amsterdam/Philadelphia, PA: John Benjamins.

Díaz Cintas, J. (2012a) *Los subtítulos y la subtitulación en la clase de lengua extranjera* [Subtitles and subtitling in the foreign language class]. *Abehache* 3, 95–114.

Díaz Cintas, J. (2012b) Subtitling: Theory, practice and research. In C. Millán and F. Bartrina (eds) *The Routledge Handbook of Translation Studies* (pp. 285–299). London: Routledge.

Díaz Cintas, J., Orero, P. and Remael, A. (eds) (2007) *Media for All: Subtitling for the Deaf, Audio Description and Sign Language*. Amsterdam: Rodopi.

Film in Language Teaching Association (FILTA). See http://www.filta.org.uk (accessed on 12 June 2017).

Film, Languages and Media in Education (FLAME) Research Group. See http://windows.microsoft.com/es-es/windows/movie-maker (accessed on 2 June 2015) (*The software is not available any longer).

Mayoral, R. (2001) Campos de estudio y trabajo en traducción audiovisual. In M. Duro (ed.) *La traducción para el doblaje y la subtitulación* (pp. 19–46). Madrid: Cátedra.

Orero, P. (2007) La accesibilidad en los medios: Una aproximación multidisciplinar. *TRANS. Revista de Traductología* 11, 11–14.

Rica Peromingo, J.P. (2014) La traducción de marcadores discursivos (DM) inglés-español en los subtítulos de películas: Un estudio de corpus. *Journal of Specialised Translation* 21, 177–199.

Rica Peromingo, J.P. (2016) *Aspectos lingüísticos y técnicos de la Traducción Audiovisual (TAV)*. Frankfurt am Main: Peter Lang.

Rica Peromingo, J.P. and Braga Riera, J. (2015) *Herramientas y técnicas para la traducción inglés-español: Los textos literarios*. Madrid: Babélica Herramientas. Escolar y Mayo.

Rica Peromingo, J.P., Albarrán, R. and García, B. (2014) New approaches to audiovisual translation: The usefulness of corpus-based studies for the teaching of dubbing and subtitling. In E. Bárcena, T. Read and J. Arús Hita (eds) *Languages for Specific Purposes in the Digital Area* (pp. 303–322). Series: Educational Linguistics 19. Berlin: Springer-Verlag.

Sokoli, S., Zabalbeascoa, P. and Fountana, M. (2011) Subtitling activities for foreign language learning: What learners and teachers think. In L. Incalcaterra McLoughlin, M. Biscio and M.Á. Ní Mhainnín (eds) *Audiovisual Translation: Subtitles and Subtitling. Theory and Practice* (pp. 219–242). Oxford: Peter Lang.

Talaván, N. (2013) *La subtitulación en el aprendizaje de lenguas extranjeras*. Barcelona: Octaedro.

Part 4
Teacher Training and Resources

10 Towards an Inclusive Model for Teaching Literature in Multimodal Frameworks: The Case of a Film-Based Workshop in the Complutense EFL/ESL Teacher Training Programme

Jelena Bobkina and Elena Domínguez

This chapter outlines the work carried out following a research project titled Innovative Teaching in Higher Education at the Complutense University of Madrid (UCM) in Spain. A four-week, film-based workshop was developed for a UCM master's degree course aimed at training secondary school teachers of English as a foreign language (EFL) and English as a second language (ESL). The main motivation for introducing the workshop was the fact that literature has recently become an essential part of the curriculum in bilingual secondary schools in Madrid. In addition, the reality that the use of film adaptations of literary texts facilitates the implementation of literature in the EFL/ESL classroom was an important factor in the design of the workshop. This chapter describes an experiment – framework, methodology and results – in which a group of UCM students participated in the four-week workshop. In the fourth week, an interview was conducted so that students could share their views on video-literary practices in the EFL/ESL classroom. As they are the teachers of the future, their opinions are important when it comes to anticipating eventual practices of teaching literature through film in the EFL/ESL classroom.

Introduction

The master's degree for training secondary school teachers of English as a foreign language (EFL) and English as a second language (ESL) was launched in the Spanish university system during the 2009–2010 academic year in response to the new demands of the Education Organic Law 2/2006 of 3 May, which requires new teachers to take a course in pedagogical skills (Ministry of Education, Culture and Sport, 2006). As lecturers in a master's course aimed at training secondary school teachers of EFL and ESL at the Complutense University of Madrid (UCM), we present part of our teaching proposal for this course. Moreover, to add to the value of our students' work, we share the film-based teaching plans that they developed to meet the requirements of the course in question.

Learners are increasingly being exposed to a large number of multimodal texts that combine written words with visual images, sound effects, music and complex graphic design (Kress, 2003; Kress & van Leeuwen, 1996). Our proposal focuses on raising the students' awareness of the role of multimodal texts in second language acquisition within the context of instruction. Special emphasis is placed on text-based teaching and, more specifically, on the supremacy of the multimodal text as a starting point for developing teaching tasks and activities (Burns, 2012). That is to say, we focus on the teaching of language through literature as much as through its audio and film modes. Spanish–English bilingual secondary education governed by the Regional Government of Madrid (known as Comunidad de Madrid) is regulated by Decree 3331/2010 of 11 June 2010 that specifies, for the bilingual sector, that content must focus equally on English language and English literature (Madrid Regional Government, 2010). The decree strongly recommends the use of literary texts that have been adapted for film, since film adaptations facilitate the comparative analysis of written and visual language. Literary workshops are the preferred teaching format, as they lead to a deeper approach to literary texts.

Teaching Based on Printed Texts

The emphasis on working with culturally authentic texts is central to curriculum reform in EFL/ESL teaching today (e.g. Arens & Swaffar, 2000; Dupuy, 2000; Gilmore, 2004; Roberts & Cooke, 2009). The latest developments in text-based teaching also point to a curriculum 'in which language, culture, and literature are taught as a continuum' (Modern Language Association of America, 2007). Alongside these advances, the incorporation of literary texts into the language curriculum is now considered a must (Van, 2009). Nevertheless, teaching literature in the second language classroom is a challenge. Many linguists refer to literature content as being extremely demanding for teachers and students alike (McKay, 2001; Savvidou, 2004). Not surprisingly, many teachers tend to avoid using literary texts for this reason.

Yet, the film format can facilitate the use of literature in the classroom. As stated by Caixia (2013), many literary texts, including novels, short stories and plays, have been adapted for film; thus, they have become easily accessible language products. As students and teachers commonly associate films with entertainment, they are highly motivating teaching tools. When properly selected and implemented in the classroom, film adaptations play an important role in the language teaching and learning process (Baddock, 1996; Stemplinski & Tomalin, 1990). Indeed, when it comes to comparing novels and films, most researchers admit that films are more accessible for students. Furthermore, Montgomery *et al.* (1992) affirm that films ensure an easier understanding of written texts. In addition, according to Caixia (2013), visual images seem to establish a more direct relationship with the depicted objects, resulting in film narratives (usually) being more understandable than written narratives. Sound and light are additional characteristics of the film format that tend to contribute to general understanding. In certain situations, these sound and light effects alone are sufficient to tell a story (Bo, 2008).

A close look at the recent literature published in the field of EFL/ESL teaching and media studies demonstrates clearly that the use of authentic, not dubbed, English and American media forms and video materials brings multiple advantages to the classroom. According to Brown (2009: 45), English language foreign films are 'the most direct resource available to learning a target language and culture'. For Yassaei (2011), original video is a motivating tool for teaching grammar. Rucynski (2011) defends the use of television series, focusing on *The Simpsons* (1989–) as an example, to activate the students' background knowledge of the target culture and society, and Eken (2003) explores the use of films as a way to develop students' critical thinking skills. Furthermore, films and video materials allow for an exploration of the literary texts through visual imagery, sound, light and the actors' performances (Caixia, 2013; Eken, 2003).

Teaching Based on Multimodal Texts

Learners are increasingly exposed to a large number of multimodal texts, which combine written words with visual images, sound effects, music and complex graphic design (Kress, 2003; Kress & van Leeuwen, 1996). These texts are inseparable from modern student life and dominate their reading preferences today. Nevertheless, there is a marked distance between the texts that students read at school and the texts that they encounter in everyday life. As an obvious consequence of this, many educators now claim that there is a need to increase the presence of multimodal texts in the language curriculum and to elaborate on specific strategies, glossaries and knowledge to train students to succeed in the age of technology (Anstey & Bull, 2006). The textual or 'paradigm' shift (Bearne,

2003) towards the dominance of multimodality has been described by a number of researchers (Cope & Kalantzis, 2000; Kress & van Leeuwen, 1996). Nevertheless, print-based texts continue to be the most common means of instruction (Lankshear & Knobel, 2006), with monomodal texts, such as classic novels and short stories, still monopolising the contemporary language classroom (Serafini, 2012a). In this context, although there have been different, and often controversial, definitions of reading in the field of education, 'these have been traditionally applied to the reading of print-based and mostly monomodal texts' (Walsh, 2006).

Serafini (2012a) explains that in the modern world the reader's role is that of a 'reader-viewer'. This dual position of the new reader requires the acquisition of alternative reading skills, such as inferring, asking questions, summarising and interpreting visual images and design elements. These premises made, and in the light of the model developed by Freebody and Luke (2003), Serafini (2012b) offers a reconceptualised notion of the reader as a reader-viewer navigator, interpreter, designer and interrogator, as outlined below:

(1) **Reader as navigator.** The role of the reader as navigator implies that students must master the codes and conventions associated with design, images and other visual elements (Kress & van Leeuwen, 1996). In particular, students are expected to follow the grammar of visual design alongside the traditional elements associated with written language.

(2) **Reader as interpreter.** The reader as interpreter is involved in the complex process of constructing meaning and making sense of the text. Usually, interpretations draw as much on multiple experiences of other visual texts as they do on personal experiences. This interpretative framework 'requires attention to the perceptual, structural and ideological aspects of the multimodal texts' (Serafini, 2012b).

(3) **Reader as designer.** The concept of reader as designer goes far beyond the classic constructivist claim that readers construct meaning out of what is depicted or represented. Multimodal texts are meant to provide a unique experience of interaction with the reader (Kress, 2010).

(4) **Reader as interrogator.** Meanings constructed by the reader during the act of reading not only depend on personal experiences but also are socially embedded. During the reading process, texts are framed according to social, historical and political aspects.

These four notions are inseparable and coexist in the act of reading multimodal texts. Understanding and interpreting multimodal texts draw on the personal experiences and social practices of readers in sociocultural, political, historical and economic contexts. Ultimately, reading is a social practice that depends on a particular social context, a reader and a text (Gee, 1996).

The role of the new reader as a reader-viewer is closely related to the procedure to be followed to deal with multimodal texts. There have been numerous attempts to design a procedure to ensure valid interpretations of works of art. Art historian and critic Panofsky (1955) developed a model for the interpretation of visual works of art, which is based on the following three levels: pre-iconographic, iconographic and iconological. The model begins with recognition of the primary meaning perceived at the denotative level. The second level shifts the reader's focus to the connotative meaning. Meanwhile, the third level involves the interpretation of the intrinsic meaning of the texts, where philosophical ideas are revealed. Some decades later, O'Toole (1994) suggested a systemic-functional semiotic model for the analysis of paintings and visual forms. He refers to four ways of approaching visual forms: (1) a historical approach, which focuses on the historical circumstances of the work's creation; (2) an iconographic approach, which centres on the subject matter itself from a philosophical perspective; (3) a textual approach, which deals with the study of the compositional elements; and (4) a semiotic approach, which is based on the text metafunctions proposed by Halliday (1978).

As a further development of O'Toole's (1994) model, Serafini (2014) proposes a tripartite framework for the analysis of multimodal texts. The framework focuses on the following three textual dimensions.

(1) **Perceptual**. This dimension deals with the image itself, navigating and naming those elements of multimodal texts that are visually perceived (Panofsky, 1955).
(2) **Structural**. This dimension is based on the analysis of visual grammar and design (Kress & van Leeuwen, 1996) and on semiotic theories of meaning. Readers are expected to find meanings, themes and messages through the interpretation of visual images and multimodal elements.
(3) **Ideological**. This dimension includes the analysis of the context, culture and history of an image. Text and image are treated as social artefacts within the framework of social semiotic theories of meaning (O'Toole, 1994).

The model presented by Serafini (2014) can be taken as a starting point to facilitate students' approach to multimodal texts.

Teaching Based on Printed and Multimodal Texts: Towards an Inclusive Model

Multimodal texts, contrary to printed texts, construct meaning through a set of visual resources, such as layout, size, shape, colour, line, angle, position, perspective, frames, icons, links and hyperlinks, sound, movement and graphic animation (Kress, 2003). The narrative voice is usually achieved in these texts by a set of visual means, such as camera position, angle and perspective, while the visual imagery is mainly attained through the use of various visual and sound elements: colour, voice and music. Beyond sight, though, these multimodal-based texts involve a holistic perception of the textual reality: visual, aural and kinaesthetic. Moreover, in the case of films, multimodal texts induce non-sequential, non-linear narratives by means of extensive flashbacks and flash-forwards within the storyline: a technique that contributes to the process of making meaning (Walsh, 2006). Multimodal texts and printed texts, however, are not mutually exclusive (Walsh, 2006). As explained by Avgerinou and Pettersson (2011), visual language often requires some verbal support. For this reason, the traditional aspects of a literary work (language, culture and personal growth) need also to be approached from different perspectives.

Four-stage inclusive model for the analysis of films

These premises made, and the need to use different modes to teach literature having been revealed, we present our four-stage inclusive model for the analysis and implementation of films adapted from literary works in the EFL/ESL classroom (see Figure 10.1). This model was put into practice during the UCM four-week workshop in question.

Stage 1: Focus on context/pre-viewing. The first stage of the model is focused on context analysis. The students analyse a film poster and other available images. They also watch a trailer to identify the most salient elements of the film. The ultimate goal is to predict the genre of the film and discuss the elements that they expect to find in it.

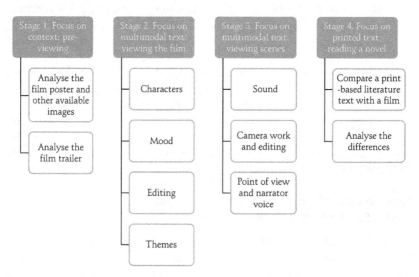

Figure 10.1 Inclusive model for film analysis, with multimodal basis

Stage 2: Focus on multimodal text/while viewing the film. The second stage focuses on the multimodal text as a whole. Students watch a film and analyse its main characters, the mood of the film and the way in which this mood is created, the style of editing, the types of shots used, the main themes and topics, and the values conveyed.

Stage 3: Focus on multimodal text/while viewing scenes. The third stage involves the analysis of a selection of scenes from the film. Students make a list of the most memorable parts of the film and, after a second viewing, analyse the way in which each particular scene is filmed. Aspects to be taken into consideration include the use of sound effects, music, camerawork and editing, camera angles and narrative voice.

Stage 4: Focus on printed text/reading a novel. The fourth stage is centred on the printed text. Students are asked to read what they consider to be the most significant moment of the novel and look at how this has been adapted for the film. They try to justify the changes that have been introduced, with a focus on the scenes and characters that have been excluded from the film script.

A Film-Based Workshop

The workshop involved 19 students enrolled on the master's degree course in foreign language teaching at UCM. It aimed to familiarise students with the implementation of literature-based films in the EFL/ESL classroom. With this purpose in mind, we presented our model for film analysis (based on a multimodal framework) during the first week of the workshop. Following this guide, subsequent weeks were devoted to group work and classroom presentations. At the end of the workshop, we conducted an interview with each of the groups in order to evaluate the work done. Students were asked to reflect on the following questions.

(1) Do you think that literature should be part of the English language curriculum in secondary education in Spain? Justify your answer.

(2) Do you consider that videotexts facilitate the use of literature as a language teaching tool?

(3) What makes literary-based videotexts appealing to young adult learners of English?

(4) Which videotexts based on literary works would you use in the EFL/ESL classroom? Why?

(5) Have you ever had the opportunity to work with literature in any English language learning or teaching context before this course? If your answer is yes, describe your first experience.

(6) Has the workshop changed your mind about the use of literary-based multimodal texts in the EFL/ESL secondary classroom in Spain? Would you like to implement the multimodal framework in your future teaching practice?

Procedure

Week 1. During the first week, we discussed the aims of the workshop with our UCM students, paying special attention to the possible contributions of film to their future students' understanding of literature. We also introduced the inclusive model for film analysis that we developed especially for this workshop in order to provide students with the theoretical framework that they would need in the following weeks. The first week finished with a viewing of Rob Reiner's (1986) *Stand By Me*, a film based on Stephen King's (1982) short novel *The Body*. Some extracts from the novel were also read in the classroom. The aim was to implement our model for film analysis in a multimodal framework, in order to provide an example.

Week 2. The class was divided into five groups of four students. Each group was asked to choose a literary text with a film adaptation. Following this, the students were invited to develop a set of activities to be implemented with their future secondary school students in line with the four-stage model for film analysis.

Weeks 3 and 4. Each group worked towards leading a microteaching session based on the activities that they had developed to implement the literary text of their choice. More specifically, the texts selected by the groups included Chaucer's (1400 [1976]) *The Wife of Bath*, Shakespeare's (1623 [2000]) *Henry VIII*, Oscar Wilde's (1891) *The Picture of Dorian Gray* and Suzanne Collins' (2008) *The Hunger Games*. The students' activities based on the latter are included as an example of the resulting pedagogical proposals from the workshop. The choice of this example was influenced by the success of Collins' trilogy among young adults today, which makes it a perfect model for implementation in the EFL/ESL classroom. The UCM students' presentations were followed by group discussion and feedback from the lecturer. Special emphasis was placed on what methods they could use to motivate their future students.

Week 4. At the end of the final session, an interview was conducted with each of the working groups to evaluate their response to the use of film as a tool to teach literature in bilingual education. As mentioned previously, the usefulness of the workshop was also assessed.

Example of students' pedagogical proposal

This section presents an example of how our inclusive model was used by new teachers to develop a teaching proposal based on Suzanne Collins' (2008) *The Hunger Games*.

(1) Focus on context/pre-viewing
  (a) Look at the poster for *The Hunger Games* film. Discuss the elements you can see on the poster. How is the title presented? What visual and design elements are used (photographs, lines,

colours, shapes, borders)? How do you think the visual elements help to transmit the message of the poster (*The Hunger
Games* – Poster, 2012)?

(b) Watch the trailer for the film. What are the most salient elements of the film that are highlighted in the trailer?

(c) The film is an example of dystopian fiction. What kind of elements do you expect to find in a dystopian novel? Make predictions. Can you think of any other dystopian novels?

(2) Focus on multimodal text/while viewing the film

  (a) Characters:

    (i) Katniss Everdeen, the 16-year-old 'hunger games' warrior,
has been referred to as 'the most important female character in recent pop culture' (Lewit, 2011). Do you agree with
this statement? Give your reasons.

    (ii) Katniss Everdeen and Peeta Mellark are the main char-
acters in the film. What do they look like? How are they
dressed? What do we know about their background? What
do they do and say in the film?

    (iii) What personality traits of these two characters do not con-
form to gender stereotypes? In what way do they break the
traditional concept of gender stereotypes?

  (b) Mood:

    (i) Describe the mood of the film. Do you find it humorous,
sad, depressing, serious, uplifting, amusing, gloomy, or
thoughtful? What makes you feel that?

    (ii) How does the director create the mood and the atmo-
sphere in the film?

- Reflect upon the use of lighting, setting, make-up and
clothing to depict life in the capital city vs life in the
districts.
- Consider the combination of close-up and long shots
from different levels and heights used throughout the
film.
- Most of the film is shot from a subjective point of view.
However, there are also some scenes that are shot from
an objective point of view. Identify the different points
of view and reflect upon their function in the film.
- What kind of music and sound effects are used in the
film? How do they help to create the mood? Are there
any songs?

  (c) Editing:

    (i) Is the film shown in chronological order? Are there any
flashbacks? If your answer is yes, identify them and reflect
upon their function in the film.

(ii)   What kinds of shots prevail for scene editing? Are there any cutaway shots or dissolve shots? If your answer is yes, what are they used for?

(iii) Consider the kind of shots that are used in the following scenes: 'depicting the games', 'describing the moment when Katniss was hallucinating in the forest' and 'when the tribunes first arrived in the forest'. Why do you think these scenes have been edited in this particular manner?

(d) Themes:

(i)   These are some of the major themes that can be found in the film. Reflect upon the way in which they are represented in the story:
- Survival and maintaining humanity and dignity.
- Human rights and the equality of citizens.
- Suffering as entertainment.
- The importance of appearance.

(ii)   What do you think are the moral and ethical problems that are raised in *The Hunger Games*?

(iii) What are the life lessons that you have learned from the film?

(iv)   How does the film make you feel?

(3) Focus on multimodal text/while viewing scenes

(a) According to *The Christian Science Monitor* (2015), the top 10 scenes in *The Hunger Games* include the following:

(i)   Katniss volunteers in Primrose's place.
(ii)   Madge gives Katniss the mockingjay pin.
(iii) Katniss wears her dress of fire.
(iv)   An arrow startles the Game judges.
(v)   Peeta makes an on-air confession.
(vi)   Rue helps Katniss when she is under attack.
(vii) Katniss decorates Rue's body.
(viii) District 11 thanks Katniss.
(ix)   Thresh saves Katniss out of gratitude for Rue.
(x)   Katniss and Peeta threaten the Capitol.

(b) Choose your favourite scenes and, after a second viewing, analyse the following aspects: sound effects and music, camerawork and editing, point of view and the narrator's voice.

(c) Table 10.1 describes the scene (i) and needs to be completed. Consider the use of camera shots, sound, lighting, music, dialogue and costumes.

Katniss volunteers in Prim's place (THG Fansite, 2012). Link to image: https://bit.ly/2AyhhKg

Table 10.1 Description and analysis of the scene (i)

Description	Analysis
The camera shows the Hall of Justice where the reaping ceremony takes place.	
Effie Trinket, the escort of the District 12 tributes, is choosing the name of a female tribute from a glass ball. There is a close-up shot of her hand choosing a piece of paper from the glass ball.	
There is a close-up of Primrose Everdeen hearing her name announced.	
The camera turns towards Katniss Everdeen, Primrose's sister.	
The camera pulls back to show Primrose walking from behind.	
There is a sudden cry from Katniss, Primrose's sister, who proposes herself as a volunteer.	
The camera shows Katniss Everdeen stepping up to the stage. There are several cutaway shots to depict Katniss from different angles and points of view.	
The camera switches from Katniss to her sister and mother.	
Effie Trinket starts clapping her hands and asks the rest of the tributes to give a big hand for Katniss.	
Nobody else is clapping. There is a close-up shot of the tributes' hands in the air.	
The music starts to sound.	
Effie Trinket is reading the name of a male tribute, Peeta Mellark.	
The camera offers a close-up shot of Peeta Mellark.	
The camera cuts between Peeta and Katniss. The music is getting louder and louder.	
There is a flashback that takes us back to the past.	
Close-up shot of Katniss and Mellark shaking hands.	

(4) Focus on the printed text/reading a novel
   (a) This film is based on the novel *The Hunger Games* by Suzanne Collins. To adapt a novel for the big screen, changes are inevitable: characters are removed, dialogues are edited out and certain scenes are deleted or modified. Why do you think this happens? Can you think of any examples?
   (b) Here is a list of some differences found between the book and the film. Reflect upon them and explain the possible reasons that the screenplay writers chose to introduce these changes.
      (i) The book is written in the first-person from the perspective of Katniss Everdeen. In the film the first-person narrative is changed to a third-person narrative.
      (ii) There are some changes of perspective. For example, the riot in District 11 after Rue's death is not mentioned in the book. It is mentioned in the second part of the trilogy. In the film, the official flag of Panem appears in various scenes, but this is not mentioned in the book.

    (iii) Some pieces of clothing have been changed. Effie Trinket's reaping suit, described as 'spring green' in the book, is magenta pink in the movie. In the book, Katniss' interview dress is covered in precious gems. They reflect the light, creating the effect of fire when she spins the jewels on her dress. In the film, however, she is wearing a simple red dress with some false fire.

    (iv) There are some differences in how District 12 is shown. Some characters are omitted in the film, as is the case for Madge Undersee, the mayor's daughter, and Peeta's father. In the book, there are both male and female miners in District 12, whereas in the film all the miners are male.

    (v) In the film, it is not clear that Katniss and Peeta had to pretend to be in love to gain sponsors. In fact, in the book, they have an argument on the train home and Peeta realises that Katniss' love for him was not real. This scene is not present in the film.

(c) Sometimes, the film creators opt to make changes to scenes in the film adaptation. Below is an example of a scene from the book that has been modified in the film, which is clear when you watch the film adaptation of the chariot scene and read the same scene in the book (Collins, 2009: 64–65). Answer the following questions:

    (i) Which one do you prefer? Why?

    (ii) Why do you think the filmmakers changed it?

    (iii) Do you think both scenes transmit the same message to the reader/audience?

    (iv) Which one is more powerful?

(d) Are there any scenes from the novel that have not been included in the film script? Why? Choose one and design a storyboard for the scene you have chosen.

(e) Read the opening chapter of the novel and compare it with the opening of the film. Do they have a similar opening? If your answer is no, reflect upon the possible reasons.

The Students' View

Following the group interviews in the fourth week, it can be first concluded that 100% of the students involved in the workshop agreed on the need to include literature as part of the English language curriculum in secondary education in Spain. They referred to literature as a source of cultural enrichment, a good way to approach authentic texts in the classroom and an entertaining tool with which to teach languages. In the case of bilingual education, literature was considered to contribute to the immersion process. The need to use adapted, abridged versions of the texts was emphasised for non-bilingual education, though.

With regard to the use of videotexts aimed at supporting the implementation of literature as a tool for language teaching, the vast majority of the UCM students (95%) mentioned the suitability of these texts for meeting their future students' motivational needs.

As for the main characteristics that literary-based videotexts should have in order to be appealing to young adult learners of English, diversity was considered a must. According to 90% of the participants interviewed, a variety of literary genres should be chosen in order to reflect diverse reading preferences. Literature should provide readers with the opportunity to learn about themselves and their world. Among the videotexts recommended by the UCM participants, film adaptations of series and franchised books for young adults were preferred. *Harry Potter* (Columbus, 2001, 2002; Cuarón, 2004; Newell, 2005; Yates, 2007, 2009, 2010, 2011), *Twilight* (Condon, 2011, 2012; Hardwicke, 2008, 2009; Slade, 2010) and *The Hunger Games* (Lawrence, 2013, 2014, 2015; Ross, 2012) were recurrent examples.

In response to the fourth interview question, 75% of the students said they had been exposed to graded readings of classic literary texts in their secondary school years. Nevertheless, as reported, the focus was always on traditional reading comprehension, with no specific framework for the implementation of multimodal materials. The exception was an additional 7% of participants who had attended international schools, where literature was given an important role in the EFL/ESL curriculum. The remaining 18% had no contact with literature as a language learning tool prior to their graduate studies.

Students gave positive feedback on the use of this workshop format for teaching literature and film in the EFL/ESL classroom. They found the suggested combination of multimodal films and printed texts especially interesting. In addition, they appreciated being given the opportunity to implement a model for film analysis that allows for a structured approach to films. This model was considered to be an effective tool for developing strategies to tackle multimodal texts in the classroom.

As for the use of multimodal texts for teaching literature, the majority of the participants confirmed that they did not have any previous experience of using multimodal texts as a tool to work with literary texts. Nevertheless, all of the participants reported that films enhance the implementation of literature. They all agreed on supporting the use of videotexts, given their usefulness for engaging and entertaining students and for clarifying those issues within the written texts that may be obscure to students with the lowest levels of English. According to the vast majority of the participants (98%), videotexts, therefore, may be useful for attracting students' attention and then consolidating content information, while reinforcing listening skills and integrating all of the language acquisition skills.

Conclusions

This chapter has critically presented and evaluated an example of the four-week workshop that was carried out with students enrolled on UCM master's degree courses aimed at EFL/ESL secondary teachers. The inclusive four-stage method that we developed for this workshop, aimed at including and analysing films adapted from literary works in the EFL/ESL classroom, has been presented after being positively received by the students. Indeed, our main focus was on the results obtained, which is why we have shared examples of the activities developed by the students using our inclusive method. As reported by the majority of the participants, who will become EFL/ESL secondary school teachers in the near future, the workshop experience was highly positive and contributed to their understanding of the importance of literature and its film mode as a useful tool for teaching English.

Among the limitations of the study that may challenge the validity of our results, the length of the study and the number of participants must be mentioned. The workshop needs to be implemented repeatedly in the forthcoming academic years. This will increase the number of participants and facilitate the possibility of a diachronic approach informing the evolution of the use of literature in the EFL/ESL classroom. Moreover, in consecutive workshops, students will be provided with one teacher-developed example for each of the major literary genres – novels, short stories, poetry and plays – even if this means that the duration of the workshop increases to six weeks. We would also like to encourage our students to work with more pedagogically convenient, shorter pieces of video.

References

Anstey, M. and Bull, G. (2006) *Teaching and Learning Multiliteracies: Changing Times, Changing Literacies.* Newark, NY: International Reading Association.

Arens, K. and Swaffar, J. (2000) Reading goals and the standards for foreign language learning. *Foreign Language Annals* 33 (1), 104–122.

Avgerinou, M.D. and Pettersson, R. (2011) Toward a cohesive theory of visual literacy. *Journal of Visual Literacy* 30 (2), 1–19.

Baddock, B. (1996) *Using Films in the English Class.* Hemel Hempstead: Phoenix ELT.

Bearne, E. (2003) Rethinking literacy: Communication, representation and text. *Reading Literacy and Language* 37 (3), 98–103.

Bo, B. (2008) The differences between novels and films: Enhance literature teaching by using films. *US-China Education Review* 5 (7), 58–71.

Brown, K. (2009) *Teaching Literary Theory Using Film Adaptations.* Jefferson, NC: McFarland.

Burns, A. (2012) Text-based teaching. In A. Burns and J.C. Richards (eds) *The Cambridge Guide to Pedagogy and Practice in Second Language Teaching* (pp. 140–148). Cambridge: Cambridge University Press.

Caixia, H. (2013) Film and novel: Different media in literature and implications for language teaching. *Cross-Cultural Communication* 9 (5), 87–91.

Chaucer, G. (1400 [1976]) *The Wife of Bath's Prologue and Tale and the Clerk's Prologue and Tale from the Canterbury Tales*. Gloria Cigman (ed.). New York: Holmes & Meier.

Christian Science Monitor (2015) The Hunger Games: 10 favourite scenes, 28 December. See http://www.csmonitor.com/Books/2012/0227/The-Hunger-Games-10-favorite-scenes/Katniss-volunteers-in-Prim-s-place (accessed 26 May 2017).

Collins, S. (2008) *The Hunger Games*. New York: Scholastic.

Collins, S. (2009) *Catching Fire*. New York: Scholastic Press.

Columbus, C. (2001) *Harry Potter and the Philosopher's Stone* [DVD]. USA/UK: Warner Bros. Pictures.

Columbus, C. (2002) *Harry Potter and the Chamber of Secrets* [DVD]. USA/UK: Warner Bros. Pictures.

Condon, B. (2011) *The Twilight Saga: Breaking Dawn – Part 1* [DVD]. USA: Summit Entertainment and Temple Hill Entertainment.

Condon, B. (2012) *The Twilight Saga: Breaking Dawn – Part 2* [DVD]. USA: Summit Entertainment and Temple Hill Entertainment.

Cope, B. and Kalantzis, M. (2000) *Multiliteracies: Literacy Learning and the Design of Social Futures*. Melbourne: Macmillan.

Cuarón, A. (2004) *Harry Potter and the Prisoner of Azkaban* [DVD]. USA/UK: Warner Bros. Pictures.

Dupuy, B.C. (2000) Content-based instruction: Can it help ease the transition from beginning to advanced foreign language classes? *Foreign Language Annals* 33 (2), 205–223.

Eken, A.N. (2003) You've got mail: A film workshop. *ELT Journal* 57 (1), 51–59.

Freebody, P. and Luke, A. (2003) Literacy as engaging with new forms of life: The 'four roles' model. In G.A. Bull (ed.) *The Literacy Lexicon* (pp. 51–66). Frenchs Forest, NSW: Pearson Education.

Gee, J. (1996) *Social Linguistics and Literacies: Ideology in Discourses*. London: Taylor & Francis.

Gilmore, A. (2004) A comparison of textbook and authentic interactions. *ELT Journal* 58 (4), 363–374.

Halliday, M. (1978) *Language and Social Semiotics: The Social Interpretation of Language and Meaning*. London: Edward Arnold.

Hardwicke, C. (2008) *Twilight* [DVD]. USA: Summit Entertainment and Temple Hill Entertainment.

King, S. (1982) *The Body*. New York: Viking Press.

Kress, G. (2003) *Literacy in the New Media Age*. London: Routledge.

Kress, G. (2010) *Multimodality: A Social Semiotic Approach to Contemporary Communication*. London: Routledge.

Kress, G. and van Leeuwen, T. (1996) *Reading Images: The Grammar of Visual Design*. London: Routledge.

Lankshear, C. and Knobel, M. (2006) *New Literacies: Everyday Practices and Classroom Learning*. Maidenhead: Open University Press.

Lawrence, F. (2013) *The Hunger Games: Catching Fire* [DVD]. USA: Color Force.

Lawrence, F. (2014) *The Hunger Games: Mockingjay – Part 1* [DVD]. USA: Color Force.

Lawrence, F. (2015) *The Hunger Games: Mockingjay – Part 2* [DVD]. USA: Color Force.

Lewit, M. (2011) Casting 'The Hunger Games': In praise of Katniss Everdeen. *The Atlantic*, 9 March. See https://www.theatlantic.com/entertainment/archive/2011/03/casting-the-hunger-games-in-praise-of-katniss-everdeen/72164/ (accessed 26 May, 2017).

Madrid Regional Government (2010) Decree 3331 of 11 June 2010, on bilingual Education in the Region of Madrid. *Official Gazette of the Region of Madrid* (in Spanish).

McKay, S. (2001) Literature as content for ESL/EFL. In M. Celce-Murcia (ed.) *Teaching English as a Second or Foreign Language* (pp. 319–332). Boston, MA: Heinle & Heinle.

Ministry of Education, Culture and Sport (2006) Organic Law 2/2006, 3 May, of Education, Official State Bulletin, 106, 4 May 2006, 17158-17207 (in Spanish).

Modern Language Association of America (2007) Foreign Languages and Higher Education: New Structures for a Changed World, pdf. See http://www.mla.org/pdf/forlang_news_pdf.pdf (accessed 26 May, 2017).

Montgomery, M., Durant, A., Fabb, N., Furniss, T. and Millis, S. (1992) *Advanced Reading Skills for Students of English Literature. Ways of Reading.* London: Routledge.

Newell, M. (2005) *Harry Potter and the Goblet of Fire* [DVD]. USA/UK: Warner Bros. Pictures.

O'Toole, M. (1994) *The Language of Displayed Art.* Leicester: Leicester University Press.

Panofsky, E. (1955) *Meaning in the Visual Arts.* New York: Doubleday.

Reiner, R. (1986) *Stand By Me* [DVD]. USA: Columbia Pictures.

Roberts, C. and Cooke, M. (2009) Authenticity in the adult ESOL classroom and beyond. *TESOL Quarterly* 43 (4), 620–642.

Ross, G. (2012) *The Hunger Games* [DVD]. USA: Color Force.

Rucynski, J. (2011) Using *The Simpsons* in EFL classes. *English Teaching Forum* 49 (1), 8–17.

Savvidou, C. (2004) An integrated approach to teaching literature in the EFL classroom. *The Internet TESL Journal* 10 (12), 1–6. See http://iteslj.org/Techniques/Savvidou-Literature.html (accessed 11 April 2017).

Serafini, F. (2012a) Reading multimodal texts in the 21st century. *Research in the Schools* 19 (1), 26–32.

Serafini, F. (2012b) Expanding the four resources model: Reading visual and multimodal texts. *Pedagogies* 7 (2), 150–164.

Serafini, F. (2014) *Reading the Visual.* New York: Teachers College Press.

Shakespeare, W. (1623 [2000]) *King Henry VIII.* G. McMullan (ed.). London: Thomson.

Slade, D. (2010) *The Twilight Saga: Eclipse* [DVD]. USA: Summit Entertainment and Temple Hill Entertainment.

Stemplinski, S. and Tomalin, B. (1990) *Video in Action.* London: Prentice Hall.

THG Fansite (2012) *The Hunger Games* #1. *Movie clip – Volunteer as tribute* (24 August). (Video File). See https://www.youtube.com/watch?v=iTyyKROkC3E (accessed 12 June 2017).

Van, T. (2009) The relevance of literary analysis to teaching literature in the EFL classroom. *English Teaching Forum* 47 (3), 2–9.

Walsh, M. (2006) The 'textual shift': Examining the reading process with print, visual and multimodal texts. *Australian Journal of Language and Literacy* 29 (1), 24–37.

Weitz, C. (2009) *The Twilight Saga: New Moon* [DVD]. USA: Summit Entertainment and Temple Hill Entertainment.

Wilde, O. (1891) *The Picture of Dorian Gray.* London: Ward Lock.

Yassaei, S. (2011) Using original video and sound effects to teach English. *English Teaching Forum* 12 (1), 12–16.

Yates, D. (2007) *Harry Potter and the Order of the Phoenix* [DVD]. USA/UK: Warner Bros. Pictures.

Yates, D. (2009) *Harry Potter and the Half-Blood Prince* [DVD]. USA/UK: Warner Bros. Pictures.

Yates, D. (2010) *Harry Potter and the Deathly Hallows – Part 1* [DVD]. USA/UK: Warner Bros. Pictures.

Yates, D. (2011) *Harry Potter and the Deathly Hallows – Part 2* [DVD]. USA/UK: Warner Bros. Pictures.

11 An Analysis of the Success of the 'Cultural Topic' at A Level through the Study of Spanish Film Directors

Mark Goodwin

As the A level[1] in modern foreign languages in existence in England since 2009 drew to a close in 2016, this chapter reviews how successful the cultural topic has been in meeting the objectives of the A-level Spanish syllabus through the teaching, learning and assessment of Spanish national cinema. The chapter investigates current provision in schools and universities in north-west England concerning the use of Spanish cinema in the teaching and learning of Spanish language, history, society and culture. Focusing on the AQA examination board in the UK, examination reports from 2010 to 2014 and questionnaire responses from 20 A-level Spanish students will be used as qualitative evidence to analyse the outcomes of the cultural topic. With new A-level specifications in place since 2016, questions will be answered surrounding improvements, particularly regarding how the integration of Spanish film into the new A-level curriculum is able to enhance students' understanding of Spain's linguistic, historical, social and cultural identity.

Introduction

This chapter evaluates the impact of current practice on students' linguistic, historical, social and cultural understanding of Spain. The findings presented are an integral first step towards answering two main research questions (as part of a wider study on the teaching and learning of Spanish through film):

(1) How successful is the study of a Spanish director at A level (through the cultural topic) in teaching Spanish language, history, society and

culture and, in this regard, does the current assessment structure benefit students?

(2) How can the use of Spanish cinema be developed and further exploited in the teaching and learning of Spanish?

Specifically, this chapter aims to evaluate the success of the outgoing A-level Spanish specification of the UK examination board AQA in meeting the specification's objectives through the study of Spanish cinema. It covers the period from September 2009 to September 2016, when the reformed Spanish A level and new specifications were introduced. Such 'success' will be measured according to AQA examination reports and a sample of questionnaire responses from current and recent A-level students in the north-west of England. There were a total of 20 respondents: 8 of my own students (a mixture of current and past students) and 12 from two other local schools. My current students completed the questionnaires during class time; my former students were sent the questionnaires by email and the other students received and returned their questionnaires by post. The research, therefore, uses a mixed methods approach alongside relevant theory surrounding viewer response, motivation and visual literacy and my own observations as both a researcher and teacher. In addition to providing an overview of what exactly students are supposed to be learning from the cultural topic and, crucially, the films selected by teachers, this chapter incorporates a much-needed student voice in order to establish what learners think of current practice and to shed initial light on students' opinions of the works to which they are exposed. Finally, it seeks to establish the obstacles and challenges in the teaching and learning of Spanish cinema within the cultural topic and the extent to which the practice is, if at all, enhancing students' learning of Spanish and their continued interest in the subject.

Context

The importance of the cultural topic is reflected in the high proportion of marks it carries – up to 75/160 if discussed in the speaking examination and in the assessed essay. One of the most popular topic areas involves the study of 'a director, architect, musician or painter from a target language-speaking country/community' (AQA, 2014b specification, updated version). Some educationalists would agree that this area of study is not only advisable but also imperative. For example, Álvarez Mennuto (2009: 1) reveals that 'the power of media [including film] has shifted from communication to education to the point where it has become an **essential** [my emphasis] tool in the teaching of foreign languages'. Teachers and students are advised that this detailed study of at least one work of an artist could include: 'the influences on the artist; the ideas or techniques of the artist; the importance of the artist both in his/her own lifetime and later; [or] a personal evaluation' (AQA, 2014b). If studied as one of two topic areas, students are encouraged to speak about the director for a significant part of the conversation element of their A2 (second half of A-level study) speaking examination (worth 35 marks). Students also have the option of writing an essay about aspects of the director's work (40 marks). To be able to evaluate all aspects referred to in the introduction, I will now consider the objectives of the cultural topic that are most relevant to this study, which I have grouped into three categories: enjoyment, language and history/society/culture.

Objective 1: Enjoyment

The AQA (2014b: 19) specification states that, through the A-level course, including the cultural topic, students should 'derive enjoyment and benefit from language learning'. The specification also aims to provide 'a sufficient basis for the further study of languages at degree level or equivalent' and to encourage students to 'develop a [general] interest in, and enthusiasm for, language learning' (AQA, 2014b: 19). It is difficult to draw conclusions based on enjoyment from the examination reports, although it is telling that the study of a director is consistently the most popular choice of topic in both the essay and the speaking examination. To begin explaining the reasons behind students' preference for discussing cinema (and, therefore, to a significant extent, teachers' preference), Bazalgette (2009: 14), in reference to using film and media in lessons, notes that learners welcome and enjoy most novelties that offer 'time out' from the daily grind of the curriculum, which can stimulate them to learn more effectively. Wilkinson and Head (2009: 28) go further by explaining that such classroom activity involves, engages and motivates students and gives them control over their own learning. AQA examiners were quick to confirm the popularity of this method of cultural learning (and teaching), noting in the 2011 examination report that, 'this (question 14 – A director, architect, musician or painter from a Spanish-speaking country/community) was by far and away the most popular choice of topic, with most students choosing to study a film director' (AQA, 2011); an observation that was echoed in subsequent years' reports. In terms of recurring directors, year on year, many candidates have shown a keen interest in Pedro Almodóvar's techniques and can express informed views and opinions on his work. Other popular directors according to the examiners include Guillermo del Toro (from Mexico) and Carlos Saura, Alejandro Amenábar and José Luis Cuerda (from Spain). More consideration of why some of these directors are chosen will be explored later in this chapter.

The analysis of students' questionnaires confirms their preference for this topic. In response to the question, 'How much would you say watching this/these Spanish film(s) has increased your interest in Spanish as a subject?', 70% of the respondents said 'a lot' or 'quite a lot' and only two said 'not much' or 'not at all'. These figures not only suggest that a significant proportion of students derive enjoyment from watching Spanish film but also that it is an aspect of Spanish studies that is of particular interest and is one that dramatically enhances the appeal of the subject to young people.

Perhaps even more exciting for Spanish teachers is the extent to which film can make a difference to the popularity of the subject at higher levels of study. Students were asked, 'How much would you say the cultural topic has encouraged you to continue studying Spanish at university?': 90% responded that it had influenced their decision to continue their studies 'a little', 'quite a lot' or 'a lot', with only one student saying 'not at all'. With ever-dwindling numbers of languages graduates and 'strong evidence that the UK is suffering from a [general] growing deficit in foreign language skills at a time when global demand for language skills is expanding' (British Academy, 2013), data such as these, which point to increased interest and motivation, should not be ignored if we are determined to regain strong university language departments and produce British linguists for the future.

Film is, however, more than just an enjoyable activity and a change from the norm; it stimulates a variety of powerful cognitive processes in a learning context and develops visual and sound banks of reference that, in turn, facilitate the contextualisation and extended understanding of Spanish as a subject. In short, it is an absolutely essential part of learning Spanish. Therefore, it should not only be reinforced at A level but also be inserted into all stages of the curriculum, from the very beginning. Gee (2008) looks at one aspect of this importance in his consideration of 'primary discussion' and 'secondary discussion', whereby 'secondary' concerns the power of film to maintain interest and encourage further discussion and investigation. To further reinforce the potential of film at all stages of modern foreign language learning, the British Film Institute (2013: 22) advises that 'if children get the chance to experience a literacy curriculum that respects and extends their knowledge of moving image media, they are likely to do better at school'. This collective evidence points to a broadly accepted association between the enjoyment of language learning through film and an expectation of raised attainment, with the A-level cultural topic being in the best position to facilitate such an association. As we will now see, however, this potential is far from being fully achieved.

Objective 2: Language

Through the cultural topic and the AQA A-level Spanish course, students should 'develop an understanding of the language in a variety of contexts and genres' and learn to 'communicate confidently, clearly and effectively in the language for a range of purposes' (AQA, 2014b: 19). The June 2010 examination report[2] noted that in the written essay, students had used 'generally good Spanish' and that the level of language was 'generally quite reasonable'. However, examiners also noted that it was a shame that so many candidates seemed not to have practised writing in the foreign language on these cultural topics and were short of appropriate topic-orientated vocabulary. There are clear signs of the difficulty that the students faced in comments such as, 'it is worrying to see how many candidates appear not to know how to plan and write an essay' and that 'all too often, such candidates did not access the higher marks for the language categories because of their lack of focus on the question, **which directly affected their language marks**' (my emphasis). In the first year of assessment for the cultural topic, one of the biggest problems surrounding it became clear. Factors outside true linguistic ability, which mainly concern expectations relating to examination technique, were preventing large numbers of students from reaching the top marks. Consequently, we may infer that the teachers were not yet comfortable with teaching complex elements surrounding the content of the films in the target language, or, at least, they were not successful in equipping students with the knowledge and strategies to do this. Therefore, students were unable to demonstrate sufficient cultural understanding because of linguistic restrictions.

In the speaking examination of the same year (2010), the overall impression of grammatical competence was generally positive. Examiners commented on the wide range of vocabulary, tenses and constructions used. Despite this, marks reached the top band in only a minority of cases 'because the effect was mitigated by recurrent, familiar errors'. It is evident that suddenly, students were having to deal with high expectations in terms of complex written structures, sound grammatical awareness and a wide and often technical range of vocabulary, in addition to demonstrating a clear and detailed understanding of a director's work. Not surprisingly, for many students this was a jump too far and too quick.

There was little improvement one year later when examiners noted in June 2011 (AQA, 2011) that there were still some students who appeared not to know how to plan or write an essay. In the speaking examination, fluent speakers were able to use a variety of tenses and moods in addition to a wide range of vocabulary and idiomatic expressions. However, even the more able students sometimes failed to achieve a mark in the top band. Examiners again reported that many students had learned answers containing complex structures by heart and were then unable to use them appropriately to suit the question asked. At this point, there seems to be enough evidence to suggest that the demands of the cultural topic, when added to those of other topics (such as the impact of technology on society and renewable energies), are such that teachers (and, therefore, students) suffer from a lack of time to explore the complexities – and, apparently, some of the more basic areas – of Spanish grammar.

Examiners were pleased to note that in June 2012 the quality of essays showed some sign of improvement (AQA, 2012). Basic language errors were still evident, and there were many pre-learned 'stereotyped' phrases, such as *si fuera*, but the most able students used more complex language effectively to express their thoughts in a spontaneous way. The highest marks were gained by essays that had a clearly focused and short introduction, followed by a series of clearly identifiable and structured paragraphs, each addressing one aspect of the question with an in-depth analysis supported by good textual justification. Once again, technique is key. This brings us back to the questions surrounding students' expected skills in writing essays in Spanish about an aspect of Spanish culture when they have probably never had to do so before. It also raises questions about whether teachers have sufficient knowledge to most effectively guide students in this regard.

Despite this growing need to train teachers in how to teach effectively through film, there is evidence to suggest that the level of training is not matched by the growing demand. In a sample of modern foreign language teaching colleagues at varying stages of their career, to whom I spoke during a departmental meeting, only two out of eight had ever received any training on teaching through foreign film. Perhaps even more worryingly, in a larger sample of 22 local trainee teachers of modern foreign languages, 77% described the training they had received to teach through film as less than 'good', including 41% who went as far as to describe it as 'inadequate'. It is not entirely surprising, then, if students are not equipped to effectively demonstrate their interpretations of the films and directors to which they have been exposed.

Examiners' comments continued to suggest in the 2012 and 2013 reports that teachers, in a bid to improve the quality of language used by students in the examinations, seemed to be encouraging students to memorise chunks of language that could be applied to virtually any question (AQA, 2012, 2013). This is perhaps an inevitability of an examination of this kind, especially when considering the time limitations for teachers of A-level Spanish. However, if the purpose of incorporating film, and, in fact, any of the potential cultural topics, into the curriculum is to allow students to access authentic materials as part of being able to, according to the specification, 'communicate confidently, clearly and effectively in the language for a range of purposes' and, in the speaking, to sustain 'a meaningful exchange with very little prompting' while 'responding well to regular opportunities to react spontaneously' (AQA, 2014b: 19) (to achieve a mark in the top band for 'Interaction'), then clearly these objectives are still far from being fully achieved.

The students' response to 'How much would you say your understanding of Spanish language has improved by watching this/these film(s)?' is somewhat reassuring: 65% felt that their understanding of Spanish language had improved 'quite a lot' or 'a lot' by studying Spanish cinema within the cultural topic. Some of the students specified that this was down to the fact that they were listening to 'real Spanish voices' in 'an authentic context'. Looking at the questionnaire responses, it is perhaps not surprising that most of the students felt that their 'general listening skills' had improved. It is also encouraging that 75% of the students recognise the value of the moving image with sound to enhance attainment in listening. This finding supports theoretical claims such as that of Ortí Teruel *et al.* (2011: 2), who state that 'it is the images of cinema [along with sound] that allow for the comprehension of linguistic messages and the development of sociolinguistic and pragmatic competence'.

Interestingly, half of the students asked noted 'slang' as the aspect of Spanish language in which they felt they had made most progress. There is clearly great potential in the use of film to teach students popular and often humorous slang, although it is questionable how many marks a good knowledge of slang is actually worth. Examiners do not praise students' use of slang in any of the reports; nor do they mention it as something they are looking for. Pleasingly, the majority of the students asked mentioned vocabulary or range of expression as two further areas of noted progress; 60% and 55%, respectively. These figures and my own observations support the arguments proposing that the strength of studying film in the cultural topic lies in its ability to expand students' linguistic range for a variety of purposes, with dialogue components often providing handy, poignant or memorable points of reference for new words, expressions and linguistic constructions.

Objective 3: History, Society and Culture

The AQA (2014b: 19) specification outlines that in addition to allowing students to 'consider their study of the language in a broader context', the cultural topic should allow students to 'develop an awareness and understanding of the contemporary society, cultural background and heritage of countries or communities where the language is spoken'. In June 2010, the examiners commented positively on most candidates' breadth of knowledge of the cultural topics that they had studied (AQA, 2010). However, they commented that there were too many prepared essays and answers to 'the question I hoped to get', and there were some 'fairly weak essays which described rather than analysed the chosen films'. In the speaking examination, the work of Almodóvar was very popular, in particular, *Volver* (Almodóvar, 2006), *Todo sobre mi madre* (Almodóvar, 1999) and *Hable con ella* (Almodóvar, 2002). Many candidates showed a keen interest in the director's techniques and could express informed views and opinions.

In June 2011, the examiners commented that there were, once again, too many 'all-purpose' essays and that students seemed to have reproduced teachers' notes with little attempt to mould them to the specific requirements of the question (AQA, 2011). Many of these responses lacked a clear focus on evaluating the director's contribution to the popularity of the work. Conversely, the examiners noted that there were also students whose answers displayed excellent knowledge and a high level of discipline in the sense of producing well-planned and well-reasoned essays. In the speaking examination, Almodóvar was again the most popular director. According to the examiners, the students talked knowledgeably about a range of his films but the most frequently discussed were, again, the three films mentioned above. For now, suffice to confirm that, among the reasons cited in an essay for Almodóvar's success in June 2012 were themes, plot, connections to his background, choice of actors, cinematographic artistry and cinematic intertextuality.

In June 2013, echoed again in 2014, examiners noted that 'there were many very poor essays on *Volver*: with too many hackneyed responses about the use of the colour red, strong women and the traditions of La Mancha' (AQA, 2013, 2014a). Alejandro Amenábar (2004) was also popular, with responses mostly on the theme of euthanasia, characters and landscapes in relation to his film, *Mar adentro*. As ever, many candidates wrote about Guillermo del Toro, with the focus on special effects, the worlds of fantasy and reality and the theme of the Spanish Civil War. In the speaking test, the examiners noted that the majority of students had a very good knowledge of their cultural topics and reported hearing many interesting discussions.

In the questionnaires, students were asked, 'How much would you say your understanding of Spanish history has improved by watching this/these film(s)?'. Before looking at the students' responses, in strong support of Spanish film's potential here, Stephens (2001: 3) explains how film furnishes an accessible window into Spain that would otherwise be blocked or unavailable to undergraduate students who are unable to read novels or plays (or to read enough of them) to gain a broad understanding. Assuming for now that this is accurate, for the majority of the students, it was, perhaps predictably, the Spanish Civil War and the Franco dictatorship that provided the main subject of the historical context. More specifically, students highlighted that some of the films helped to teach them about the 'causes and consequences' of the war and the notion of 'social oppression'. Students said that the films gave them a valuable insight into 'the position of women and civilians at the time and their treatment by the military' while highlighting 'the importance of female role models for young people at the time'. There is evidently a good basis here in the broad historical issues raised by some of the films, which, presumably, some students would not otherwise have access to if directly following the specification.

In terms of figures, it is pleasing to note that 75% of the students asked felt that their understanding of Spanish history had improved 'a little', 'quite a lot' or 'a lot'. However, how much of Spanish factual history can we be confident that students gain knowledge of from studying popular fictional films such as *El laberinto del fauno*? When considering this great responsibility of film, one must remain conscious of the feature filmmakers' inevitable subjectivity, desire for artistic expression and, certainly in the cases of the directors mentioned so far, 'auteurship' – all of which can and do prevent feature films from being completely historically accurate. For assessment purposes this dilemma may not be detrimental to students' writing and speaking within this particular topic: after all, they are, first and foremost, studying 'the work of a director'. However, as the motivations of the creators of any authentic resource go beyond simply educating an audience within the classroom context, all parties involved must take lengths to differentiate factual accuracy and artistic expression. Moreover, film must not be considered a complete replacement for more traditional resources for educating students about the history and heritage of the target language country. To echo these warnings, Champoux (1999: 12) brands all films as fiction and notes that fiction writers and directors have much flexibility in how much 'reality' they want their films to show. However, according to Talty (2002), 'the control is not in the writer's words, but with the reader's choices'. It is evident that opinions differ on the reliability and other potential obstacles concerning the subjectivity of cinema within an educational context. To this end, the New London Group (1996: 11–12) appears to find a balanced middle ground in its suggestion that, in order to be relevant, learning processes need to recruit, rather than attempt to ignore and erase, the different subjectivities that students (and others) bring to learning. The group goes on to describe the role of pedagogy to develop an 'epistemology of pluralism that provides access without people having to erase or leave behind different subjectivities'.

In response to the question, 'How much would you say your knowledge of Spanish society has increased by watching this/these film(s)?', it is pleasing to note that 75% students asked felt that their knowledge of Spanish society had improved 'a little', 'quite a lot' or 'a lot', with over one-third of the total respondents saying 'quite a lot'. One student noted, 'The film shows the societal values of the time, and how they differ from modern Spanish values, which shows a contrast in values between the fascist regime and democratic approach'. The same student said, '*El laberinto del fauno* helped me to understand the lives of different demographic groups of people (e.g., women and children) in the context of a civil war'. Finally, the student commented that 'the film has some aspects of hierarchy such as the male characters being "above" the female characters in terms of rank and importance'. In response to these more detailed comments, there is some evidence here that at least some of the films being used are able to map significant movements in Spanish society; how groups fitted into that society then, and how they fit into it now. In this case, I use the word 'then' to refer to a generic unspecified period of time, as historical films will differ greatly in terms of when exactly they are set and how the director chooses to represent said society. Caution, as always, must be applied to make the most of Spanish cinema as a window into periods and particularities of Spanish society. The real challenge for the Spanish teacher is to somehow convey and classify the identity of Spanish society, or indeed, societies, while ensuring that students understand it/them as complex, conflicted and 'unstereotyped'.

Finally, students were asked, 'How much would you say your knowledge of Spanish culture has increased by watching this/these film(s)?'. Beginning with a theoretical viewpoint, Ortí Teruel *et al.* (2011: 2) discuss how cinema 'allows for the development of communicative competence and intercultural consciousness as it permits the understanding of similarities and differences between one's own culture and the culture represented in the film'. Such a concept is featured in the Common European Framework of Reference for Languages (Council of Europe, 2001: 103), which states that intercultural competence involves the understanding of the existing relation between the country of origin and the target culture. But what do students think?

In terms of questionnaire responses, perhaps ironically (given that film is a cultural product), fewer students studying cinema within the cultural topic felt that they had increased their knowledge of Spanish culture than their knowledge of aspects of Spanish language, history or society. Only 30% felt that their knowledge of Spanish culture had increased 'quite a lot', with a significant 40% of students choosing the 'not much' category. Of those who did recognise the cultural value of learning Spanish through film, one of the most interesting comments describes *El laberinto del fauno* as a film that 'strikes many contrasts between oppression and the lack of free will under Franco's regime, and highlights how modern Spanish culture, by contrast, is one filled with innovation and freedom of expression'. This comment reminds us of the inherent potential of film to allow its audience to compare national culture at different times. This can be achieved either through films set in the present day but made in different years or through historical films, such as *El laberinto del fauno*, which give the audience the opportunity to look at Spanish culture in the past and present and to experience culture as interconnected with historical fact and/or perspective and changes in societal views. The disadvantage of such films is summarised by one student, who noted, 'Culturally, Spain is very different from what it was during the Civil War, mainly due to the dark period of censorship under Franco that Spain endured. As such, the film doesn't teach us much about current culture'. Some students, it would seem, miss out on learning about contemporary Spanish culture via the cultural topic, which in many ways would seem to be the most significant era for today's A-level students. Compressing this cultural element into just one part of the final year of A-level study appears to be not only insufficient but also counterproductive, as it provides students with a highly limited and likely biased representation at various levels – from the stance of the director to the cultural experiences and knowledge of the teacher, which includes such basics as their choice of film. To reflect this, Castiñeiras Ramos and Herrero Vecino (1999: 1) speak of the 'complexity of cultural experience', as 'culture' is clearly a hugely diverse aspect of national identity and one that could be seen as more complex to 'teach' to a foreign audience. Consequently, the curriculum must provide sufficient space for a meaningful and varied appreciation of Spanish culture, which I believe is currently lacking due to the unbalanced focus on the production of regurgitated target language. If we really want to know what students have learned about Spanish culture, why not let them express it in English?

A second interesting point concerns the study of a Spanish film within the context of the national industry as being part of learning about Spanish culture. One student commented, 'Studying the film provided an insight into Spanish cinema and I learned about the most prominent directors in the industry, with whom I was previously unfamiliar'. By simply watching and appreciating a Spanish film, students naturally absorb an element of Spanish culture, which has its own very important value. However, if restricted to one film it is necessary to choose a film that contains a maximum amount of national cultural content to avoid a missed opportunity for students to explore, contextualise and link the cultural identity of the language they are studying, which, unfortunately, is all too often 'alienised'.

Conclusion

In conclusion, the cultural topic has in many ways been a great success, as it has added to the enjoyment of studying Spanish at A level and has been a motivational factor in students' decision to continue their study at undergraduate level. It has encouraged a much-needed modernisation of modern foreign language learning in a subject that has often struggled to convince students of its relevance and contemporary nature, with students frequently suffering from a detachment of authenticity, diverse resources and tangible points of reference, despite teachers' best efforts. Students, by and large, do recognise the value of Spanish film to enhance their understanding of Spanish language and Spanish history, society and culture, often noticing and appreciating elements that perhaps no one else, including the teacher, had processed in the same way. Subjectivity should not be feared or discouraged, but rather embraced; indeed, many of the assessment requirements of the cultural topic are designed so that every viewpoint and opinion is considered equally important. However, the lack of consistency and, for some, transparency, of the assessment requirements is highly problematic, especially when they fail to measure students' true ability in the subject or, indeed, their actual understanding of a film as a cultural text and, therefore, of 'the work of a director'.

In order for the cultural topic, or what is now the study of set cultural texts (including film within the reformed A level), to be a true success, students and teachers must first receive adequate training and have ample practice over an appropriate timescale. Secondly, schools need to be provided with the means and the confidence to facilitate a modern foreign language curriculum that prioritises 'culture' (encompassing history and society) and includes film much earlier, much more consistently and in much greater depth. For that to happen, it must be prioritised in the national curriculum at primary level, Key Stage 3 and GCSE,[3] in addition to the A-level specifications: this would permit consistency in students having sufficient knowledge and the skills required to critically appreciate and understand foreign cultural identity. Finally, specification objectives and mark schemes must be designed so that modern foreign languages examinations are able to reflect students' true abilities, rather than penalising students through what is, for many, an overly ambitious assessment structure that shows little consideration for the inadequacies of cultural studies and related assessment at all previous levels.

Notes

(1) An 'A level' (Advanced level) is a British higher education qualification, usually taken at the end of what is called 'Key Stage 5' in either a school or a college when students are 18 years old. Students usually take three A levels and the combination of subjects varies greatly. University undergraduate course offers are often based on A-level results. The first part (usually lasting a year) of A-level study is known as 'AS' (Advanced Subsidiary) and the second part is often called 'A2'. Until 2016, an AS was the equivalent of half an A level, although from 2017 the AS will be a stand-alone qualification, meaning that the A-level assessment is based on the full (usually two-year) A-level course.
(2) The link to the report is no longer available on the AQA website.
(3) British school education is divided into four 'Key Stages'. Key Stage 3 begins at the start of secondary education and normally lasts for three years. Students then study a number of subjects for 'GCSE', with English, maths and science being compulsory or 'core', and other subjects being optional.

References

Álvarez Mennuto, A. (2009) ¿Cómo puedo usar material audiovisual auténtico con principiantes? In R. Bueno Hudson, M. Abad and A. Valbuena (eds) *Actas de las II Jornadas Didácticas del Instituto Cervantes de Mánchester* (pp. 21–28). Manchester: Instituto Cervantes de Manchester.
Almodóvar, P. (1999) *Todo sobre mi madre/All about my Mother*. Spain: El Deseo.
Almodóvar, P. (2002) *Hable con ella /Talk to Her*. Spain: El Deseo.
Almodóvar, P. (2006) *Volver*. Spain: El Deseo.
Amenábar, A. (2004) *Mar adentro*. Spain: Sogepag and Sogecine.
AQA (2011) Unit 3 Examination report (own copy). UK: AQA.
AQA (2012) Unit 3 Examination report (own copy). UK: AQA.
AQA (2013) Unit 3 Examination report (own copy). UK: AQA.
AQA (2014a) Unit 3 Examination report (own copy). UK: AQA.

AQA (2014b) GCE AS and A level specification: French/German/Spanish (version 1.6). See http://filestore.aqa.org.uk/subjects/specifications/alevel/AQA-2650-2660-2695-W-SP-14.pdf

Bazalgette, C. (2009) *Impacts of Moving Image Education: A Summary of Research*. Scottish Screen.

British Academy (2013) *Languages: State of the Nation*. Report prepared by T. Tinsley. Alcantara Communications. See http://www.britac.ac.uk/publications/languages-sta te-nation (accessed 2 June 2015).

British Film Institute (2013) *Reframing Literacy*. Report. See http://www.bfi.org.uk/sites/bfi.org.uk/files/downloads/bfi-education-reframing-literacy-2013-04.pdf (accessed 12 October 2015).

Castiñeiras Ramos, A. and Herrero Vecino, C. (1999) Más allá de las imágenes: El cine como recurso en las clases de español. In T. Jiménez Juliá, M.C. Losada Aldrey and J.F. Márquez Caneda (eds) *Español como Lengua Extranjera: Enfoque comunicativo y gramática* (pp. 817–824). Santiago de Compostela: ASELE and Universidad de Santiago de Compostela.

Champoux, J.E. (1999) Film as a teaching resource. *Journal of Management Inquiry* 8 (2), 240–251.

Council of Europe (2011) *The Common European Framework for Languages: Learning, Teaching, Assessment*. See http://www.coe.int/t/dg4/linguistic/Source/Framework_EN.pdf (accessed 2 June 2015).

del Toro, G. *El laberinto del fauno*. Mexico and Spain: Estudios Picasso and Tequila Gang.

Gee, J.P. (2008) *Social Linguistics and Literacies: Ideology in Discourses* (3rd edn). London: Routledge.

New London Group (1996) A pedagogy of multiliteracies: Designing social futures. *Harvard Education Review* 66 (1), 60–92.

Ortí Teruel, R., García Collado, M.A. and Bendriss, N. (2011) El desarrollo de la competencia intercultural a partir del cine. Celda 211. See http://comprofes.es/sites/default/files/slides/garcia_collado_angeles.pdf (accessed 12 October 2015).

Stephens, J.L. (2001) Teaching culture and improving language skills through a cinematic lens: A course on Spanish film in the undergraduate Spanish curriculum. *ADFL Bulletin* 33 (3), 22–25.

Talty, C. (2002) Teaching a visual rhetoric. Northern Illinois University (blog). See http://kairos.technorhetoric.net/7.3/response/Visual_rhet/ctalty2002 (accessed 2 June 2015).

Wilkinson, J.E. and Head, G. (2009) *Evaluation of the Moving Image in Education Project*. Final report. Glasgow: University of Glasgow.

12 Audiovisual Activities and Multimodal Resources for Foreign Language Learning

Stavroula Sokoli and
Patrick Zabalbeascoa Terran

Language teachers often resort to video for various foreign language learning (FLL) purposes. Since learning by doing is considered to be more effective than learning by viewing, this valuable asset can be enhanced through hands-on activities. This chapter focuses on the integration of multimodal activities in FLL. It also discusses elements of the ClipFlair conceptual framework and how they are relevant to the broader context of language learning. The ClipFlair project's main premise is that FLL can be enhanced by using activities that require learners to work from a video by inserting their own writing (captioning) or speech (revoicing). This framework opens up a whole range of possible activities to teachers, using standard subtitling and dubbing models and alternative options adapted to FLL, within and beyond ClipFlair.

Introduction

The advantages of using video in the foreign language classroom have been widely acknowledged and explored by a number of specialist scholars in this field (e.g. Allan, 1985; Baltova, 1994; King, 2002; Stempleski & Tomalin, 1990; Tschirner, 2001) and this interest is continuing to increase. The associated benefits include variety, flexibility, adaptability to learning needs, enhanced learner motivation, exposure to non-verbal elements and the ability to present authentic linguistic and cultural aspects of communication in context.

There are multiple applications of video in foreign language learning (FLL). Therefore, when one embarks on such a large-scale project as ClipFlair, which is based on the notion that video can be used to enhance FLL, there seems to be a pressing need to revise the state of the art of what is on offer and the notions and concepts that are associated with video-orientated FLL. It is essential to promote effective communication in this area. The ClipFlair project, therefore, does more than provide off-the-shelf activities and clips in a free and open online environment for a large number of languages, levels and interests. We have also situated ClipFlair and its potential applications and usefulness in the context of what has been done in the field so far and what is yet to be done. By putting a finer point on certain definitions and terms, we aim to improve understanding of what we are doing and how new contributions can be made. Given that we have no customers and no aim to make a profit, there is no vested interest in luring prospective customers through advertising rhetoric rather than providing a coherent system of related terms. This means that ClipFlair focuses, among others, on two important goals: sustaining the results beyond the funding period and offering findings and contributions that may be useful for other pedagogical projects and courses, as a contribution to FLL studies. The ClipFlair conceptual framework (Zabalbeascoa et al., 2012) reflects this, providing terminology and ideas for learners, teachers, course designers and educational authorities who are interested in a pedagogical rationale for using video (actively) in FLL.

This chapter focuses on aspects that can be (and have been successfully) used in the ClipFlair environment or as part of a different kind of course design or syllabus for a variety of settings and scenarios. Ultimately, we intend to be relevant to FLL as a whole by providing ideas and concepts that necessarily relate to each other and are practical as well as theoretical.

Teaching and Learning Objectives, Profiles, Styles and Settings

First and foremost, we must state that the proposal in this chapter falls within the boundaries of FLL. Translation and language are so closely related that their overlapping areas sometimes cause confusion. Moreover, certain approaches and attitudes towards FLL frown upon the use of any language other than the one being learned (second language [L2]) in exercises and tests or for communication. Another source of possible confusion is that trainee translators are also often involved in language learning, which gives rise to the notion of language learning for translators. This is not to be mistaken for translation exercises for language learners, given the different goals and profiles in each case. A broad notion of translation may not actually involve interlingual transfer if we accept the possibility of intralingual rewording, whereby translation can be viewed along the lines of conveying a message 'in other words'.

The practice of audiovisual (AV) translation constitutes a meaningful task, set in a well-defined context, whose outcome, unlike those of watching or viewing techniques, is a tangible, shareable student product: a video with subtitles or dubbed voices. Researchers have found that subtitling improves trainee translators' language skills. Until recently, this conclusion had been reached incidentally, as a side benefit of courses that use professional subtitling software designed for future professionals (Klerkx, 1998; Neves, 2004; Williams & Thorne, 2000). Subsequent empirical research focused specifically on language learning has highlighted the positive effects of subtitling on vocabulary learning (Incalcaterra McLoughlin & Lertola, 2011; Lertola, 2012; Talaván, 2013), the retention and recall of idiomatic expressions (Condinho Bravo, 2008) and intercultural skills (Borghetti & Lertola, 2014). To a lesser extent, researchers have also focused on dubbing (Burston, 2005; Chiu, 2012; Danan, 2010; Sánchez-Requena, 2018; Sokoli, 2018), audio description (Herrero & Escobar, 2018; Martínez, 2012; Navarrete, 2018) and motivation (Baños & Sokoli, 2015).

Despite the advantages, the practical integration of AV activities into language learning can be daunting. The high costs of professional software and limited technical knowledge have discouraged teachers and learners alike. In 2004, an initial effort was made to overcome these obstacles with the development of subtitling software and activities designed specifically for language education: the Learning via Subtitling (LeViS) project (Sokoli, 2006). According to the LeViS survey (Sokoli *et al.*, 2011), learners not only consolidated and improved their language skills but were also enthusiastic about the innovative nature of the approach. The ClipFlair project was developed after LeViS, as a next step. That was when it was decided that revoicing could be added (conceptually and technologically), while also taking advantage of the new project to broaden the scope that LeViS had had by shifting from subtitles to captioning, as this term covers a broader concept, for all forms of screenwriting (including subtitles, of course).

Learners

It is clear, then, that the learners we have in mind wish to improve their foreign language skills, communicative competence and overall proficiency. Having established this as their common denominator, we need to address the variety of their profiles. Learning can be incidental (as a by-product of other activities, such as travelling abroad or watching foreign films), informal (intended but largely unstructured) or formal (e.g. a structured course). A learner's setting can vary depending on the amount of guidance provided by a teacher or tutor and the number of peers or fellow course members. According to the ClipFlair conceptual framework (Zabalbeascoa *et al.*, 2012), students are learners in formal settings with teachers or tutors, in contrast with independent learners (i-learners). Another important variable is the number of face-to-face contact hours with either the teacher or fellow course members. 'Distance learning' is the term used when course exercises and explanations are sent (almost) entirely through the post or provided online. Blended learning refers to a situation where a course is balanced between face-to-face contact and distance learning. Technology is another variable that cuts across all the others in different ways; that is, distance learning is not necessarily dependent on information and communication technology, just as formal learning may not entail the presence of a teacher, and so on. A platform like ClipFlair is able to cater for distance, blended and face-to-face learning, largely because of its awareness from the beginning of the difference between these three cases. Likewise, it can cater for learners guided by teachers in addition to those who are more independent. This is because step-by-step instructions are built into the activities. These instructions can be adapted or ignored when there is someone to guide or teach learners.

Teachers, Course Designers and Activity Creators

ClipFlair can be seen as a resource for teachers as much as for those who are learning a language without a teacher. Teachers can use ready-made activities as they are presented or adapt them to their own specifications (Zabalbeascoa *et al.*, 2015). We understand that just as there are different learning styles, there are also different teaching styles, methods and approaches. Teachers may – but need not – be overwhelmed by the apparent need to know languages, computer skills and translation principles. Such requirements depend very much on the nature of the activity, but much can be done with a very rudimentary knowledge of such matters. Some things can be learned as one goes along; others are not necessary, since all one needs to do is to follow clear instructions. There is much to be said in favour of collaborative learning among students, and teachers learning (or pretending to learn) from their students. The concepts of translation, subtitling and dubbing can be applied to activities even within a single language, if that is how a teacher feels most comfortable or if it is how they wish to design their activities.

There is no claim that video captioning and revoicing activities are popular among all teachers. ClipFlair does not include a fully fledged FLL course, although it could if it had enough activities connected to each other in such a way. This means that i-learners and teachers can use the videos and activities provided in the ClipFlair Gallery as part of their course materials and resources. Another option is to create one's own activities, either from scratch or by making minor or major changes to existing activities. Activity creators or authors are the people who create or adapt FLL activities. Anyone can play this role, including learners, teachers and their students, and course designers who are interested in creating activities, even if they do not work as teachers. Teachers always need to invest some time in preparing materials, resources and activities for their courses. The principle is to maximise this investment by choosing materials and activities according to criteria that will make them 'pay off'. In this sense, the ClipFlair conceptual framework helps teachers to become aware of how and why certain items can pay off more than others, for them.

Materials and Resources

A course is built up from a justifiable sequencing of the following components: resources, materials and activities. A digital environment, such as ClipFlair, has software that can be used online or offline. The basic materials offered by ClipFlair are video clips, which can be found in the gallery. Each activity is a combination of a video clip and a set of pedagogically guided instructions and any further materials needed to carry out the activity (e.g. files, templates, links and documents). The resource offered is the ClipFlair software, which allows the user to inter-act appropriately with the materials and activities. Activities are carried out in the ClipFlair Studio (http://studio.clipflair.net). This is a container window with a variable number of components (including clips, text files, captioning and/or revoicing templates, images and links) that can be arranged visually in many different ways.

An activity forms part of a lesson, which is part of a didactic unit within the structure of formal learning (a course). The principles of flex-ibility and contingency stress the fact that (prototypical and reusable) activities can be well suited to different didactic units and even different courses – sometimes unchanged, and at other times by adapting one or more of the components (instructions or materials). Activities can also be done in a freer sequence in the context of informal learning.

Given that materials and activities are related but not bound by a one-to-one dependency, the ClipFlair Gallery includes two sections: one for clips and one for activities. This allows ClipFlair users to adapt exist-ing activities and/or create new ones by combining clips with activities (in their instruction component) in different ways, which highlights the potential for multiple uses of a given clip in different activities, and mul-tiple applications of certain activities across a number of clips. ClipFlair follows a principle of efficiency for course materials, meaning that a posi-tive factor of materials (and activities) is how (much) they can be reused in different lessons, courses and settings (Figure 12.1).

All activities, clips, texts and images are accessible through the Clip-Flair Gallery (http://gallery.clipflair.net). Each resource category has its own gallery (Activity Gallery, Video Gallery, Image Gallery, etc.). Given the component-based nature of the platform, the same material can be combined in multiple ways to create an array of different activities in different languages. For example, the same clip may be exploited differ-ently for learners with different levels of proficiency, and the same set of instructions can be used with different clips. For example, a clip used for

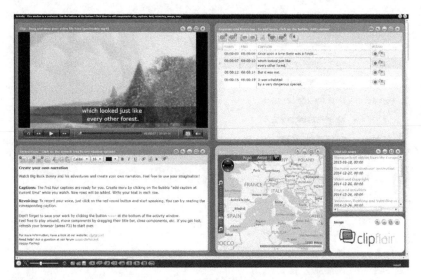

Figure 12.1 Components of a sample ClipFlair activity

a B2 activity (intermediate) can be exploited differently in an activity for learners at the A2 level (beginner), by asking them, say, to identify certain words and write them in the captions. Accordingly, instructions used in an activity – provided that they are not clip specific – can be copied in an activity based on another clip.

By the end of 2015, the gallery offered 650 selected video clips and 440 activities in 17 languages (see Figure 12.2). Some of the activities can be used to learn any language, as they include non-verbal clips; thus, they are language independent.

Each item in the gallery is accompanied by relevant metadata, which facilitates searching for and identifying clips and activities. When activity authors have an activity ready to upload to the gallery, they are asked to provide information about each component of the activity in the form of metadata. Activity metadata include the following items:

- language to be learned;
- language combination;
- language level (A1–C2);
- estimated time to complete the activity;
- skills promoted;
- kind of response required by the learner (repeat, react or rephrase);
- kind of task (revoicing or captioning);
- learner type (independent, guided or teacher dependent);
- age group;
- keywords;
- author's name.

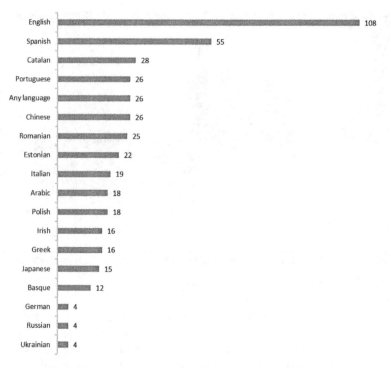

Figure 12.2 Number of activities per language in the ClipFlair Gallery

Users can search the Activity Gallery using these metadata as filters to narrow their search. There is also a search field, where keywords of interest can be entered.

Multimodal Combinations of Activity Components for Audiovisual Literacy and Richness

ClipFlair is multimodal in that it brings together components in a single window on the screen. There is an AV component (the clip) and at least one text component (the instructions) in the 'prompt' stage, and the outcome will produce at least one other component: either captions (writing) or a voice recording (audio). Today, multimodality is becoming increasingly popular in daily life and in education, especially with the widespread use of tablets, e-books, laptops and smartphones for leisure, work and education. ClipFlair is driven by educational goals, such as literacy, independent critical thinking, communication competence (including semiotic awareness) and respect for diversity and other languages and cultures. AVs are no longer just an extracurricular activity, purely motivational, a filler for the end of a class, a substitute teacher or for use on a rainy day. We take a similar stance to that of de Beaugrande and Dressler (1981), who proved in 1981 that textual communication can be defined by such factors as coherence, cohesion and intertextuality but not unavoidably by the presence of spoken or written words. We regard literacy as a feature of social education that is not restricted to reading written words but also reaches out to AV texts, which tend to combine verbal signs with non-verbal signs in order to create meaning and communicate feelings and intentions. We do not wish to accelerate the demise of the written word: on the one hand, we want to promote it through new forms of communication; on the other, we want to prepare learners to cope with language settings that increasingly involve AVs and multimodal communication as a sign of the times we live in.

'Literacy' according to the ClipFlair conceptual framework, refers to the ability to read for knowledge, write coherently and think critically about the written word (Zabalbeascoa *et al.*, 2012). Visual literacy also includes the ability to understand all forms of communication, be it body language, pictures, maps or video. Literacy encompasses a complex set of abilities to understand and use the dominant symbol systems of a culture for personal and community development. In a technological society, the concept of literacy is expanding to include the media and electronic text in addition to alphabet and number systems.

What is a good clip for FLL? We would say that there are two important features to take into account. The first is the clip's reusability in different settings, as noted above. Another major finding, not only for our project but for all FLL using multimodality and AVs, is the notion of AV richness, which we find to be a more important variable than whether an AV is animated or not, its genre or other traditional typologies.

If we categorise the elements of an AV text (Figure 12.3a–d) according to the combinatory possibilities of two channels (audio and visual), with a binary option of verbal signs (words) or any other type of sign (images and sound effects), we can assess how 'rich' a clip is in each of these four sectors.

Figure 12.3 shows how video can be assessed for its usefulness in FLL, and probably in other areas of filmic appreciation. The scale from 0 to 3 can also be applied to other relevant criteria for clip selection in FLL (e–h): 0 = lacking/irrelevant; 1 = unimportant/uninteresting; 2 = somewhat varied or important; and 3 = varied, important and dynamic.

(a) **Pace.** There is a sense of action or movement. The camera moves a lot, with changes of shots and angles. There are changes and variations in the weight and importance of the AV components (a–d).

(b) **Talking heads.** Faces can be seen speaking. There is mouth movement and/or verbal interaction can be seen, with paralinguistic and non-verbal elements (e.g. body language, distance between speakers).

(c) **Characters interact and do things.** People can be seen moving and behaving in different ways (apart from talking); for example,

	Audio	Visual
Verbal	**(a) Speech** (audio-verbal) 0 – No words can be heard 1 – Unimportant/uninteresting 2 – Somewhat varied/important 3 – Varied, important, dynamic speech	**(b) Writing** (visual-verbal) 0 – No words can be read 1 – Unimportant/uninteresting 2 – Somewhat varied/important 3 – Varied, important, dynamic writing
Non-verbal	**(c) Music and sound effects** (audio-semiotic) 0 – Music/sound is lacking or completely irrelevant 1 – Semiotically/culturally unimportant/uninteresting 2 – Somewhat varied/important 3 – Varied, dynamic, semiotically interesting and important	**(d) Picture** (visual-semiotic) 0 – Picture lacking or completely irrelevant 1 – Semiotically/culturally unimportant/uninteresting 2 – Somewhat varied/important 3 – Varied, dynamic, semiotically interesting and important

Figure 12.3 Criteria for audiovisual richness by four semiotic signs

eating, running, swimming, dancing, walking or reacting to some stimulus.

(d) **Narratively rich.** A plot, a story or an argument is developed. A clip may have no words and still offer great potential for creative captioning and revoicing because of its narrative quality.

We believe that these 'richness' factors are relevant when using video in FLL, no matter what the approach, level or purpose.

FLL Prompts and Productions: Combinations of Skills

ClipFlair is a flexible tool that can host a wide range of activities. What can it do and what can it not do? Part of the answer lies in the nature of the prompts and outcomes that are ClipFlair specific and those that are not. A prompt is an instruction or stimulus that triggers an activity and its outcome. For example, it is usually what teachers ask their students to do at a specific time (read, write, speak, listen, watch or mime). Subtler prompts may be implicitly expressed; for example, by a silence or by holding up a picture. Different FLL methods and approaches can often be distinguished by differences in the kinds of prompts and outcomes that they promote or ignore. In this section, we will concentrate on the range of prompts that the conceptual framework has developed into a useful typology for FLL.

Let us consider 'from X to Y' or simply 'X to Y' as shorthand for 'eliciting an outcome (Y) by means of a prompt and preliminary action (X)'. 'Read to speak' is shorthand, then, for asking students to read (methodology) in order to get them to speak (goal). Now we have a means of considering ClipFlair-like activities (captioning and revoicing) in the context of many other FLL activities (e.g. dictation, role play and guided composition). ClipFlair is characterised by the nature of students' output, or outcome, which is restricted to one of the following: repeat, rephrase or react (the three Rs). *Repeat* activities include such exercises as transcription (e.g. dictation) or very close translation (lexicosemantically). *Rephrase* is a label for exercises involving a rather creative, 'free', pragmatic, adapted or localised rendering or rewording of the source text provided (as in 'retell in your own words'). *React* is a label that includes other types of responses, such as answering questions, or guided composition. All three can be either intralingual (L2 → L2) or interlingual (e.g. first language [L1] → L2 or L2 → L1). The possible kinds of activities are multiplied depending on combinations of learner inputs and outputs (X to Y), language combinations (L0, L1, L2, third language [L3]; see the definitions below), types of learner response (the three R's) and AV skills developed (more than 'the four skills', reading, writing, listening and speaking). We wish to highlight the rich possibilities for combining the intra- vs interlingual variable with repeat-rephrase-react options.

L0 – Language of instructions/description: This can be L1, L2 or a lingua franca. For example, the same intralingual activity for learning Polish can be used for learners with different L1s by using a common language.

L1 – Learner's language: Any language that the learner knows well enough to work 'from' (the prompt).

L2 – Language being learned: The target language to learn.

L3 – Other language: Any other language that might appear in a clip being used in an activity (when it might be important to know such information). There may be different language combinations in an activity.

We also envisage the possibility of *multilingual* scenarios and combinations that are not strictly L1-to-L2 or L2-to-L1 interlingual exercises, either because an L3 (some other language) is involved (e.g. in the clip) or because the learner's expected output is a mixture of L1 and L2. 'Multilingual' can also signal that the clip is not entirely monolingual, even if it only includes the learner's L1 and L2 (when X is not a purely monolingual clip *to* a purely monolingual learner output Y).

Audiovisual Skills (Beyond Reading, Writing, Listening and Speaking)

(1) **Watch**: AV interpreting skill for AV texts (e.g. film) as a whole, single, complex semiotic communicative act, in order to find

meaning and sense in a combination of verbal and non-verbal signs (Figure 12.3). It includes interpreting non-verbal pictures, icons, symbols, metaphors, cultural elements, etc., and any combination of verbal and non-verbal textual items.

(2) **AV listen**: Listening combined with the effect of other elements of the AV text.

(3) **AV read**: Reading combined with the effect of other elements of the AV text, and the ability to read according to the requirements of the screen (speed, focus, etc.).

(4) **AV speak**: Revoicing (dubbing, karaoke, voice-over and free commentary), adapting to speed, voice quality, performance, character portrayal, etc. Includes a variety of prompts, such as improvising, reading from a script, repeating and mimicking.

(5) **AV write**: Effective scriptwriting or captioning in its various forms. A specific component of 'full' AV production skills. Includes storyboard skills and visual narrative skills involving the use of the camera.

(6) **AV produce**: Filmmaking and film-directing; for example, learners being able to produce films and clips, displaying AV literacy production skills.

All of these skills, in addition to the traditional four, can be worked on in ClipFlair. The following examples illustrate the combinatory possibilities of X-to-Y prompts and outcomes for the various skills with no interlingual translation required.

Intralingual Repeat. Repeat someone's words as closely as possible.

- Listen to write: Dictation.
- Watch to AV write: *Captioning* for FLL or for the hard-of-hearing.
- Watch to AV speak: Dubbing the same words or an audio description of the picture. *Karaoke* (AV read to sing).
- Watch to speak: Intralingual *dubbing for FLL pronunciation* practice.
- Listen to speak: As in cassette, teacher's voice or digital audio-file 'listen and repeat' *drills.*

Intralingual Rephrase. Put what you read/heard/watched into your own words.

- Read to write: Summary, report or notes.
- Listen to write: Note-taking from a lecture or speech.
- Watch to AV write: Monolingual captions. Intralingual subtitles, conforming to strict norms of number of characters per line, etc., to force rephrasing (gist). Picture is a factor.
- Watch to AV speak: Dubbing paraphrases while taking the picture into account.

Intralingual React. Beyond repeat or rephrase, and more creative.

- Listen to speak: Learners answer questions orally, for instance, as they might respond to an interlocutor over the telephone.
- Watch to AV speak: The lines of one of the characters in a clip are silenced, so the learner must fill in that character's dialogue according to what the other characters are saying or what is happening.
- Free-commentary revoicing for a silent video.

Activity Samples and Prototypical Activities: Beyond the Lesson Plan

Although a project like ClipFlair is committed to education and conceives the activities as being part of a lesson (and, hence, a lesson plan), the activities also have a life beyond the lesson plan, especially when used with more independent learners, for motivational or introductory purposes, as supplementary material or as 'rainy day' games for the class. The added value of ClipFlair consists of ways to:

- promote learner (or student) independence;
- have fun while learning, by being creative;
- become semiotically and communicatively aware and pragmatic, by integrating the four skills;
- social interaction with peers;
- provide ClipFlair with a life after its funding ends.

In any teaching project, proposal or curriculum, a pool of activity samples is a way of providing guidelines and suggestions for activities without 'tying' learners or teachers to just one material (or clip, in the case of ClipFlair) per activity. This is for teachers and experts who wish to guide i-learners and for teachers who are looking for alternative ways to exploit popular clips (or other materials). Such activity samples serve the purpose of highlighting ClipFlair's added value. These would also seem to be generally desirable features of other FLL projects. This kind of approach reduces the tension of feeling that one has to discard every aspect of previous foreign language teaching methods when presented with a new one. What we are claiming here is that good activities can survive changing trends in education and adapt to different methodologies. Video and its related activities do not constitute an FLL method but are a tool like a Swiss army knife, which, among other advantages, helps to raise awareness of the nature of teaching and learning. The question, then, is not so much 'Are video activities like ClipFlair any good for me as an FLL teacher/learner?' but rather 'How can I best use and adapt these resources to my specific needs?'. Activity samples can help to answer this and other related questions.

Activity sample

Role play the director's comments on a DVD.

Revoice instruction: You are the director of the film/clip (or you made the home video). Explain how you made the scene, the purpose of the scene in the context of the film or something about the actors taking part (e.g. Are they really like the characters they are playing? Did they have to repeat the scene many times? Is there anything to look out for within the scene, such as hidden meanings in the wardrobe or props? Are there any cameos? Did you have to hire your mother?).

Pedagogical rationale: This is actually an exercise in guided composition (if prepared in writing first), pronunciation and oral fluency, and semiotic awareness. It is creative and fun. It can be done by i-learners and any other type of learner.

Prototypical activities

By 'prototypical' we mean that an activity can be applied to most video clips. These activities give learners who want to explore the Clip Gallery as if it were a library (an AV library promoting AV literacy) a 'guide' or list of things to do with the clips they like. This means that such prototypical activities could even be used in other FLL environments; thus, constituting ideas for FLL. Teachers, as ClipFlair users, can get students to collaborate with them in collecting new materials by giving the instruction that they must find clips that are suitable for the prototypical activity. This makes it more likely that students will bring to the course materials that are more relevant to them, saving the teacher the trouble of guessing what their interests might be.

Example A. Subtitle this clip in two different ways and compare the differences in the results.

(A1) Transcribe or translate as many words as possible.
(A2) Summarise as much as possible.

Note: If the clip is in the language you are learning (L2) then do this exercise in the same language (L2 → L2 transcription). If the clip is in a language you already know well, then write the subtitles in the language you are learning; that is, translate L1 → L2.

Pedagogical rationale: This is an exercise in guided composition. It involves comparing repeat (A1) and rephrase (A2). It develops the competence of gist translation and summarising, in the case of A2, thereby working on the competence of synthesis. In some cases, it will demonstrate the need for summarising in professional subtitling, thereby enabling the learner to appreciate subtitles more when watching them.

It is an active way of listening repeatedly. A1 develops the same skills as traditional dictation (when the exercise is intralingual), and A2 develops lexicosemantic equivalence. A2 may also develop more pragmatic awareness and interpretative skills.

Follow-up instruction (prompt): Think about how the picture influenced your choice of words or word order in A1 and A2.

Example B. Subtitle this clip in two different ways and compare the differences in the results.

(B1) Write down (or translate) as much as you can hear without looking at the screen.
(B2) Write down (or translate) as much as you can while watching the screen.
(B3) Compare the results.

Prompts: How (much) does the picture affect your understanding or interpretation of the words? How (much) does the picture influence your choice of words for the subtitles? For example, which words did you decide to omit in B2, because they would be redundant when seen with the picture?

Pedagogical rationale: An exercise in listening comprehension (B1) and watching, which is AV, by definition, (B2), and for the learner to become more aware of the differences between the nature of these two skills. It is also an exercise in AV literacy and in guided composition (writing skills). Ultimately, it is an exercise in integrating all of these skills. It is important to note that this exercise was created from an idea arising from Activity A1, which demonstrates that the nature of prototypical activities is to act as a catalyst for new ideas for activities.

Example C. Have fun, be creative and playful. Three ideas.

(C1) Revoice the clip using different voices and different types of voice. Use female voices for male characters and vice versa.
(C2) Write subtitles that create a new interpretation of the picture.
(C3) Write subtitles in different languages for different characters (e.g. L1 and L2).

Example D. Have fun by breaking the rules. Three ideas.

(D1) Write 'too many' words for the subtitles. Notice the effect it has.
(D2) Revoice in superfast speech ('too many words'); for example, the *Big Bang Theory* title song. Revoice in superslow speech ('too slow') or with a supersummary (very few words).

(D3) Write subtitles (or revoice) mixing L1 and L2 within the same utterance (code-switching). Subtitle some characters and revoice others.

Examples of Audiovisual Activities

Having presented the fundamental features of ClipFlair and how it can help teachers and course designers to think of new activities by building on ideas suggested by ClipFlair's conceptual framework and its existing activities, we now present some examples of repeat, rephrase and react activities sorted by input (prompt) and output (learner production), expressed as input-to-output (e.g. read-to-speak, below). The list is meant to clarify the concepts presented herein and, hopefully, to inspire readers to think of new activities or how to apply these ones to their specific needs and interests.

Read-to-speak

(a) **Repeat/verbatim**: Intralingual read aloud or interlingual 'sight translation'.
(b) **Rephrase/gist**: Oral report or summary.
(c) **React/respond**: Answer, analyse, criticise, agree, etc.

Listen-to-speak

(a) **Repeat**: Intralingual or interlingual (more or less verbatim); for example, traditional 'listen and repeat' exercises. Liaison and consecutive interpreting.
(b) **Rephrase**: Also intralingual or interlingual; simultaneous interpreting, relay, paraphrase or report (reported speech).
(c) **React**: Answer questions, turn-taking in spontaneous conversation or debate. Dialogue would involve a minimum of two instances of listen-to-speak by two people to each other.

Read-to-write

(a) **Repeat**: Copying; intralingual or interlingual translation/rendering; intertextuality (as in quoting or parodying).
(b) **Rephrase**: Summarise, report, adapt.
(c) **React**: Book review or film analysis.

Listen-to-write

(a) **Repeat**: Intralingual dictation, transcription and on-the-spot translation.
(b) **Rephrase**: Intralingual and interlingual note-taking.

(c) **React**: Radio listener's letters to the editor or programme; viewers' texts or tweets during a television or radio programme.

Conclusion

Teachers and scholars consider video to be a valuable resource in the foreign language classroom because it is appealing, it offers variety and flexibility, it provides exposure to non-verbal cultural elements, it contextualises linguistic aspects and it is closer to natural ideal communication than the written mode. Despite these and other advantages, the practical integration of AV activities into language learning can be demanding, because of technical requirements and potential lack of expertise in various areas. The ClipFlair project, partially presented in this chapter, aims to meet the need for ready-to-use AV resources by providing a web platform with the necessary tools and materials and a conceptual framework. The framework promotes a common understanding of terms and, most importantly, widens the range of possibilities for such activities beyond the traditional AV translation modes of subtitling and dubbing. This framework proposes the concept of AV skills, including AV writing (a synonym for captioning) and AV speaking (also called revoicing). New ideas for activities are inspired by combining the kind of skill with the type of response required by the learner (repeat, rephrase, react) and by combining the language of the clip with the learner input (interlingual or intralingual).

This chapter has also presented the ClipFlair web platform, including the studio and its tools, as well as the gallery, with 460 ready-to-use activities for 17 languages at various levels. The ClipFlair project was funded under the Lifelong Learning Programme of the European Commission. Although the funding period has come to an end, the platform will be maintained for at least five years and can be accessed free of charge. The aim of the partnership has been to consolidate existing research and pave the way for future research, projects and applications, contributing tangible results. It is hoped that ClipFlair has provided beneficial resources and a flexible and user-friendly platform in order to exploit the great potential of captioning and revoicing for language learning.

References

Allan, M. (1985) *Teaching English with Video*. London: Longman.

Baltova, I. (1994) The impact of video on the comprehension skills of core French students. *Canadian Modern Language Review* 50 (3), 507–532.

Baños, R. and Sokoli, S. (2015) Learning foreign languages with ClipFlair: Using captioning and revoicing activities to increase students' motivation and engagement. In K. Borthwick, E. Corradini and A. Dickens (eds) *10 Years of the LLAS Elearning Symposium: Case Studies in Good Practice* (pp. 203–213). Dublin: Research-publishing. net. doi:10.14705/rpnet.2015.000280

Borghetti, C. and Lertola, J. (2014) Interlingual subtitling for intercultural language education: A case study. *Language and Intercultural Communication*, 14 (4), 423–440.

Burston, J. (2005) Video dubbing projects in the foreign language curriculum. *CALICO Journal* 23 (1), 79–92.

Chiu, Y.H. (2012) Can film dubbing projects facilitate EFL learners' acquisition of English pronunciation? *British Journal of Educational Technology* 43 (1), 24–27.

ClipFlair. See http://clipflair.net

Condinho Bravo, M.C. (2008) *Putting the reader in the picture: Screen translation and foreign language learning.* Doctoral thesis, Rovira i Virgili University, Spain. See http://tdx.cat/bitstream/handle/10803/8771/Condhino.pdf?sequence=1 (accessed 7 May 2017).

Danan, M. (2010) Dubbing projects for the language learner: A framework for integrating audiovisual translation into task-based instruction. *Computer Assisted Language Learning* 23 (5), 441–456.

De Beaugrande, R. and Dressler, W. (1981) *Introduction to Text Linguistics* (Longman Linguistics Library, No. 26). London/New York: Longman.

Herrero, C. and Escobar, M. (2018) A pedagogical model for integrating film education and audio description in foreign language acquisition. *Translation and Translanguaging in Multilingual Contexts* 4 (1), 30–54.

Incalcaterra McLoughlin, L. and Lertola, J. (2011) Learn through subtitling: Subtitling as an aid to language learning. In L. Incalcaterra McLoughlin, M. Biscio and M.Á. Ní Mhainnín (eds) *Audiovisual Translation Subtitles and Subtitling. Theory and Practice* (pp. 243–263). Bern: Peter Lang.

King, J. (2002) Using DVD feature films in the EFL classroom. *Computer Assisted Language Learning* 15 (5), 509–523.

Klerkx, J. (1998) The place of subtitling in a translator training course. In P. Sewell and I. Higgins (eds) *Translation in Universities. Present and Future Perspectives* (pp. 259–264). London: CILT.

Lertola, J. (2012) The effect of subtitling task on vocabulary learning. In A. Pym and D. Orrego-Carmona (eds) *Translation Research Projects 4* (pp. 61–70). Tarragona: Intercultural Studies Group.

Martínez, S. (2012) *La audiodescripción (AD) como herramienta didáctica: Adquisición de la competencia léxica* [Audiodescription (AD) as a didactic tool: Acquisition of lexical competence]. In S. Cruces Colado, M. Del Pozo Triviño, A. Luna Alonso and A. Álvarez Lugrís (eds) *Traducir en la Frontera* (pp. 87–102). Granada: Atrio.

Navarrete, M. (2018) The use of audio description in foreign language education. *Translation and Translanguaging in Multilingual Contexts* 4 (1), 129–150.

Neves, J. (2004) Language awareness through training in subtitling. In P. Orero (ed.) *Topics in Audiovisual Translation* (pp. 127–140). Amsterdam: John Benjamins.

Sánchez-Requena, A. (2018) Intralingual dubbing as a tool for developing speaking skills. *Translation and Translanguaging in Multilingual Contexts* 4 (1), 101–128.

Sokoli, S. (2006) Learning via subtitling (LvS): A tool for the creation of foreign language learning activities based on film subtitling. In M. Carroll and H. Gerzymisch-Arbogast (eds) *Audiovisual Translation Scenarios: Proceedings of the Marie Curie Euroconferences MuTra Multidimensional Translation.* Copenhagen, Denmark, 1–5 May.

Sokoli, S. (2018) Exploring the possibilities of interactive audiovisual activities for language learning. *Translation and Translanguaging in Multilingual Contexts* 4 (1), 77–100.

Sokoli, S., Zabalbeascoa, P. and Fountana, M. (2011) Subtitling activities for foreign language learning: What learners and teachers think. In L. Incalcaterra McLoughlin, M. Biscio and M.Á. Ní Mhainnín (eds) *Audiovisual Translation Subtitles and Subtitling. Theory and Practice* (pp. 219–242). Bern: Peter Lang.

Stempleski, S. and Tomalin, B. (1990) *Video in Action: Recipes for Using Video in Language Teaching*. London: Prentice Hall.

Talaván, N. (2013) *La subtitulación en el aprendizaje de lenguas extranjeras [Subtitling in Foreign-Language Learning]*. Barcelona: Octaedro.

Tschirner, E. (2001) Language acquisition in the classroom: The role of digital video. *Computer Assisted Language Learning* 14 (3–4), 305–319.

Williams, H. and Thorne, D. (2000) The value of teletext subtitling as a medium for language learning. *System* 28 (2), 217–228.

Zabalbeascoa, P., Sokoli, S. and Torres, O. (2012) ClipFlair Conceptual Framework and Pedagogical Methodology. See http://hdl.handle.net/10230/22701 (accessed 5 March 2015).

Zabalbeascoa, P., González-Casillas, S. and Pascual-Herce, R. (2015) Bringing the SLL project to life: Engaging Spanish teenagers in learning while watching foreign language audiovisuals. In Y. Gambier, A. Caimi and C. Mariotti (eds) *Subtitles and Language Learning* (pp. 105–126). Bern: Peter Lang.

Conclusion: Present and Future Directions for Video, Film and Audiovisual Media in Language Teaching

Carmen Herrero

The studies included in this volume advocate different theoretical backgrounds, and explore a range of relevant practices. They present research studies for the use of film and audiovisual media, including television, and the impact made by the increased accessibility of online video. The pedagogical applications and related research that permeate the theoretical bases of these works are underpinned by a three-axis approach: first, multiliteracies practices, including multimodal literacy and the development of critical thinking skills; second, a global perspective, including enhancing intercultural awareness and empathy; and, finally, translingual and transmodal practices.

The term 'multiliteracies' was coined by the New London Group (1996) to account for the new interpretations associated with the concept 'literacy', due to the impact of globalisation, technology and increasing linguistic, cultural and social diversity.[1] As noted by Kern (2000: 16), literacy 'is the use of socially-, historically-, and culturally-situated practices of creating and interpreting meaning though texts. It entails at least a tacit awareness of the relationships between textual conventions and their contexts of use'. Thus, it is not surprising that implementing the framework of multiliteracies, which has been a particular influence on education over the past decade, calls for infusing a wider range of literacies in all learners (Paesani *et al.*, 2016). One cannot help but notice that the moving image is becoming the primary mode of online communication (Cisco, 2016) and, therefore, visual literacy represents an essential process in the language classroom (Chan & Herrero, 2010; Donaghy & Xerri, 2017; Herrero, 2018a, 2018b). As noted by Goodwin (Chapter 11), this is one of the challenges in second language (L2) teaching due to the lack of appropriate teacher training in this field.

The undeniable significance of multimodal texts to account for the varied forms of meaning-making beyond print language (Bezemer &

Kress, 2016; Kress, 2003; Kress & van Leeuwen, 2001) elevates the role of audiovisual texts in language learning and teaching. On the one hand, multimodal literacy (Jewitt & Kress, 2003) comprises the development of learners' skills to analyse and produce multimodal materials, making use of different semiotic resources. On the other hand, it refers to the ways in which teachers use multimodal resources, and also to their understanding of the pedagogical and educational possibilities of multimodal resources. The latter is exemplified by Bobkina and Domínguez's application of multimodal theories to support the teaching of literary texts through films (Chapter 10). An excellent example of how to integrate multimodal activities in the L2 is provided by Sokoli and Zabalbeascoa Terran using the ClipFlair project (Chapter 12). Furthermore, as pointed out by Chan and Herrero (2010: 11), 'films are rich multimodal texts containing linguistic meaning, but they also contain other modes that are sometimes more difficult to illustrate or provide in the standard language lesson, such as the gestural component'. Reclaiming the importance of body language communication, Dubrac (Chapter 4) calls for making more use of the moving image as a tool to develop oral skills integrating gestural and verbal communication.

The rise of a participatory culture in the 21st century has also shifted the focus of literacy from individual expression to community involvement and has enhanced the value of new multiliteracy skills in the digital media environment. These involve social skills developed through collaboration and networking (Jenkins et al., [2006] 2009). There are relevant examples of research and teacher training projects that apply the principles of the new media literacies and film education to the L2 classroom (accessing, analysing, interpreting, understanding and creating visual messages in multimedia environments) (Anderson & Macleroy, 2016; Chan & Herrero, 2010; FILTA; FLAME; Herrero, 2016; Herrero et al., 2017; Herrero & Escobar, 2018; Thaler, 2014). However, this is still an underdeveloped area in the language curriculum that calls for new research projects (Herrero, 2018a, 2018b).

The volume reflects how language pedagogy is taking on board the tools and devices with which today's students are familiar. Video cameras in tablets and mobile phones provide language learners with opportunities to develop video projects as there is a strong interest among young learners to engage with film and media, not just as consumers, but also as producers, curators and critics (Anderson & Macleroy, 2016; Bahloul & Graham, 2012; Donaghy, 2015; Goldstein & Driver, 2015; Herrero et al., 2017; Herrero & Escobar, 2018; Herrero & Valbuena, 2009, 2011; Keddie, 2014; Video For All, 2015). Different studies (Donaghy in Chapter 1, Seeger in Chapter 3 and Alonso Pérez in Chapter 8) included in this book exemplify this creative and participatory approach of film in the language classroom. They all draw attention to the relevance of filmmaking projects in the language learning environment, namely the creative dimension of film education applied to language teaching.

Learning a foreign language represents a communicative experience intrinsically linked to the acquisition of language skills and verbal competence. It also develops cultural knowledge and promotes related skills that enrich the process of interlingual and intercultural communication (Council of Europe, 2001, 2018; Dervin, 2017; Puren, 2002; Sercu, 2004, 2006; Shaw, 2000; Windmüller, 2011). In an era of global interconnectivity and persistent political instability, it is of paramount importance to develop students' intercultural mindset and professional skills. The recommendations of the report *Foreign Languages and Higher Education: New Structures for a Changed World* (Modern Language Association [MLA], 2007) were designed for the USA but are applicable to other contexts. They call for strategies to raise language learners' translingual and transcultural competences. In the UK, the position statement *Language Matters More and More* (British Academy, 2011) also confirms that:

> understanding the languages, cultures and societies of others, as well as the way in which languages interact with each other and with English, is an important means of improving intercultural interactions and enhancing social well-being at home as well as overseas. (British Academy, 2011: 5)

Therefore, the comparative nature of the acquisition of intercultural skills should not be underestimated when devising language teaching materials, which do not necessarily focus entirely on the L2 and its culture, but also on a comparative approach. The intercultural attitude can manifest itself as the transfer of knowledge, as the active understanding of cultural acts or speech and as the ability to respond to intercultural situations. It also refers to comparative evaluations and discussions of culture-related elements, ranging from habits and traditions to attitudes and behaviour. However, because learners tend to relate new cultures to their own culture (ethnocentrically), comparing L2 cultures is not sufficient for fostering an open-minded observation of cultural manifestations (Risager, 2006, 2007). Beyond focusing on multilingualism and intercultural awareness, a set of core competences to complement language acquisition has been promoted at European institutional level in the training of language students and teachers (e.g. new version of the Common European framework guidelines updated and released in 2018). This confirms Tomlinson's argument in his contribution to this volume about including intercultural competence into curricula (Chapter 2). Tomlinson recognises intercultural awareness as the first step towards intercultural competence. For this author, effective interaction in the target language fosters the development of intercultural awareness; but also films and other visual media are among the most valuable materials 'to facilitate the development of intercultural awareness and/or competence'. Dubrac's project (Chapter 4) also proved to be successful in developing student intercultural awareness through film-related activities.

The increase in interactions across nations, cultures and borders, and the global flow of ideologies and media are a mark of the 21st century (Appadurai, 1996, 2013; Castells, 1996, 2009). Nowadays, there is compelling evidence of the complex dynamic forces of multilingual realities in super-diverse societies (Vertovec, 2007). As noted by Seeger in Chapter 3, films and videos can also provide answers to challenges arising from the profiles of students in Europe (i.e. migrants). Seeger proposes creative and pragmatic resources mapped against Common European Framework of Reference for Languages (CEFR) levels to address this 'super-diversity' in the language classroom. The kaleidoscopic phenomenon of multilingualism has been analysed by language scholars under different terms, such as 'flexible bilingualism', 'code-meshing' and 'polylingual languaging' (Creese & Backledge, 2010). Translingual practice (Canagarajah, 2013) and translanguaging (García, 2009; García & Wei, 2014) are two notions that aim to capture 'an epistemological change that is the product of acting and languaging in our highly technological globalized world' (García & Wei, 2014: 20).[2] Thus, the demands of the real world outside the classroom require a broadening of conceptions of essential literacy 'to include translingual, transmodal, and trans-presentational practices, which include creating, negotiating, transforming, and sharing texts across multiple codes, channels, and symbol systems' (Lizárraga et al., 2015: 118). Audiovisual translation (AVT) applied to language learning and teaching offers multiple possibilities of working with multimodality and transmodality. A real breakthrough of the book is to demonstrate the validity of AVT in activities such as audio description, dubbing, subtitling and voice-over for improving oral comprehension, fostering autonomous learning and enhancing motivation and active participation by students (Frumuselu in Chapter 7). Another significant development in AVT presented in this volume is the use of case studies that are informed by the principles of project-based learning (Alonso Pérez in Chapter 8). The results of innovative empirical studies in the use of captioned videos for vocabulary acquisition (Cokely & Muñoz in Chapter 5) and eye-tracking studies (Mora & Cerviño-Povedano in Chapter 6) can guide teachers when using video with captions in L2 activities. Other chapters have reported research on testing learners' linguistic accuracy using different modes of AVT with professional and non-professional software (Rica Peromingo & Sáenz Herrero in Chapter 9).

The authors, who have all been practising teachers themselves, approach the integration of film into the language syllabus in different ways and contexts, but what really emerges from the book is how these resources and ideas are flexible and easily transferable to a range of educational contexts. Indeed, it would not be difficult to see in the contributions examples of how language educators should theorise from and about their practice. This particular aspect of the inductive approach can be found in the chapters by Seeger (Chapter 3), Dubrac (Chapter 4) and Goodwin (Chapter 11).

Activities based on film, video and audiovisual media have been used for several decades in the L2 classroom. This reflected the evolution of language teaching methodologies and approaches. Looking forward, the rapid changes in today's media landscape will have a significant impact on the way media texts are used to support teaching, learning and the assessment of students' competences. Trying to anticipate future evolution in this area is extremely difficult because of the ever faster-changing needs in communication. This is particularly relevant at a time when education is increasingly enhanced by information and communication technologies. Video-based learning, which is driven by learner's interest and motivation, is also becoming the norm particularly in informal learning. A good starting point is to consider the disruptive effects of technology and innovation in media organisations and audiences. There are three significant trends that are relevant and will impact on the interdisciplinary field of language education, media literacy and media technology: first, the increase in video consumption as a ubiquitous practice (i.e. on mobile phones) for the millennial generation (age 21–34) and Generation Z or the post-millennial generation (age 15–20); secondly, the exponential growth of video content and associated practices, including sharing video on social media; and thirdly, the growth of delayed TV viewing and streaming services such as Netflix, Amazon and Hulu.

The impact of the above trends on the learning practices of millennial and post-millennial learners is starting to be visible. It is possible to envisage how innovative education models (flipped learning, blended learning and distance learning) rely on the use of education videos and other social media-related tools to support the learning-teaching processes and assessments. New research has explored how technology and video enhance higher education student learning experience in the UK (Panopto, 2018). The study's results emphasise, for example, the way in which video has become the preferred learning medium for the majority of students, with 78% using online video platforms (i.e. YouTube or Vimeo) to learn new skills or to inspire independent study. Findings from the study show that more students prefer to learn via a video compared to a book (25% chose to learn from a video over reading a book and 15% choose to learn from a book over a video). The study also reports that a growing number of students record their own video content (33% had created video content for personal content and 10% had recorded video for educational purposes).

It is possible to see how these trends are already impacting on language learners' motivation. Young learners, particularly, prefer a blend of formal and informal learning. The positive response to the new experiments presented in this volume should also encourage language teachers to be more confident in adopting and developing interactive learning strategies when using video in the L2 classroom (e.g. mobile learning, peer collaboration and video assessments). Thus, it is vital that the governmental bodies and institutions that support and promote language learning programmes take into consideration the research findings addressed here. Furthermore, there is also a need to undertake wider research on the changing role of the educational video in the design of L2 learning activities (Laaser & Toloza, 2017).

YouTube has produced new video genres that redefine the way we consume, enjoy and learn with moving images. From video blogs (or vlogs) to how-to videos, the rise of new short format video genres is facilitating the expansion of microlearning, a learning approach linked to content of short duration and mobile learning (Hugh, 2005). The educational potential of microlearning for language learning in formal and informal settings is only starting to be apprehended, let alone evaluated. However, its practical applications and potential impact on the language classroom and also independent study modes are evident, particularly with the creative pedagogical use of short films in the language classroom (see Donaghy, Chapter 1; Donaghy, 2015; Junkerjürgen *et al.*, 2016; Thaler, 2017).

The complex convergent and participatory nature of popular culture is contributing to the phenomenon of genre hybridity and media fusion. Consequently, the term 'video' now encompasses a number of shifts that have taken place in contemporary media culture, moving away from rigid conceptions of television, film, digital media and video games. New ways of approaching video viewing and, in some cases, more immersive experiences, such as 360-degree video content, augmented reality and virtual reality,[3] are already transforming the educational landscape and their positive effects on learning are starting to be assessed (Observatory of Education, 2018). Language learning and teaching in formal and informal settings are already affected by these shifts and, inevitably, language pedagogy has to realign itself to respond to the requirements derived from these new learning experiences (See Transmedia in Education).

Transmedia storytelling is used to denote products that are simultaneously created or distributed across various media channels 'for the purpose of creating a unified and coordinated entertainment experience' (Jenkins, 2007). It also implies that 'each medium makes its own unique contribution to the unfolding of the story' (Jenkins, 2007). Transmedia storytelling, which has been successfully introduced in television series (*The Sopranos, Lost, The Wire* and *Game of Thrones*), offers creative opportunities in four areas (Jenkins, 2009): backstory, mapping the world, displaying other character's perspectives on the action and expanding audience engagement. A recent analysis of the trends in education, focused on transmedia storytelling, illustrates how the shifts in media consumption are also impacting on today's ever-changing educational landscape (Observatory of Education, 2017). It highlights several actions for the application of transmedia storytelling in education: '1) study the storytelling and cultural practices carried out in the network to learn what can be replicated in schools; 2) explore storytelling, games and simulation; and 3) transform diverse commercial narratives into case studies for learning purposes' (Observatory of Education, 2017: 22). With regard to the use of digital storytelling in the foreign language classroom, most of the current studies involve English with fewer studies related to other languages (Anderson & Macleroy, 2016).

The blend of research and practice presented in this volume is very relevant to language teachers and trainers, as well as researchers in education. Each chapter has highlighted in its own way the importance of elaborating video and audiovisual media pedagogies supported by interdisciplinary theoretical frameworks and using primary research carried out in international language classrooms. The research-based chapters have demonstrated the scope of video use for language teaching and learning across different languages, age groups and curricular areas and identified a range of exciting areas for further research.

Acknowledgments

The work for this chapter was supported by the UK Arts and Humanities Research Council's Open World Research Initiative (OWRI, https://ahrc.ukri.org/research/funded themesandprogrammes/themes/owri/), under the programme 'Cross-Language Dynamics: Reshaping Community', and the Manchester Metropolitan University.

Notes

(1) The New London Group refers to the 10 leaders in the field of literacy pedagogy who met in 1999 in the small town of New London, New Hampshire, in order to discuss the growing importance of cultural and linguistic diversity and multimodal literacy due to the power of new communication technologies. The outcome of their discussions was encapsulated under the term 'multiliteracies'.

(2) Applied to bilingualism, the term 'translanguaging' 'extends the repertoire of semiotic practices of individuals and transforms them into dynamic mobile resources that can adapt to global and local sociolinguistic situations' (García & Li, 2014: 18).

(3) Using an omnidirectional camera or a collection of cameras, 360-degree video offers a view in every direction; 360-degree videos can be watched and uploaded in YouTube. Augmented reality relies on the integration of digital information with the user's environment in real time. The information that can be 'augmented' includes multiple sensory modality elements (visual, auditory, haptic, olfactory and somatosensory). Finally, virtual reality is an artificial environment that is created with interactive software and hardware. This realistic and immersive simulation is experienced in a real environment.

References

Anderson, J. and Macleroy, V. (2016) *Multilingual Digital Storytelling*. London: Routledge.

Appadurai, A. (1996) *Modernity At Large: Cultural Dimensions of Globalization*. Minneapolis, MN: University of Minnesota Press.

Appadurai, A. (2013) *The Future as Cultural Fact: Essays on the Global Condition*. London: Verso.

Bahloul, M. and Graham, C. (eds) (2012) *Lights! Camera! Action and the Brain: The Use of Film in Education*. Cambridge: Cambridge Scholars Publishing.

Bezemer, J. and Kress, G. (2016) *Multimodality, Learning and Communication: A Social Semiotic Frame*. London/New York: Routledge.

British Academy (2011) *Language Matters More and More* (position statement and transcript of launch event, 9 February 2011). See https://www.thebritishacademy.ac.uk/publications/language-matters-more-and-more (accessed 7 December 2018).

Canagarajah, S. (2013) *Translingual Practice: Global Englishes and Cosmopolitan Relations*. London: Routledge.

Castells, M. (1996) *The Information Age. The Rise of the Network Society*. Oxford: Blackwell.

Castells, M. (2009) *Communication Power*. Oxford: Oxford University Press.

Chan, D. and Herrero, C. (2010) *Using Film to Teach Languages*. Manchester: Cornerhouse Education. See https://goo.gl/oP4t3A (accessed 7 December 2018).

Cisco (2016) Visual Networking Index: Forecast and Methodology, 2016–2021 (White paper). 15 September 2017. See https://www.cisco.com/c/en/us/solutions/collateral/service-provider/visual-networking-index-vni/complete-white-paper-c11-481360.html (accessed 15 September 2017).

Council of Europe (2001) *Council European Framework of Reference for Languages: Learning, Teaching, Assessment*. Cambridge: Cambridge University Press.

Council of Europe (2018) *Common European Framework of Reference for Languages: Learning, Teaching, Assessment. Companion Volume with New Descriptors*. See https://rm.coe.int/cefr-companion-volume-with-new-descriptors-2018/1680787989 (accessed 18 December 2018).

Creese A. and Blackledge, A. (2010) Translanguaging in the bilingual classroom: A pedagogy for learning and teaching. *Modern Language Journal* 94, 103–115.

Dervin, F. (2017) *Compétences interculturelles*. Paris: Editions des archives contemporaines.

Donaghy, K. (2015) *Film in Action: Teaching Language Using Moving Images*. Peaslake: Delta Publishing.

Donaghy, K. and Xerri, D. (eds) (2017) *The Image in English Language Teaching*. Malta: ELT Council.

Film, Languages and Media in Education (FLAME) https://www2.mmu.ac.uk/languages/flame/

Film in Language Teaching Association (FILTA). See http://www.filta.org.uk (accessed 23 May 2018).

García, O. (2009) *Bilingual Education in the 21st Century: A Global Perspective*. Malden, MA: Wiley/Blackwell.

García, O. and Wei, L. (2014) *Translanguaging: Language, Bilingualism and Education*. New York/Basingstoke: Palgrave Macmillan.

Goldstein, B. and Driver, P. (2015) *Language Learning with Digital Video*. Cambridge: Cambridge University Press.

Herrero, C. (2016) Film in Language Teaching Association (FILTA): A multilingual community of practice. *English Language Teaching Journal* 70 (2), 190–199. See https://doi.org/10.1093/elt/ccv080 (accessed 21 December 2018).

Herrero, C. (2018a) El cine y otras manifestaciones culturales en ELE. In M. Martínez-Atienza de Dios and A. Zamorano Aguilar (eds) *Iniciación a la metodología de la enseñanza de ELE* (Vol. IV; pp. 65–85). Madrid: EnClaveELE.

Herrero, C. (2018b) Medios audiovisuales. In J. Muñoz-Basols, E. Gironzetti and M. Lacorte (eds) *The Routledge Handbook of Spanish Language Teaching: metodologías, contextos y recursos para la enseñanza del español L2* (pp. 565–582). London/New York: Routledge.

Herrero, C. and Valbuena, A. (2009) Nuevos alfabetismos en la clase de ELE a través del cine. In R. Bueno Hudson, M. Abad and A. Valbuena (eds) *Actas de las II Jornadas Didácticas del Instituto Cervantes* (pp. 52–66). Manchester: Instituto Cervantes.

Herrero, C. and Valbuena, A. (2011) Cultura participativa y alfabetización multimodal aplicadas a la enseñanza de lenguas. In M. Buisine-Soubeyroux and J. Seguin (eds) *Image et education* (pp. 277–286). Lyon: Le Grihm/Passages XX-XXI and Université Lumiere-Lyon 2.

Herrero, C. and Escobar, M. (2018) Pedagogical model for integrating film education and audio description in foreign language acquisition. In L. Incalcaterra McLoughlin, J. Lertola and N. Talaván (eds) Special issue on Audiovisual Translation in Applied Linguistics: Beyond Case Studies. *Translation and Translanguaging in Multilingual Contexts* 4 (1), 30–54. http://dx.doi.org/10.1075/ttmc.00003.her

Herrero, C., Sánchez-Requena, A. and Escobar, M. (2017) Una propuesta triple: análisis fílmico, traducción audiovisual y enseñanza de lenguas extranjeras. In J.J. Martínez Sierra and B. Cerezo Merchán (eds) Special Issue: Building Bridges between Film Studies and Translation Studies. *InTRAlinea*. See http://www.intralinea.org/specials/article/2245 (accessed 7 January 2018).

Hugh, T. (2005) Microlearning: A new pedagogical challenge. In *Microlearning: Emerging Concepts, Practices and Technologies after e-Learning: Proceedings of Micro-Learning Conference* (pp. 7–11). Innsbruck: Innsbruck University Press.

Jenkins, H. (2007) Transmedia Storytelling 101. *Confessions of an ACA-FAN*. See http://henryjenkins.org/blog/2007/03/transmedia_storytelling_101.html (accessed 9 January 2018).

Jenkins, H. (2009) *Confronting the Challenges of Participatory Culture: Media Education for the 21st Century*. Cambridge, MA: MIT Press.

Jewitt, C. and Kress, G. (eds) (2003) *Multimodal Literacy*. New York: Peter Lang.

Junkerjürgen, R., Scholz, A. and Álvarez Olañeta, P. (eds) (2016) *El cortometraje español (2000–2015). Tendencias y ejemplos*. Madrid/Fráncfort del Meno: Iberoamericana Vervuert.

Keddie, J. (2014) *Bringing Online Video into the Classroom*. Oxford: Oxford University Press.

Kern, R. (2000) *Literacy and Language Teaching*. Oxford: Oxford University Press.

Kress, G. (2003) *Literacy in the New Media Age*. London: Routledge.

Kress, G. and van Leeuwen, T. (2001) *Multimodal Discourse: The Modes and Media of Contemporary Communication*. Oxford: Oxford University Press.

Laaser, W. and Toloza, E.A. (2017) The changing role of the educational video in higher distance education. *The International Review of Research in Open and Distributed Learning* 18 (2), 264–272.

Lizárraga, J.R., Hull, G.A. and Scott, J.M. (2015) Translingual literacies in a social media age: Lessons learned from youth's transnational communication online. In D. Molle, E. Sato, T. Boals and C.A. Hedgspeth (eds) *Multilingual Learners and Academic Literacies* (pp. 105–132). New York: Routledge.

Modern Language Association (MLA) (2007) *Foreign Languages and Higher Education: New Structures for a Changed World*. See https://eric.ed.gov/?id=ED500460 (accessed 23 September 2017).

New London Group (1996) A pedagogy of multiliteracies: Designing social futures. *Harvard Educational Review* 66 (1), 60–92.

Observatory of Education (2017) *Edu Trend: Storytelling*. Monterrey: Tecnológico de Monterrey. See http://observatory.itesm.mx/edu-trends-storytelling (accessed 13 February 2018).

Observatory of Education (2018) *Edu Trends: Augmented and Virtual Reality*. Monterrey: Tecnológico de Monterrey. See http://observatory.itesm.mx/edu-trends-augmented-and-virtual-reality (accessed 19 December 2018).

Paesani, K., Allen, H.W., Dupuy, B., Liskin-Gasparro, J.W. and Lacorte, M. (2016) *A Multiliteracies Framework for Collegiate Foreign Language Teaching*. Upper Saddle River, NJ: Pearson.

Panopto (2018) 10 Video Trends You Should Know About to Enhance the Student Learning Experience. See https://www.panopto.com/blog/10-video-trends-that-can-enhance-the-student-learning-experience/ (accessed 19 December 2018).

Puren, C. (2002) Perspectives acionnelles et perspectives culturelles en didactique des langues cultures: vers un perspective co-actionnele-co-culturrelle. *Les Langues Modernes* 2, 55–71.

Risager, K. (2006) *Language and Culture: Global Flows and Local Complexities*. Clevedon: Multilingual Matters.

Risager, K. (2007) *Language and Culture Pedagogy: From a National to a Transnational Paradigm*. Clevedon: Multilingual Matters.

Sercu, L. (2004) Assessing intercultural competence: A framework for systematic test development in foreign language education and beyond. *Intercultural Education* 15 (1), 73–89.

Sercu, L. (2006) The foreign language and intercultural competence teacher: The acquisition of a new professional identity. *Intercultural Education* 17 (1), 55–72.

Shaw, S. (ed.) (2000) *Intercultural Education in European Classrooms*. Stoke on Trent/ Sterling, VA: Trentham Books.

Thaler, E. (2014) *Teaching English with Film*. Paderborn: Schöningh.

Thaler, E. (ed.) (2017) *Short Films in Language Teaching*. Tübingen: Narr Francke Attempto.

Transmedia in Education. http://transmediaineducation.com.

Vertovec, S. (2007) *New Complexities of Cohesion in Britain: Super-Diversity, Transnationalism and Civil Integration*. Wetherby: Communities and Local Government Publications.

Video for All (2015) See http://videoforall.eu/ (accessed 12 September 2017).

Windmüller, F. (2011) *Français Langue étrangèr: L'approche culturelle et interculturelle*. Paris: Belin.

Index

CPSIA information can be obtained
at www.ICGtesting.com
Printed in the USA
LVHW051818131121
703258LV00009B/404